From Bangkok to Bishkek, Budapest to Bogotá

The compelling story of International Congregations

2nd Edition

Kenneth D. MacHarg

English Methodist Church (today, Methodist International Church), Hong Kong—circa 1964

ISBN: 978-1-63199-577-4
eISBN: 978-1-63199-578-1

EnerPower Press
P. O. Box 841
Gonzalez, Florida 32560

enerpowerpress.com
EnerPower Press is an imprint of Energion Publications

Ken MacHarg has organized the largest collection of International Church history in print. This reservoir of inspiration demonstrates that the International Church reaches all kinds of **people** in all kinds of **places**. Ken broadcasts the strategic **position** of International Churches reaching **persons** of every tribe, tongue and nation. The stories told within motivate us to be **prudent,** investing time, effort and personnel in the International Church around the globe. Ken's compendium testifies that Jesus will build His Church! Have a read, experience where God is at work.

Rev Dr. Warren Reeve, Missional International Church Network Founder/Lead Pastor of the Martin Luther King English Speaking International Church in Paris

Ken MacHarg knows the international church. His research is an invaluable tool to help understand the multicultural church phenomena, which from the day of Pentecost onward, been a powerful factor in world evangelism. These churches play a very important role in the spiritual growth of individuals and families and in spread of the gospel around the world, and as important tools of God need to be understood better. I recommend this book to you as a helpful resource as a source of encouragement in the work of God in the world and to help understand the history, the reality, and the future of the international church.

Dr. David Packer, Senior Pastor of the International Baptist Church of Stuttgart, Germany

Having had the privilege to serve a total of 18 years at two of the oldest and largest American international congregations, the *Union Evangelical Church in Mexico City* and the *American Church in Paris*, I was impressed to read of so many more congregations with varying degrees of similar history and diversity around the world. Indeed, the international and union churches are a sign of the Kingdom of God in-breaking into our world. I am grateful for MacHarg's extensive research and pray for greater understanding of and learning from these congregations as they show us the way forward and the true meaning of *e pluribus unum.*

Dr. Scott Herr, Senior Pastor, The American Church in Paris

Other Books by Kenneth D. MacHarg

- *Tune in the World, The Listener's Guide to International Shortwave Radio*, Miller Publishing Company, Media, Pennsylvania, 1983
- *Introducing International Radio,* Global Village Press, Jeffersonville, In, 1987
- *A Haven By The Side Of The Road, The Story of Wayside Christian Mission*, Wayside Christian Mission, Louisville, Kentucky, 1997
- *Don't Rush the Lord, A Pilgrimage to God's Purpose*, Wm. Carey Library, Pasadena, California, 1997
- *Inside Track: Latin America Through the Eyes of a Missionary Journalist,* Editorial Buena Semilla, Bogotá, Colombia, 2001
- *Proclaiming the Gospel; Guidelines for Local Christian Radio Programming Around the World,* Latin America Mission, Miami, Florida, 2003. Published in Spanish as: *La proclamación del Evangelio; Pautas para programadores locales de radio cristiana alrededor del mundo*, Latin America Mission, Miami, Florida, 2003 and in Portuguese as: *Proclamando o Evangelho no rádio*, Transcultural Editora e Livraria Ltda., Anápolis, Brazil. 2004
- *Not in Vain*, with David M. Howard, Latin America Mission, Miami, *Florida, 2005. Also available in Spanish*
- *From Rio to the Rio Grande; Challenges and Opportunities in Latin America,* Global Village Press, Miami, Florida 2007
- *Radio Survives and Thrives, The History of Kentucky Broadcasting from 1945-1970,* Global Village Press, Carrollton, Georgia 2011
- *Singing the Lord's Songs in a Foreign Land; Biblical Reflections for Expatriates,* Global Village Press, Carrollton, Georgia, 2011

Dedication

This book is dedicated to the following who helped me grow in my love for and commitment to service of the Lord through International (Union) Churches:

The late *Dr. Norman A. Horner*, Dean and Professor of Missions at the Louisville Presbyterian Theological Seminary. His brief, almost off-hand, mention one day in a missions class of what were then known as Union Churches turned on a light for me that has never dimmed.

The late *Rev. Gregory Seeber*, pastor of international congregations in Panama, Turkey and Poland. Greg came by to introduce himself to us our first day at the Margarita Union Church in Panama. He helped me to learn international churches and opened up the exciting nature of the world-wide fellowship of such congregations.

The late *Rev. J.R. "Jack" Collins*, who, through the office of International Congregations and Lay Ministries in New York City, served in a position similar to an Association Minister (District Superintendent, Executive Presbyter, Bishop) of the global network of ICs, wisely advised me on how to seek my first pastorate in one, and continued as a friend and encourager through correspondence and visits for many years.

Thank you

It would be impossible to name all of the people and institutions that have helped me in the preparation of this book. They go back to those cited in the Dedication and to people and agencies in more recent times that have encouraged me, provided information and helped with the writing, editing and publishing process.

Among those who cheered me on are Warren Reeve the founder of MICN, Jimmy Martin of the International Baptist Convention, Jim Dwyer formerly of the Network of International Congregations and others.

My good friend and missionary colleague, Ralph Kurtenbach, was very encouraging and provided a thorough editing of my work.

There are dozens of others who provided books, pamphlets, and other resources—far too many to remember or mention here.

I would be remiss not to thank those nine international churches in seven countries which allowed Polly and me to serve them. Those are Treasure Cay Community Church, Treasure Cay, Abaco, the Bahamas, Escazú Christian Fellowship in San Jose, Costa Rica, International Church of Prague in Prague, Czech Republic, First (International) Baptist Church and English Fellowship Church in Quito, Ecuador, International Christian Fellowship in San Pedro Sula, Honduras, International Church of Bishkek in Bishkek, Kyrgyzstan, Margarita Union Church, Margarita, Gatun Union Church, Gatun, Panama Canal Zone (Panama).

And then there is my dear wife Polly who fully shared in these ministries and, as with all of my other books, listened to me chatter on and patiently allowed me to spend voluminous hours on the computer.

Table of Contents

"Consequently, you are no longer foreigners and strangers, but fellow citizens with God's people and also members of his household, built on the foundation of the apostles and prophets, with Christ Jesus himself as the chief cornerstone. In him the whole building is joined together and rises to become a holy temple in the Lord. And in him you too are being built together to become a dwelling in which God lives by his Spirit."

Ephesians 2:19-22

Introduction

How can we sing the songs of the Lord while in a foreign land? Psalm 137:4 NIV

Consider these statistics: There are 9,161 churches in the Presbyterian Church in the United States of America (PCUSA), over 6,939, the Disciples of Christ, 3,627, the Southern Baptists over 47,000, the Church of Scotland (Presbyterian) 1,353, and the international churches number well over 3,000.

Wait a minute—international churches? Is that a denomination? Who are they? Why haven't I ever heard of them? Three-thousand churches?

One should not be surprised if they didn't recognize the name "international churches." In fact, these congregations would be easy to miss because they are not a denomination, but are part of an existing network or fellowship or, perhaps, movement of congregations spread around the globe.

However, their obscurity should not hide their immense influence around the world with people from multiple denominations and just about every nation on earth.

The assumption that someone from an English-speaking nation might make is that when locating to another country they either will have to attend church in the language of the host nation where they are visiting or working, or they might just have to skip going to church while they are abroad.

Think again. For over 450 years, British, Scottish, Canadian, Australian, Filipino, Nigerian, Ghanaian, South African, American and other English-speaking expatriates (those who live outside of their own country) have attended

English-language churches in foreign lands while on vacation, studying or working.

Most likely, those congregations have been multi-national, multi-denominational churches meeting in their own buildings, a rented church, a hotel banquet room or school auditorium, a borrowed hall or gymnasium or someone's expanded home. They have ranged from a handful of people squeezed into a living room to thousands who attend each Sunday in multi-campus congregations.

For the most part, they have met in small to medium-sized gatherings in a variety of venues, worshipping, studying and sharing in fellowship with people who share their common language and a firm belief in Jesus Christ.

And, while these congregations are somewhat hidden from church-goers back in their home country, they number in the thousands and have been a mighty force in the expansion of the Kingdom of God and the evangelization of people in countless countries.

While many of them were most often known as Union Churches, or occasionally American Churches in the past, today they go under the general description of International Congregations and they are unique gatherings of Christians with a wide influence.

This description from the website of the Missional International Church Network best describes these unique congregations:

What is an International Church?

International churches (ICs) are those churches around the world that primarily serve people of various nationalities (expatriates) and church backgrounds living outside their passport (home) countries.

Main Characteristics:

- *They function in a language (mostly English) not normally spoken in the host country. Usually, there is a significant proportion of the church (which has) English as a second language.*

- They have a majority of people from other countries – expatriates / people of the global diaspora / foreign passport holders. (In some major cities, the growing numbers of nationals who have been internationalised through substantial overseas experience has resulted in some international churches with a majority of nationals who are culturally more at home here than in the national church. In some others, it is illegal for nationals to attend.)
- They have a cultural flavouring and rich diversity, with stronger more global and global-nomad perspectives, which reflects the mix of nationalities and cultures involved. Typically, multi-national, multi-cultural, multi-denominational. Very intentional in preserving a focus on this diversity with a primary concern to serve (or minister to) expatriates.

Other typical characteristics include …

- *There are well over a thousand*[1] *international churches across the globe. They can be found in nearly all major cities, especially where English is not the main language. Most major and capital cities have several international churches.*
- *They are usually interdenominational, though a proportion is denominationally based. Denominational international churches may not always have the same breadth of multi-denominational expression*
- *They tend to have a high turnover of people as people transition in and out of the country.*
- *They tend to have fewer retirees (and a younger leadership) and fewer post high school students as these usually go back to home country. Otherwise they are multi-generational.*

---

[1] A more recent accounting puts the total number of international, English-speaking congregations at more than 3,000.

- *They range from very small gatherings with volunteer leadership through to large mega-churches with multiple sites and multiple pastoral staff.*
- *They have a concern to reach out to and serve the wider expatriate community and, depending on the local context, often also have various roles in supporting the national church and contributing to the wellbeing of the city in which they are placed.*
- *The practical challenges of living far from home country tend to be a significant part of the international church agenda.*
- *There are English speaking international churches in English speaking countries. The emphasis in these is on cultural diversity and the concerns typical of expatriates.*
- *Some international churches may have a majority of nationals but are very intentional in preserving a focus on cultural diversity with a primary concern to minister to expatriates.*

But not…

- *There are many expatriate churches that serve a single ethnic, national or language group. These too can be found in most cities across the world. They are not usually included in what we mean by international church. Ethnocentricity may be a challenge to overcome on the missional journey.*
- *There are also churches that include the word "international" in their name who do so to reflect the international character of the Kingdom but are not international churches as described here. Some do so as a fund raising strategy!*
- *There are many national churches that include amongst their services an English speaking congregation. The church may not be international but the congregation may reflect the main features of an international church –*

language, passport and cultural diversity. (http://micn.org/defined/)

In another document, MICN describes those who attend IC's as *an assembly of Christians that are inordinately adventurous, highly educated, entrepreneurial, Biblically literate and living effectively outside their countries of origin.* (https://micn.org/story/)

Another umbrella organization, the Network of International Congregations offers this description:

Millions of people are living in lands other than their own, struggling to understand another language, culture, way of life. They seek community, support, a grasp of hope and reality. Persons in such situations can be lost, uncertain, confused.

For these and all who might be touched by the Good News in Jesus Christ, there are oases where Living Water is to be found. Christians abroad find fellowship in International Congregations, gatherings of like-minded and like-experienced people who seek God's presence and seek to follow God's leading.

These assemblies of believers focus their lives and activities together under six significant common characteristics.

***EVANGELICAL** is the chief and theological characteristic for an International Congregation. It sees the "Gospel," the Evangel, as the principle sign, idea for a Christian. It points to Jesus Christ, the center and key for God's church. "Evangelical" says that a church focuses on Jesus, who He is and what He does and means for us. Being evangelical means that Jesus is first, that He is Lord and Savior of all.*

***ECUMENICAL** is the sociological characteristic. In these churches each person [left and right, liturgical and non-liturgical, fundamentalist and liberal, traditional and experimental] finds the welcome mat out. The affirmation "one, holy, catholic and apostolic Church" takes on a new depth as openness, and inclusiveness, gives a truly "Pentecostal" flavor to International Churches.*

INTERNATIONAL *is the political characteristic. If there is content to the current phrase, "New World Order," then International Congregations have been an advance party of awareness. Vast changes are erasing old boundaries and diluting old ideologies. International Congregations witness to a reality transcending "the American way of life;" they testify to a willing embrace of all persons into one community in Christ.*

ENGLISH *is the linguistic characteristic. The English language now ties people within and among nations together. International airline communication is in English. Scientific and professional organizations use English as the prime language. Libraries want literature and reference works in English. Some nationals affiliate with an English-speaking congregation because they married an English-speaking spouse, or studied in English, or are more at home in English than any other language. As language was a key for a diverse company of people on the first Pentecost, so it continues to weld men and women into community.*

CONTEXT *is the cultural characteristic. The Christian faith is always wrapped in a cultural robe. There is no way to receive the faith outside of a cultural context. Congregations seek to connect individuals to a faith that acknowledges an inter-cultural reality by being part of a trans-cultural experience. The joy and amazement derived from association with these congregations stem from the fact it is possible to transcend human differences that often divide people.*

MISSIONAL *is the functional characteristic. It is for mission that the church exists: "As the Father has sent me, so I send you." Mission is expressed in word and deed, in telling and doing, in acting and being. Churches do not live only to perpetuate themselves, but to be servants of their Servant Lord. A mission-minded International Congregation reaches out to English-speaking persons even when they are not within the normal social or economic circle of the congregation.*

International Congregations visualize the united, world-wide church of Jesus Christ without regard to separations of confession, race, culture, or nation. Diversity and unity are seen as complimentary qualities.

Some International Congregations are related through the agency of the Network for International Congregations (NIC). It is a network of congregations in more than 65 countries. They are instruments of God for demonstrating that barriers can be overcome, that faith binds believers into one company.

Congregations related to NIC fall into two styles of accountability: independent and confessional. "Independent" churches are frequently called "Union" or "Community" or "International," reflecting an inter-/multi-denominational posture; they have no ecclesiastical base, or responsibility toward or benefit from a churchly source. "Confessional" churches are tied to a single Protestant denomination, but intentionally direct their ministry in an ecumenical or non-denominational manner; such congregations have a responsibility toward and receive benefits from their sponsoring church body. **(https://tinyurl.com/y257ajag)**

In a more succinct form, Dr. Warren Reeve describes some of the characteristics of these churches:

- ✓ ***PEOPLE in the International Church:*** *Rockstars, reformers, royalty, artists, ambassadors, academicians, military, mavericks, missionaries, politicians, professionals and pundits all engaged with the International Church.*
- ✓ ***PLACES of the International Church:*** International Churches are first responders answering in close proximity to global crisis assisting where there is geopolitical turmoil, natural disasters and displaced people challenges.
- ✓ ***POSITIONS of influence:*** *Located and functioning in open and limited access nations, nothing can penetrate closed countries, tight cultures and the kaleidoscope of classes like an International Church.*

✓ ***PERSONS of every tribe, tongue and nation:*** *The International Church plays a significant role in gathering the scattered diaspora and reaching persons from least reached people groups around the globe.*

✓ ***PRUDENT investment produces synergistic impact:*** In our ever increasing globalized world, properly positioned personnel in the International Church will catalyze national redemptive lift for countries and regions around the world.

– Rev Dr Warren Reeve, Missional International Church Network Founder

IC pastor James Carlson offers a fourth description, less extensive and complex, but helpful:

An International church is a church where at least half of the congregation does not live in their passport country.

An International Church can be found anywhere in the world. It specializes in ministry to people who are not living in their passport country for a variety of reasons. International churches use the lingua franca of the world as the language of communication, which in today's world is English. They may offer translation into the local language or other languages found in the congregation, but English will always be used. International Churches are often different characteristically from local churches because of their congregation's greater diversity nationally, theologically, denominationally, economically, educationally and linguistically. Because of these characteristics, demographically International Churches tend to have younger and more highly transitional congregations than the other churches around them.

(James Carlson, *International Church Assessment,* privately published, available at www.amazon.com, 2019)

Each of these differ in understanding as well as experience and while some may question the assumptions voiced, particularly in the third description, taken together they help to define and describe these churches in particular as they are different from congregations in the homeland.

There are many common characteristics among the more than 3,000 such congregations, however, one can easily say that each of those is distinctly different and difficult to compare to others. While many may classify themselves as multi-denominational, each congregation's theological and ecclesiastical profile is shaped by the denominational background of those who formed it or those who have influenced it in more recent times. Therefore, although a church founded by Presbyterian missionaries or lay people may bear a resemblance to its roots, eventually, with the frequent turn-over of leadership and membership, it may change to reflect a more formal liturgical style or adapt to a more evangelical theology. Given that many churches call pastors from a variety of denominational backgrounds over the years, it is no wonder that some will eventually become a melting pot of various denominational backgrounds or change their characteristics with the ebb and flow of pastors and lay leadership.

Thus, while ICs are frequently characterized as being multidenominational and multinational, a particular church may reflect a North American way of doing things under the influence of leadership from that region. Years later, however, one could be excused for thinking its background is British or Australian as others come in and bring with them their practices and understandings of what a church might be.

For the purposes of this book, we will include under the title "international congregations" those churches in, primarily but not limited to, non-English speaking countries which serve third-culture people (i.e. primarily expats as well as locals with international experience). These churches are largely characterized as being multinational and multi-denominational individual supporting church.[2]

So, why write a history of a movement that, while global, is little known in the home countries of those who make up their constituencies?

First, this history is important because the international congregations reflect a long trajectory of ministry which has had a global impact, even when known only to a few.

Second, as will be illustrated, these churches have roots in not only ecclesiastical settings, but in the political, cultural and religious nature of English-language cultures going back for over four centuries. The establishment of British Anglican international churches goes hand in hand with the development of the British Empire which dates back to the late 1500s and expanded to the four corners of the earth. After all, the expression that the sun never sets on the British Empire denotes its global outreach and the spread of the gospel to those lands. In turn, the development of American global influence and expansion which began in the early 1800s was strongly tied to the planting of Union or American churches from Europe to Latin America, Asia, Africa and points in between. Finally, the onset of globalization in modern times coincided with the rise to prominence of the American evangelical churches and their expanded missionary outreach globally which included the planting of hundreds of new, English-language, expat churches.

---

[2] While this book focuses on the various Protestant international churches around the world, it should be noted that hundreds if not thousands of English-language Roman Catholic masses are held regularly in local vernacular churches, seminaries or other Catholic institutions in all parts of the inhabited world. The location of these congregations and other Roman Catholic organizations and institutions can be found at https://www.catholicdirectory.com/maps.

Third, as I have been blessed to serve a number of ICs around the world and to attend several international gatherings of pastors, I have noted that many pastors are unaware of the history of this style of ministry. Too often they do not know that they share their work with other similar churches in the very communities where they labor.

Finally, as the baton is passed to a new generation of IC members and pastors, it is obvious that most are unaware of the length, width and depth of these ministries. As my generation retires and dies out this rich history will, I'm afraid, be lost, ignored and lose what it has to teach to those who labor in the expat field in the generations to come.

Several years ago I vowed that I would never write another book. Not that writing is that difficult—it comes rather easily to me. It's the publishing and distribution of books that is a difficult task (what I call a "royal pain" in my more private moments) and I really didn't want to go through it again.

Then, two events occurred almost simultaneously.

The first was the privilege of helping two men much younger than I explore the possibility of serving an IC. One accepted a call to serve an international church in Central America, the other who was living in Hong Kong and doing seminary work online, responded to my suggestion that he look into ICs by asking for information. It was refreshing and fulfilling to know that a new generation is stepping forward to continue and move the ministry of international congregations into the future.

The second was the opportunity to personally see the continued outreach of the three main streams of IC establishment while on a five week trip to Asia. On that journey my wife and I were able to visit buildings that once held vibrant Union Churches in cities throughout China and which now maintain a silent witness to those who served, worshipped and ministered there. In addition, we were privileged to worship in an historic English-language, Anglican church still serving one of Asia's dynamic cities. And, we were able to also visit new, vibrant ICs ministering to today's young expats in some of those same cities.

As will be explained more fully in the next section, three streams of IC development mark the worldwide expansion of English-language expat churches.

The first, the Scottish/British/Anglican stream, began over 400 years before this book was written, and has seen the planting of hundreds of English, Presbyterian and Anglican churches not only in British Commonwealth countries, but in numerous nations around the world.

In Hong Kong, we worshipped in the historic St. Andrew Anglican Church, the oldest English-language church in the Kowloon district of the island. The church's website reports that *While St Andrew's commenced its life as a church for the expatriate community, it is now an international church with 90% of those attending considering Hong Kong as their home.*

The idea of building an Anglican church in Kowloon was first suggested in 1897 but no progress was made until 1904, when Sir Catchick Paul Chater offered HK$35,000 to finance the construction. The chosen site was next to a large garden area owned by Sir Paul, covering the area between Robinson Road (now Nathan Road) and Austin Road.

The church was designed by Alfred Bryer of Messrs. Leigh & Orange. Work began in November 1904, and was completed in 1906. The church was consecrated on 6 October 1906.

The war years since 1914 had been difficult for the church, many of the early congregation having come from the military bases on Kowloon, so had left for duty elsewhere, and the church was barely able to make its way financially.

From 1942 to 1944, the congregation of All Saints Mong Kok used St Andrew's for services as their church was used as a rice store. They were allowed back to All Saints in late 1944, and took much of the furniture from St Andrew's with them, saving it from destruction when the main church building was turned into a Shinto shrine early in 1945.

Wikipedia contributors, "St Andrew's Church, Kowloon," *Wikipedia, The Free Encyclopedia,* https://en.wikipedia.org/w/index.php?title=St_Andrew%27s_Church,_Kowloon&oldid=918163401 (accessed January 25, 2020).

Later on that trip, we ran across the Union Church on the Chinese island of Xiamen, formerly known as Amoy. This was not the only Union Church that we heard of in China but was the only one we were able to visit. Dr. Bill Brown, an American who teaches at Xiamen University wrote to me about this church that was planted in the American/Union Church era which began in the early 1800s.

Union Church was given that name because it was built by foreigners of several denominations living on Gulangyu so they (and English speaking locals) could worship together. Before this church, built in 1863, they had to take the dangerous ferry across the harbor to Xinjie Church (China's first Protestant Church, 1848) or the Bamboo Church.

The Amoy Mission, unlike other missions in China, was composed of three denominations whose missionaries cooperated rather than competed (the denominational home offices fought it, and sent some home, but in the end accepted this). The Amoy Mission, in the 1850s, was also the source of the "three self" Chinese church principles adopted by the Communists in 1949.

In the 1930s, on Gulangyu was built Trinity Church (the Holy Trinity, but also, again, symbolizing by some the union of three denominations).

Union Church is not used for "worship" today but the local government and a wealthy Christian rebuilt it and it is used for weddings, music concerts, etc. The government allowed it to be used for services but local Chinese Christians opposed opening another church (because attendance has fallen in the other churches on the islet, largely due to its isolation from Xiamen Island).

The government spent about 4 million Yuan in helping to renovate it. Gulangyu was designated a UNESCO World Heritage Site status in 2017, and Union Church is an important part of that heritage.[3]

We also visited two churches that fall into the third stream of ICs which have been planted in recent decades by the new American evangelical movement. Those were the large International Christian Assembly (ICA) in Hong Kong which was started by the Assemblies of God and the Guanghou International Christian Fellowship in China itself. This new congregation fills a large hotel ballroom each Sunday with worshippers from around the world.

The Guanghou church describes itself this way: *GICF is a group of expatriate Christians living in Guangzhou who meet together regularly. Our mission is to serve English-speaking expatriates by providing a stable environment for fellowship, worship, Bible teaching, mutual encouragement, and personal spiritual nourishment and growth. We also provide people with an opportunity to contribute to the community and help each other live effectively as foreigners in China. (http://www.gicf.net/mission-statement)*

Similarly, ICA in Hong Kong provides this description: *We are a Glocal Church. We act locally and impact globally. Yes, it's a new kind of Church.*

We are A CHURCH THAT CARES to embrace all people, regardless of age, gender, class, countries, cultures and creed

---

[3] Much of the above information came in a personal letter to the author from Dr. Brown. Rev. John Abraham Otte was a Dutch missionary and medical doctor. The Island was the site of 13 foreign consulates, thus an ideal place to form an international Union Church.

because JESUS loves all people. We choose each other as friends and family and we strive to love Jesus more perfectly as a Community.

We are a House with many rooms. People from different places worshiping in their language. People of different age and life stages with different worship styles growing and serving together. Even though we are many nations and generations yet we are ONE Church. (http://www.icahk.org/our-vision)

Visiting these churches took us through an historic sweep of 400 years, demonstrating the impact and influence that these churches have had around the world and the importance of their ministries. We will explore how these came about and developed in the rest of this history.

A brief note: Writing a history of any kind is daunting when the author is neither an historian nor an academic. In fact, I am a practitioner more than anything. As a pastor, a missionary, a teacher, I have been involved with ministering to congregations and individuals, helping churches to grow and care for people. Knowing how to write a history is beyond my scope.

I trust that in telling the story of ICs as I have known them will help others to catch the vision of what they are about and to appreciate how they have not only been centers of ministry to expat and third-culture communities, but have also been facilitators, trainers, teachers and evangelists, sending people back to their home countries in all parts of the world as better trained, experienced evangelists and pastors.

History

If one desires to pinpoint where and when the first international church was founded, he/she is going to be very disappointed. Such a task is impossible and such a search would be fruitless, disappointing and totally frustrating.

No such record exists in that early attempts were most likely individual, localized efforts to form a fellowship among expats in some distant seaport or inland station far from a home country and without the support of clergy or a denominational structure.

Even today there exist many small living room groups which gather on a Sunday morning or evening for the singing of hymns, the reading of Scripture, a time of prayer, and a biblical interpretation or sermon presented by someone in the room or a pastor far away whose presentation is downloaded on an electronic device.

If one considers those informal gatherings along with the historic Anglican, Presbyterian and Union churches and today's new wave of evangelical international congregations as part of the stream, then the history goes back over 450 years.

That stream not only began with informal fellowships gathered on the front porch of a missionary home but also includes Scottish Presbyterian churches, such as that formed in Geneva in 1556 or in Amsterdam in 1607, British Anglican chaplaincies in places such as India as early as 1608 (and perhaps earlier in other locations) along with the later wave of Union churches planted primarily by U.S. missionaries, church groups or individuals which began in the early 1800s.

The development of ICs as chaplaincies and later more institutional English-language expat churches can be roughly divided into several streams or eras, some of which overlap but which, nevertheless, show the progression of these congregations over four-plus centuries.

And, just as the various colorful streams of a great river such as the Amazon flow side by side for hundreds of miles until they finally merge into one, the streams that we will read about in this book continue to maintain their individual distinctions. They also exhibit many common characteristics and third-culture nature that make them have more in common than their denominational or ecclesiastical backgrounds might indicate.

So, let us begin with the earliest streams, those of the British Anglicans and Scottish Presbyterians and move forward through the Union/International churches to those contemporary evangelical expressions which are shaping this unique ministry today.

We will follow this outline as we begin our examination:

History
British colonial era, Presbyterian and Anglican ICs 1556-1991
American colonial era and Union Churches 1816-1991
- **Serving colonial enclaves 1816-1940**
- **Interrupted by war 1940-1945**
- **Postwar Expansion 1945-1991**
- **International Congregations era 1970-1991**
- **The Baptist sub-stream**

Globalization and Evangelical era 1991-present[4]

---

[4] It should be noted that many historical documents plus material from congregations in many parts of the world are used in this book. The original spelling and name presentations are maintained whether from British or American English or representing a change of spelling in modern time—i.e., for example, Tokyo for what, in earlier times, was spelled Tokio.

Scottish Presbyterians, the British colonial era and Anglican ICs 1600-1991 –The First Stream

Scottish Presbyterians

The Church of Scotland grew out of the Protestant Reformation, which took place in the 16th century. At that time, people in many countries across Europe began to claim:

- *The freedom to read and respond to the Bible for themselves*
- *The freedom to have a direct relationship with God, without the mediation of a priest or the church authority*
- *The freedom to set their own consciences against the demands of religious institutions.*

In Scotland, the influence of Martin Luther and John Calvin gave rise to the Scottish Reformation which was led by, among others, John Knox. Throughout the 17th century, this developed into the Presbyterian system of government.

Over the years, Presbyterianism found its way to all parts of the world where Scots settled and took their distinctive form of worship and church government. In Bermuda, the first religious service conducted on the island after settlement was recorded as being conducted in the Presbyterian tradition.

The work of Scottish missionaries and expats resulted in the establishment of vibrant Presbyterian churches in Africa, India and the West Indies. Today, a number of them continue with similar characteristics of other international, English-language congregations. **https://tinyurl.com/y3gppyul**

Of particular interest is the International Presbytery (a governing body) which consists of fourteen English-language, Presbyterian churches in mainland Europe (Geneva, Paris, Amsterdam, Rotterdam, Lisbon, Rome, Lausanne, Costa Del Sol (Spain), Brussels, Budapest, Regensburg, Bochum, Malta, and Gibraltar along with Warwick, Bermuda and Colombo in Sri Lanka.)

Within that presbytery, English language, expat ministry is traceable back to at least 1556 when the Auditoire de Calvin was where the Church of Scotland in Geneva worshiped.

It is built on a site where Christian worship has taken place since at least the 5th century. At the time of the Reformation, John Calvin gave his famous lectures there, and at his suggestion the building was made available for worship by the English and Italian speaking refugees. John Knox ministered to the English speaking congregation between 1556 and 1558. The form of worship and church government that was developed there at that time became a model for Presbyterian Churches throughout the world. **https://tinyurl.com/lplnc2o**

Other early English-language, Scottish, Presbyterian churches were formed in Amsterdam in 1607, Rotterdam in 1643, Bermuda in 1719 and Colombo (Sri Lanka) in 1842.

The Amsterdam church boasts a long history and some early well-known parishioners:

Our congregation has flourished over the years, keeping English worship in the heart of Amsterdam since 1607, except for a short period during German occupation in the Second World War. The English Reformed Church was set up under the Reformed Church in the Netherlands, always with English and Scottish ministers. In the middle of the eighteenth century, the congregation established ties with Scotland; since then the minister has always come from Scotland.

The congregation is now fully part of the Church of Scotland in the Presbytery of Europe. At its twice yearly meetings the Presbytery is attended by representatives of the twelve Church of Scotland European congregations. The congregation is also represented by an elder at the Amsterdam Classis of the Netherlands Reformed Church.

We are a growing congregation of almost 400 members, and continue to reflect the international nature of Amsterdam and the world of the Christian Church. The Consistory which guides the congregation usually consists of twelve members, both deacons and elders, who represent the breadth of the congregation in age and background.

The Church Building

The first church in the Begijnhof was built as a private chapel in about 1390; it was destroyed by fire and rebuilt in the 1490s. The church was closed by the Town Council in the Reformation and lay unused for 20 years till in 1607 it was given to English-speaking worshippers in Amsterdam.

"Tomorrow morning I am going to the English church; it lies there so peaceful in the evening in that silent Begijnhof among the thorn hedges, and seems to say: In loco isto dabo pacem: In this place I shall give peace, says the Lord. Amen, so be it."– ***Vincent van Gogh***

The Congregation of the English Reformed Church has owned the building since 1607 – over 400 years! We are privileged to be the guardians of such history, welcoming a diverse range of people every week. We try and keep the church open as much as possible to enable as many people as possible the chance to see our church and experience the peace that Van Gogh wrote about. http://www.ercadam.nl/about-us/history/

The Church of Scotland in Bermuda - Founded in 1719

Another early international church planted by the Church of Scotland is Christ Church in Bermuda. From its online history we learn that *Christ Church is English in origin, taking its life from the English Puritans who colonized Bermuda in the early 17th century. Although there is evidence of much earlier association with the Church in Scotland, and preference had always been shown for Scottish ministers, it was not until 1843 that the congregation took steps to become part of the Free Church of Scotland. In 1929 Christ Church, which had been with the United Free Church of Scotland since 1900, became* *a part of the Church of Scotland, formalizing its relationship as a full member in 2001. Christ Church was built in 1719 on land given by Thomas Gilbert of the Warwick Tribe. Additions and alterations have been made but the original walls remain. In 1837, the height of the walls was increased, a new roof was constructed, larger windows were put in and the tower built. After a similar lapse of time the Church was again reconstructed in 1958. Of the three galleries, only the North remains. These were occupied at different times by the choir. During the first reconstruction the congregations worshipped at Belmont, then occupied by their minister....As the walls of the original Meeting House still stand, Christ Church has the honour of an unbroken Presbyterian descent from the earliest settlers who first set foot on the Islands.* **https://tinyurl.com/yxqst2yf**

British Anglicans

As with the early history of other international churches, the origin of Anglican work is in obscurity.

One early congregation was St Andrew's Anglican Church in Moscow. It continues the tradition of Anglican worship that started in 1553 when Tsar Ivan the Terrible first permitted the English merchants of the Russia Company permission to worship according to their own beliefs.

In the book, A History of the Church of England in *A History of the Church of England in India Since the Early Days of the East India Company* by Eyre Chatterton, Bishop of Nagpur, we read about some of the chaplains and their early work which eventually was institutionalized by the opening of Anglican churches in colonial situations such as India:

And now for a word or two about the part which the Chaplain played in the life of this strange community.

"The Chaplain," we read, "was a prominent figure in Factory life. He received £100 a year, with diet and convenient lodgings, a peon to attend him in his chamber, and the command

of a coach or horse at any time he thinks fit to use them, besides many private gifts from merchants and masters of ships, who seldom fail of some valuable oblation to him, or rarity of the place they come from, and the noble large gratuities which he constantly receives for officiating at Marriages, Baptisms, and Burials." He did not, however, live an idle life. "The Minister is obliged to a public dis- course once, and public prayers thrice on Sunday, and to read prayers morning and evening in the Chapel each other day in the week, viz. about six in the morning before the factors are called forth to business, and at eight at night, when all is past. He is engaged to catechise all the youth; to visit the subordinate Factories upon the coast of Malabar, at Carwar, Calicut, etc., and to give instructions for their administration of Divine Service in his absence." The Chapel where they meet at prayers is within the Factory, "decently embellished so as to render it both neat and solemn, without the figure of any living creature in it for avoiding all occasion of offence to the Moors, who are well pleased with the innocence of our worship." "For want of a Minister qualified for the administration of Baptism among the Dutch at Surat, they request that favour from the English, who performs it for them in their Chapel, which at first sight might be very, well taken for a guard-chamber, because they keep arms in it."

We owe to Penny, in his Church in Madras, some interesting information regarding the early Chaplains in Surat. The earliest Chaplain, he tells us, who was appointed by the Directors of the East India Company, was "one the Rev. William Leske. The Directors were well satisfied by his learning and gravity, and of his being able to contest with and hold argument with Jesuits who were then busy at Surat." He went to Surat in 1614, and stayed there for three years. Sir Thomas Roe writes of him an appreciative letter in 1616, but unfortunately later on he was relieved of his charge for unworthy conduct.

It is obvious that the atmosphere of the Factory, where everyone was absorbed in money-making, can hardly have made the task of a Chaplain particularly easy.

Great importance was attached, and naturally, to the possession of a good and equable temper on the part of their Chaplain. One can easily imagine that in the trying Indian climate, with a large body of men living together in this huge "Chummery," and especially over their evening wine-cups, there must have been frequent occasions for irritation and loss of temper, and it was above all things desirable that the Padre should be a man of peace. One reads of more than one instance of Chaplains failing in this respect.

Arnold Wright speaks sympathetically of the troubles which befell the famous Commander Downton at the hands of "a turbulent cleric named the Reverend Peter Rogers," whom he describes (we fancy mistakenly) as the first Chaplain who came to India. It is not altogether easy to decide from Wright's account, which seems unduly biassed in Downton's favour, what exactly Rogers' special faults were beyond the fact that he wrote a strong letter to the Company, speaking of Downton's "old soaked humour," "of his inveterate hatred and continuence where he once takes dislike," and of the fact that "the General is not the man you take him to be touching religion: he always ill-treats his Ministers; he neglects prayer on the week days, and very often on the Sabbath the exercises of religion to the great offence and discouragement of many. He is much given to backbiting, and he has answered my fatherly remonstrances by saying scornfully that he could tell his duty better than I could advise him, and such-like demonstrances of pride and hypocrisy."

Of one Chaplain who stayed eight years in the East, and died on his voyage home, part of which time was spent at Surat, the factors wrote to the Company on his departure in the following terms:--

"Lastly, Mr. Rund, our preacher, is the conclusive passenger of note who hath lovingly this last Sabbath included us in

his hearty prayers." "He hath lived among us peacefully without any touch of spleen or faction. His function he hath ever observed conformably and his life no way deserving public reproach, though not free from imbecilities, as in all of us might be wished a bettering."

In 1617 the Company engaged the Rev. Thomas Friday, M.A., Emmanuel College, Cambridge, as Chaplain for their Factory at Surat. After serving six years in India, he returned to England in 1623. The glamour of the East had clearly laid hold of him, for he returned to India in 1624, and died in Surat six years later. He is referred to in the Court Minutes of the Directors as one "Who came home with a good reputation--only some small touch of private trade."

Mr. Friday writes in 1625 to the Company, dwelling on the jealousy between the Dutch, Portuguese, and English who were contending for the trade of the East, and deploring the extreme measures they adopted towards one another in the Eastern seas in consequence of that jealousy. Of the Dutch, Terry the Chaplain also wrote as follows:--

"This I can say of the Dutch, that when I lived in those parts and we English there were more for the number than they and consequently could receive no hurt from them, we then used them as neighbours and brethren; but in other places, where they had the like advantage of us, they dealt with us neither like Christians nor men."

Of the Rev. Henry Goulding, another of the early Surat Chaplains, we know but little, save that his family had considerable landed property in Essex, and that before coming to India he was private Chaplain to a nobleman. He was certainly not a favourite in Surat, for the factors in their home letter, 1618, describe him as "the gentlewomen's Chaplain," and added that "so long as the Company choose preachers recommended by noblemen's letters, how can they expect to be served better?"'

Arnold Wright tells a story of him, how that "when a request which he had preferred to accompany Mrs. Hawkins and her English maid, the wife of Richard Steele, to Ahmedabad had been refused, he disguised himself in Moor's apparel and surreptitiously joined the ship in which the ladies were sailing."

One of the best known of these early Indian Chaplains was the Rev. Patrick Copeland, who made several voyages to India between 1612 and 1619. He seems to have been deeply imbued with a Missionary spirit, and is referred to in the Court Minutes as "that worthy preacher" and as "a sober discreet man." Copeland made very genuine endeavours while in the service of the Company to bring about a better feeling between the English and the Dutch, and even expostulated with the Dutch for their unfriendliness as well as for their jealousy of the English merchants. He reminded them of the assistance given to them by the English against the Spaniards at home, and added, "Now you are free from the Spaniard at home you fall out with your friends abroad."

He also was bold enough to blame the English Commanders for quarrelling with the Dutch, and preached a sermon on one of the Company's ships which caused the Commander to complain that the effect of his preaching was to imperil the fighting spirit of his crew. This charge was duly examined in London, and Copeland had to appear before the Court of Directors in Leadenhall Street. The plain fact was that any endeavour to stop the quarrels and jealousies existing between the Dutch and the English at that time was almost useless and most unpopular. The brutal murder, after torture, of a body of English sailors at Amboyna, the chief of the Spice Islands in the Dutch East Indies, by the Dutch Governor Van Speult, left such an impression of the Dutchman's callous cruelty that it took generations to efface it. The Directors were obviously on the side of the Commander, for, while acknowledging the goodness of Cope-land's intentions, they would not offer him another appointment.

During one of his voyages to India, Copeland had met with an Indian boy in Bengal whom he prepared for baptism. This boy was brought by him to England, but before baptising him he felt it right to ask for permission from the Directors of the London Company. The Court referred "this weighty matter" to no less a person than the Archbishop of Canterbury, who after due consideration gave it as his opinion that there was no reason why the Indian boy should not be baptised. King James I. was therefore asked to name the child and gave him the name of Peter. Peter was duly baptised on December 2, 1616, in one of the old City Churches, in the presence of some members of the Privy Council, the Lord Mayor and Aldermen of London and certain members of the East India Company. He was baptised by the simple name of Peter, but later on seems to have adopted the surname of Pope.

Of another of the Surat Chaplains, the Rev. Thomas Fuller, B.A., Pembroke College, Cambridge, 1612, we read that he was sent to Suwali, a small Factory close to Surat, on the Bombay coast. The Chief of the Factory had a high opinion of him, as is evident from the fact that he informed the Company that "Mr. Fuller supplied his room with the goodwill of all men," and added, "we would have kept him, but he was not very willing to stay; we are bold to entreat in his behalf, if he is willing to come back; his doctrine and life being so exemplary as we doubt of his like." In another letter of the same year they say, "Mr. Fuller our Minister has at last been persuaded to stay. We doubt not a man of his quality and demeanour will draw a blessing upon our labours surpassing the Company's charge by his detention."

Of other of the Chaplains of that early period it is to be regretted that we do not have so favourable an account. One of the Chaplains who had matriculated at Trinity College, Oxford, and had been sent to one of the Factories in Persia, was rebuked by the Chief Agent at Ispahan for dice-playing, and is referred to when writing to the Company, as "their criminal Minister, who with their critical agent Monnox and their infernal physician Strachan formed a triple conspiracy against merchantly carriage and good manners."

Of another of the Chaplains, the Rev. George Collins, who remained four years in Ispahan, the Company's Agent wrote:-- "His country travels have quite disheartened him for any longer residence, therefore he is departing, he supposes, to seek a place of more ease; not that we do not desire the conversation of an upright man that might guide us in the true way, but do not much sorrow for his miss, we have more addo to accommodate these Ministers to their desires than most the factors besides; they are so troublesome. The two that have been here in Gibson's time the tenderest chickens we ever met; and unless hereafter they are hardier, to be plain, we had rather have their room than their company."

It must have been a most difficult matter for the Directors of the Company to find the sort of Clergy suitable for the peculiar life which Englishmen had to live in India in those days. It is clear that in early days long intervals elapsed before Chaplains were appointed to fill vacancies caused by death in a country where the uncertainties of life were very great. As time went on, however, the authorities in London realised more fully the importance of the work of their Chaplains, and even appealed to the English Universities to help them in their quest for the best men.

Of the Clergy who came East some were doubtless animated by the same high motives which impelled the best men at home to enter the sacred

ministry of the Church. A few, too, were men of a scholarly type like Terry, Henry Lord, and Samuel Crook, a distinguished Fellow of Emmanuel College, Cambridge, who came East to pursue his Oriental studies. Some were of an adventurous type, prepared to run risks to see the wonders of the gorgeous East; but of others it would seem they belonged to that type of persons for whom life at home had no great attractions, and who shared the same worldly hopes as the factors to whom they ministered of shaking the pagoda tree and returning to their own native land to enjoy its fruits. **https://tinyurl.com/y4cckpxg**

While many chaplaincies undoubtedly became established English-language churches serving the British expat community, it may have taken several years for them to develop into a formal church.

The first English-language church in India was established by the Anglicans on the *"28th day of October 1680, St. Simon and St. Jude's Day, all the English inhabitants in Madras met in the new Church for the solemn event of its consecration. It was a great day in the Settlement, especially for the President, through whose faith and courage many difficulties had been overcome with regard to the erection as well as the consecration of the building.*

Shortly after this notable event Streynsham Master resigned his Presidentship owing to differences of opinion with Sir Josiah Child, who was then all-powerful with the Court of Directors in London. Later on he joined the new Company, to the serious loss of the old.

St. Mary's was not by any means the first Christian Church in India, as the Roman Catholics as

well as the Dutch Reformed had built Churches in their Settlements long before. It was, however, the first English Church in India, and it had the effect of making both Bombay and Calcutta follow its lead. Needless to say, St. Mary's is from every point of view, especially in its old monuments, one of the most interesting of our Churches in India. **https://tinyurl.com/y49v5hcb**

(It should be noted that other resources, such as Wikipedia, indicate that *from 1639, when Madras* was founded, until 1678, when *Streynsham Master* was appointed the *English East India Company's Agent at Madras, religious services were conducted in the dining-room of the Factory House. It was at Master's initiative, and without the sanction of the Directors of the Company, that a subscription was started for the construction of the church.*

The sum collected amounted to 805 pagodas with the Governor and other officers contributing. Construction was started on 25 March 1678 - *Lady Day, whereby the church acquired its name. The church was rendered the only bomb-proof building at the time, in the Fort, on account of a peculiarly designed roof.*

Construction was completed in the course of two years and the church was consecrated on 28 October 1680 by the chaplain Rev. Richard Portman. The ceremony was marked by the firing of small arms and cannon by the fort's garrison. **https://tinyurl.com/y53xftu7**)

The British East India Company entered India around 1600 AD for trading and Chennai was one of the earliest places of British occupancy in India. Fort St. George was constructed by the British in the year 1644. The fort also houses the secretariat of the Tamil Nadu state government. Besides the secretariat building there are various other offices, and the holy church revered by millions, St. Mary's Church. The St. Mary's Church, also called as the 'Westminster Abbey of the East', has its own importance. It is one of the ancient buildings of Chennai and also it is the first Anglican Church in Asia. It is also considered as the oldest Anglican Church east of Suez and has been named as St. Mary because its origin was laid down on the Annunciation day of the Virgin Mary. It is believed that on this divine day, the heavenly declaration of Jesus' birth had been announced to Mother Mary.

St. Mary's Church was constructed in 1678-1680 AD by the British East India Company. This historically very significant church has an old prayer house inside it that solemnized the marriages of important figures of East India Company like Robert Clive and Elihu Yale (Co-founder of Yale University in USA). The old church is full of commemorative inscriptions and memorials that date back to early 17th century. Baptism started to take place since 1680 and beautiful statuette adorned the fine walls of this church. The most special feature of the church is the high tower that is visible from a long distance. This tower was not part of the original structure and was rather added at the end of the seventeenth century on the orders of Sir John Goldsborough.

The church was originally built by William Dixon and designed by Edward Fowle. It is a bomb-proofed carved structure, which has the finishing touch of polished lime. The building of St. Mary's church had some later additions like the Sanctuary, Steeple, Tower and the Vestry. Colonel Gent added the church top in 1795. The interior of the church is embellished with the wooden and glass furnishings. You are bound to be overwhelmed by the intricate painting of the Last Supper, which is drawn by an unknown artist. Also, under the church's possession, are a 1660 Bible and also silver plates of the time. **https://tinyurl.com/y6h966nm**

The history of the Anglican Communion may be attributed mainly to the worldwide spread of British culture associated with the British Empire. Among other things the Church of England spread around the world and, gradually developing autonomy in each region, became the communion as it exists today.

The history of the Russia Company begins in 1553, when a *group of Londoners, said to number 240, financed an expedition to discover the north-east passage to Cathay. The expedition had mixed motives. It hoped to copy the success of the Spanish and Portuguese in discovering new markets, and especially that of the Portuguese in bringing gold and spices from the East Indies. It also hoped to discover new markets for the export of English cloth, a trade then in decline. The north-east passage was important because it would be free of Portuguese interference. Either way, the voyage failed in its original purpose, for the crews of two of the three ships froze to death during the northern winter. However the third ship, the Edward Bonaventure, under the command of Richard Chancellor, found safe anchorage in the mouth of the Dvina. Chancellor was then invited to Moscow, where Tsar Ivan IV agreed to allow English merchants to come and trade. The voyage thus led to the establishment of direct trade with all the Russias.*

The Russia Company was formally incorporated by royal charter on 26th February 1555 as the 'marchants adventurers of England, for the discovery of lands, territories, iles, dominions, and seigniories unknowen, and not before that late adventure or enterprise by sea or navigation, commonly frequented'. The Company quickly became known as the Russia Company, or Muscovy Company, or Company of Merchants Trading with Russia. The charter gave the Company a legal and corporate basis for its activities, and a monopoly. Ivan IV also granted privileges to the Company before the end of 1555, although their precise nature is disputed. However in practice the Company's monopoly of English trade with Russia included the rights to trade without paying customs duties or tolls, and to trade in the interior. The Company's principal imports from Russia were furs, tallow, wax, timber, flax, tar and hemp. Its principal export to Russia was English cloth.

The Company in London appointed agents or 'factors' in Russia, hence the term 'British Factory' for the group of British agents. The headquarters of the Factory until 1717 was Moscow, when it removed to Archangel. In 1723 the Factory moved again, this time by Imperial decree, to St Petersburg. The Company also appointed a chaplain to the Factory in Russia, and he naturally moved with the Factory, although he continued to visit Moscow to minister to British residents. With the expansion of trade in the 19th century, the number of trading posts maintained by the Company grew to include Archangel, Cronstadt, Moscow and St Petersburg. So too did the number of chaplains.

Since 1917 the Russia Company has operated principally as a charity and has given grants to English chaplaincies working within Russia. Several members of the current Court are direct descendants of families which traded in the British Factory in St Petersburg.

The early records of the Russia Company perished in the Great Fire of London in 1666. However the surviving material, including minutes of the Court of the Company from 1666, is now deposited at Guildhall Library, and available for research by the public without prior formality.

For further details, see T. S. Willan, *The Muscovy Merchants of 1555* (Manchester University Press, 1953); T. S. Willan, *The Early History of the Russia Company, 1553-1603* (Manchester University Press, 1956); and A. G. Cross, "Chaplains to the British Factory in St Petersburg, 1723-1813", *European Studies Review 2*, no 2 (1972), pp125-142. Copies of all of these are available at Guildhall Library in London, England.

The English Church in Moscow

The Russia Company was the patron of Anglican churches in Moscow, St Petersburg, Cronstadt and Archangel.

In 1825 a chapel was opened in Princess Prozorowski's house, and known as the British Chapel, Moscow. A chaplain was also appointed. Land for a permanent church was purchased in 1829, and a building completed at the beginning of 1830. In January 1885 a new church was consecrated, whose official designation was now the British Church of St Andrew, Moscow. The chaplain was appointed by the Russia Company, subject to approval by the subscribers to the chaplaincy. The Company also paid part of the costs. **https://tinyurl.com/y2e3fajq**

Embassy and Independent Churches

The British merchants (or British factory) in Russia and the Russian Company in London provided chaplains of the church of England for British factors in St. Petersburg where a church was built in 1754. The church served the British population and also served as an embassy church. By the mid-nineteenth century, the Church of England also had congregations in Moscow, Kronstadt, Archangelsk, and Riga. Busch claimed in 1862 that the Anglican congregation in St. Petersburg numbered 2,700....

In 1816 a Congregational Church or the English and American was formed around John Patterson, an agent of the British and Foreign Bible Society who also served the Russian Bible Society.

On the Edge: Baptists and Other Free Church Evangelicals in Tsarist Russia, By Albert W. Wardin, Page 16

The first Anglican service in North America was conducted in California in 1579 by the chaplain accompanying Sir Francis Drake on his voyage around the globe. The first baptisms were held in Roanoke, North Carolina, by the ill-fated Roanoke colony. The continuous presence of Anglicanism in North America, however, begins in 1607 with the founding of Jamestown, Virginia. By 1700 there were more than 100 Anglican parishes in British colonies on the mainland of North America, the largest number in Virginia and Maryland. The American War for Independence resulted in the formation of the first independent national church in the Anglican tradition.

The 1609 wreck of the flagship of the Virginia Company, the Sea Venture, resulted in the settlement of Bermuda by the Company. This was made official in 1612 when the town of St. George's, now the oldest surviving English settlement in the New World, was established. It is the location of St. Peter's Church, the oldest-surviving Anglican church outside of the British Isles (Britain and Ireland) and the oldest surviving non-Roman Catholic church in the New World, also established in 1612. It remained part of the Church of England until 1978 when the Anglican Church of Bermuda was formed. The Church of England was the state church in Bermuda and a system of parishes was set up for the religious and political subdivision of the colony (they survive, today, as both civil and religious parishes).

Throughout the 18th and 19th centuries the British Empire expanded around the world, and everywhere it went the Anglican Church could be found. The first Anglican Church in the United States was formed in the Jamestown colony of Virginia in 1607. http://staugustinehollister.org/index.php/history/

The parish of St. John the Baptist in the city of *St. John's, Newfoundland* (part of the *Diocese of Eastern Newfoundland and Labrador) is the oldest in Canada, founded in 1699 in response to a petition drafted by the Anglican* townsfolk of St. John›s and sent to the *Bishop of London, Henry Compton. In this petition the people also requested help in the rebuilding of their church, which had been destroyed, along with the rest of the city, in 1696 by the French* under the command of General *Pierre Le Moyne d'Iberville.*

On August 12, 1787, Charles Inglis was consecrated Bishop of Nova Scotia with jurisdiction over all the British possessions in North America.

In 1793 the see of Quebec was founded; Jamaica and Barbados followed in 1824 and in Toronto and Newfoundland in 1839. Meanwhile, the needs of India were met, on the urgent representations in Parliament of William Wilberforce and others, by the consecration of William Wilberforce and others, by the consecration of T.F. Middleton as Bishop of Calcutta with three archdeacons to assist him. In 1829, on the nomination of the Duke of Wellington, William Broughton was sent out to work as the Archdeacon of Australia. The first Anglican church in Latin America, St. John's Cathedral (Belize City), was built in the colony of British Honduras (Belize) in 1812.

Soon afterwards, in 1835 and 1837, the sees of Madras and *Bombay* were founded; whilst in 1836 *Broughton himself was consecrated as the first Bishop of Australia. Thus down to 1840 there were but ten colonial bishops; and of these several were so hampered by civil regulations that they were little more than government chaplains in episcopal orders. In April of that year, however, Bishop Blomfield of London published his famous letter to the Archbishop of Canterbury, declaring that "an episcopal church without a bishop is a contradiction in terms" and strenuously advocating a great effort for the extension of the episcopate.* **Wikipedia**

The first Anglican clergy to minister regularly at the Cape (South Africa) were military chaplains who accompanied the troops when the British occupied the Cape Colony in 1795 and then again in 1806. The second British occupation resulted in a growing influx of civil servants and settlers who were members of the Church of England, and so civil or colonial chaplains were appointed to minister to their needs. These were under the authority of the governor.

The first missionary of the Society for the Propagation of the Gospel arrived in 1821. He was William Wright, a priest. He opened a church and school in Wynberg, a fashionable suburb of Cape Town. Allen Gardiner, a missionary of the Church Missionary Society went to Zululand, and arranged for a priest, Francis Owen, to be sent to the royal residence of King Dingane. Owen witnessed the massacre of Piet Retief, the Voortrekker leader, and his companions, who had come to negotiate a land treaty with Dingane, and left soon afterwards.

The Anglican Church in Southern Africa at this time was under the Diocese of Calcutta, which effectively included the East Indies and the entire Southern Hemisphere. Bishops en route for Calcutta sometimes stopped at the Cape for confirmations, and occasionally ordination of clergy, but these visits wee sporadic. It became apparent that a bishop was needs for South Africa, and in 1847Robert Gray was consecrated as the first Bishop of Cape town in Westminster Abbey. The new bishop landed in Cape Town in 1848.

Intercontinental Church Society (from 1979) Church-planting

Europe experienced a new wave of immigration from all over the world which paralleled the creation of the EEC (later European Union), and then followed a period of new church-planting by some long-standing chaplaincies which both drew people abroad and caught the eye of people at home. We can identify the following: Tervuren by Brussels (1988), Liege by Tervuren (1992), Heiloo (1990) and Den Helder (1998) by Amsterdam, Amersdoort, Harderwijk and Zwolle by Utrecht, Versailles from Maisons-Laffitte, Gif-sur-Yvette from Versailles, Freiburg-im-Breisgau from Basel (2001) and Sharjah and Jebel Ali by Dubai.

1990s onward *The Society was directly involved in the establishing of: Ayia Napa (Cyprus 1993), Leipzig (1995). Warsaw (1996) and Gdansk (1999), Nord (Pas-de-Calais based in Lille 1998), Kyiv (Ukraine 1999), Prague (an Anglican church in an Old Catholic diocese -ecumenical project (2000), Klaipeda (Lithuania 2000), Poitou-Charentes (6 rural centres 1999), Brittany (rural based on Ploermel and two other centres 2000).*

Success could be noted where chaplains were visionary and entrepreneurial, sensitive to accessible worship styles, good Bible teachers with a heart for people and gentle evangelists.
https://tinyurl.com/yyduroh9

Other Anglican IC churches came about somewhat individually as British business people, educators and others settled in select locations and began their own congregation to serve British expatriates and/or local English-speaking communities.

A prime example is the historic Christ Church By-The-Sea in Colon, on the Atlantic entrance to the Panama Canal. The church was built in 1864 by the Panama Railroad, together with some private gifts at Aspinwall, Colombia, later known as Colon in the Republic of Panama. The building was consecrated on June 15, 1865 as the last official act of the Right Reverend Alonzo Potter, the Bishop of Pennsylvania who died aboard a ship in San Francisco in 1865.

Christ Church is the second oldest non-Roman Church in Central America, the oldest being the Anglican Cathedral in Belize built from 1812 to 1820 with bricks that had been used as ballast aboard ships, it was the first church to be built in the colony of British Honduras. https://www.ics-uk.org/

American colonial era and Union Churches-- The Second Stream 1816-1991

We have identified the development of international, English language churches as consisting of three streams:

1. the Scottish Presbyterian and British Anglican churches starting in the mid-1500s,
2. the American Union or International congregations beginning in the early 1800s and,
3. the contemporary stream of evangelical churches which began with the fall of communism, the increase of globalization and the rise of evangelical churches to ecclesiastical prominence in the United States from 1991.

When many Americans think of international congregations, if they think of them at all, they might recognize some of those churches which have been known variously as American churches abroad, Union churches and International Congregations.

The aforementioned Presbyterian and Anglican churches were primarily established as a deliberate act of those denominations and involved either Presbyterian missionaries or Anglican priests who were commissioned and sent out as chaplains or pastors or Anglican agencies such as the Intercontinental Church Society.

In contrast, the American-initiated churches started in a variety of ways. Those included denominational plants or others started by denominational missionaries or, in another way, by expats living in a particular country who desired a church in their own language and started one themselves or turned to missionaries already on the scene to provide leadership.

Serving colonial enclaves 1816-1940

It shouldn't surprise a serious student of the growth of the American churches that they would be involved early on with missionary outreach and especially with planting international, English-language churches.

History demonstrates that the fledgling nation quickly dispatched diplomats to various European countries. Perhaps among the best known was the American patriot and signer of the Declaration of Independence, Benjamin Franklin, was appointed as a diplomat to France before the signing of that Declaration on August 2, 1776.

The Continental Congress, formed in 1775 after the Battles of Lexington and Concord, sent Franklin to join Silas Deane to gather support from France for its independence struggle. Franklin and Deane were joined by Arthur Lee to negotiate a Treaty of Alliance and Treaty of Amity and Commerce with France. The Treaties were approved on February 6, 1778 after which Franklin was elected minister plenipotentiary to France and the sole representative of America in that country.

Franklin was, thus, the first American ambassador officially received by a foreign government. And he was an early American expatriate, the forerunner of millions to follow. **https://tinyurl.com/yygkjgzv**

With the first diplomatic representation stationed in Paris, it is easy to understand why the American Church (ACP) in Paris reports that it was the first American church established on foreign soil. "We are an inter-denominational, Protestant congregation with roots dating back to 1814," the church reports on its website.

The beginnings may be traced to the needs of American Protestants living in France in 1814, who sought a place to worship God in their native English language.

The first worship service was held in the apartment of an American merchant, and in 1814 the French Reformed Church opened the doors of its church, the Oratoire du Louvre, to these Americans, providing a place for them to hold regular services. People of all nationalities and denominational backgrounds were welcome to worship.

In 1839, a new American missionary organization, the American and Foreign Christian Union (AFCU), *(http://www.afcubridge.org)* was formed when three separate mission agencies merged. Today the AFCU includes ACP alumni who volunteer their time and energy to serve as a board of trustees, to participate in the selection of the senior pastor, and to support the church through efforts to build the endowment.

In 1857, the AFCU asked Dr. Edwin Kirk, a Presbyterian minister, to go to Paris to help the congregation become officially organized and find a permanent home. That year, the congregation chartered the American Chapel in Paris and purchased a site for a church building to be built on rue de Berri. **https://tinyurl.com/y53ynxst**

Those who began the Paris church defined the motivation for its establishment as "the needs of American Protestants living in France in 1814, who sought a place to worship God in their native English language."

Reflecting a similar description, Anna G. Edmonds wrote of the Union Church of Istanbul, "In the minutes of its committees can be seen many of the human concerns and emotions that make people seek the church: sorrow at the death of loved ones, disputes over religious beliefs, personal failures, rejoicings at births and marriages of children, a bit of envy…fear of cruelties and plain drudgery to meet the debts and taxes. The records are at times stoic in their mute acceptance of tragedy, at times puzzlingly silent on events to which the members responded." (Anna G. Edmonds, *The Union Church of Istanbul, a History*, Istanbul, 1986)

Not all of the American/Union churches were founded with the highest motivations. The history of The Union Church of Guatemala can be traced back to Guatemalan President Justo Rufino Barrios, who served from 1873-1885 and supported the development of the Protestant church to counter the power of the Catholic Church.

In August 1882, President Barrios traveled to New York, and met with the Presbyterian Council on Foreign Missions to discuss the possibility of assigning a permanent missionary to Guatemala. Reverend John Clark Hill accepted the invitation and arrived with Barrios in Guatemala on Nov. 2, 1882.

Offered police protection by the president, the missionary went to work straight away, his influence soon spreading to include not only the president but also most members of the cabinet. Within six months, Reverend Hill had established Guatemala's first English-speaking congregation, the first Protestant school (La Patria), and the first Spanish-speaking Protestant congregation.

For the next 60 or so years, regular English-language protestant services were held in the Central Presbyterian Church. In May 1943, a meeting was called on the question of formally organizing a church, and about 30 people present voted to become the charter members of the Union Church of Guatemala. **https://tinyurl.com/y63x85u5**

Still others stated their purpose in a more formal sense. The Kowloon Union Church in Hong Kong was founded in 1927 with the following fundamental aims:

i. to provide that fellowship in public worship and in spiritual communion and service which is the privilege and practice of all Christians;
ii. to spread the knowledge of the love of God in Jesus Christ, and
iii. to unite in fellowship and the worship of God, Christians of differing traditions and Nationalities. http://www.kuc.hk/history.htm

As has been pointed out earlier, the initiative for many international churches came from the local expatriate community—diplomats, missionaries, military personnel, business people, educators and others.

Their desire was to provide a place to worship, study the Bible and find fellowship among people who spoke their language—English.

Often, they would seek support from churches and denominations back home as they searched for a pastor, Sunday school material, financial resources and other assistance.

If the planting of the church involved missionaries from a particular denomination, then, quite often, the IC, while functioning to serve people from multiple backgrounds, called a pastor from that body and used their Sunday school material.

Homeland Support

In the late 1800's and early 1900's oversight of many international churches fell to a Conference of Foreign Mission Boards in the United States and Canada which met annually.

Among the denominational bodies and agencies represented at that conference were:

The Presbyterian Church, U. S. A.
The Reformed Church in America
The American Baptist Missionary Union
The American Board of Commissioners (Congregational)
The Student Volunteer Movement for Foreign Missions
The United Brethren in Christ
The Methodist Episcopal Church
The German Evangelical Society, N. A.
The Moravian Church in America
The Free Baptist Missionary Society
The American Bible Society
The China Inland Mission
The Christian and Missionary Alliance
The Reformed Church in United States
The United Evangelical Church
The Baptist Missionary Union
The Missionary Society of the Evangelical Assoc.
The American Tract Society
The Protestant Episcopal Church U. S. A.
The Evangelical Lutheran (General Synod)
The United Presbyterian Church of N. A.
The Seventh Day Baptist Missionary Society
The Presbyterian Church in Canada
The International Committee Y. M. C. A.
The Foreign Christian Missionary Society (Disciples)
The Presbyterian Church in the U. S. (South)
The Reformed Presbyterian Church
The German Evangelical Synod
The Methodist Church Canada
The United Presbyterian N. A.
The Southern Baptist Convention, and
The Free Methodist Church N. A.

A description of the work of this national committee in 1902 is instructive and encouraging. It was presented to the organization's annual assembly by John W. Wood, its chair:

To the Members of the Twelfth Conference of Foreign Mission Boards in the United States and Canada:

At its meeting in 1901 this Conference adopted the following resolution: That a Committee of three be appointed, consisting of Rev. H. C. Mabie, D.D., Rev. H. K. Carroll, LL.D., Mr. John W. Wood, to consider the question of work for British and American communities in the mission fields, and to report at the next meeting of the Conference, and that it would be well for this Committee to investigate and report on the following points: (i) The extent of these communities. (2) Their character, condition and influence. (3) What is being done for them, and by them for themselves? (4) What more, if anything, should be done. (5) If anything further should be done, how can it be provided for?

As a rule, the religious interest (with) in these communities seems to be low, and religious services for foreigners, with some encouraging exceptions, seem to be poorly attended. The general sentiment of these communities seems to be largely anti-missionary. Thus their influence hampers missionary effort, so far as the native population is concerned, and frequently arouses serious prejudice against it, so far as the Church at home is concerned.

These communities are usually cosmopolitan in character, and the people composing them are constantly changing. They represent not only great national, but great religious diversity. Although many of them may have been connected with Christian congregations in the home land, they too often display indifference to religious matters and devote themselves chiefly to business and pleasure. No doubt some of this religious indifference can be traced to the inadequate provision made in most of these communities for religious ministrations. Where services are, owing to the necessities of the case, held more or less irregularly and in unattractive halls or poorly equipped churches, there is little to command the allegiance of the man or woman whose Christian life is not of a robust type.

These drawbacks are emphasized still further when, as is the case in most of these communities, religious services have to be provided by a generally overburdened missionary. His work through the week on behalf of the native population leaves him little or no time to care in any way for the foreign community, and his teaching in an alien tongue, with his endeavor to meet alien conditions, does not, to say the least, add greatly to his qualifications for giving moral and spiritual leadership to the foreign community. As a rule, such a community needs, even more positively than a community in the home land, the strong moral and protective influence of a well-organized and well led Christian congregation. This is particularly true in the case of the thousands of young men who leave homes in this country and in England, with all their supporting associations, to live without the helps and restraints of family life in the morally vitiated atmosphere inseparable from a non-Christian city. Of the reality of the need for religious influence in such communities there can be no doubt.

The reports received indicate that these foreign communities may be grouped into three general classes:

1. *In the first class, there are the larger centres like Shanghai, Hong-kong, Manila and Valparaiso, with English-speaking communities of 5,000 or more people. In these larger communities the religious interests seem as a rule to be fairly well cared for. In all of them there are well established congregations of considerable size attached to the church of England or the American Episcopal Church. In all of them, except Manila (where denominational churches are the rule), there are good sized and well organized union congregations. The Rev. T. W. Pearee, one of the representatives of the London*

Missionary Society in Hong-kong, believes "it would not be easy to find elsewhere a proportionately greater number of religious activities making for the advantage of foreigners. Most forms of work that are possible are being attempted and there is no form of work left for me to recommend or to estimate for on a basis that would justify an appeal for aid." Bishop Graves, of the American Episcopal Mission, which maintains a foreign church in Shanghai in addition to the congregation of the Church of England, says there are good congregations in all of the churches on Sunday. The communities belonging to this class are able as a rule to provide properly for their own religious needs, and apparently are entirely ready to do so. Occasionally missionary Boards and missionary secretaries in this country might render valuable service by recommending suitable men to foreign congregations in these places looking for a pastor.

2. *In the second place, there is a group of English-speaking communities whose populations vary from 200 to 2,000; such for instance as Yokohama, Tokyo, Nagasaki, Kobe, Amoy, Canton, Hankow, Peking, etc.*

All of the communities have congregations, either of the Church of England or the American Episcopal Church, as a rule equipped with buildings, and a resident pastor or chaplain, giving the greater part, if not the whole, of his time to the work. All of these communities also have more or less well organized union congregations, but in not one instance is there at the present time such a congregation with a resident pastor, or even a missionary pastor, able to give much time or consideration to the work to be done. Tokyo has a union church building, but it is not satisfactorily located and the size and influence of the congregation are hampered accordingly. Dr. Green, of the Congregational Mission, thinks that $25,000 might well be *invested by Christians in the home land in erecting a suitable building for Christian worship in the Japanese capital.*

In Kobe there is a union congregation with a church building, which for about two years, until last September, had the advantage of a resident pastor giving his entire time to the work. Yokohama needs both building and pastor for the union congregation. These three points represent the most pressing needs, though at other Japanese and Chinese ports important work could be done if the present small and struggling union congregations could be properly equipped.

3. *In the third place, there is a group of communities with a very small English-speaking population and that chiefly composed of missionaries and their families. Osaka, Chefoo, Ningpo, Soochow, are typical of this group. The English-speaking residents, aside from the missionaries, are chiefly customs and other government officials. The opportunity and the need in places comprised within this group are alike limited and for the present, at least, there seems to be no possibility of maintaining English services other than those provided by the missionary community chiefly for its own edification, but to which the other foreign residents are always warmly welcomed.*

In practically all of the places included in groups 1 and 2, the English speaking population might be classed chiefly under three heads:

- *(a) Romanists, generally with an organized congregation and resident clergy,*
- *(b) Anglican, generally with an organized congregation and resident clergy, either of the Church of England or the American Episcopal Church,*
- *(c) Other Protestant Christians, with no one body sufficiently strong to maintain distinctively denominational services.*

Both the Roman and the Anglican congregations for obvious reasons must retain their individuality. In some instances it is found that the Anglican congregation serves to some extent at least, as a union church. In Hakodate, for instance, the service maintained by the C. M. S. missionaries appears to be the only English service in the community and is attended generally by all the members of the limited English-speaking population. At Seoul the United States' minister says "The Church of England service is attended by some who are not of that denomination, because it seems more like a Church service than the American one." But except in special cases it seems necessary and desirable under present conditions that the other Protestant Christian people should be organized into a Union Church. Your committee makes the following recommendations:

1. *It would suggest the continuance of a committee on this subject, with instructions to make further investigations.*
2. *It would suggest that this Conference consider the advisability of suggesting to Mission Boards that in communities such as those in Group 2, a missionary, presumably a representative of the strongest mission in the place, should be authorized to give so much of his time as may be necessary, for the organization and proper leadership of a union congregation, so long as it is unable to maintain its own minister. Something similar to this is done effectively by the American Episcopal Church in Hankow.*
3. *It might be well for this Conference to consider the advisability of securing from English speaking communities in mission lands, particularly from those in the larger centres, invitations to prominent Christian teachers in this land to deliver courses of sermons calculated to quicken spiritual impulses and to develop moral purpose into aggressive Christian living. Men of the type of*

the Rev. Charles Cuthbert Hall and Mr. John B. Mott, by their strong and sane presentation of Christian truth, by their appeal to the intellect as well as to the heart, have unquestionably done a vast amount of good in such communities. In this as in everything else connected with the religious interests of these communities, it seems to be of the first importance that local initiative should be encouraged. Those English speaking communities abroad have no desire to be the objects of missionary effort. As Mr. Robert E. Lewis, the efficient Y. M. C. A. secretary for Shanghai, remarks, "They do not want to be missioned and won't be."

4. *It would seem desirable that the members of this Conference should keep themselves informed, through the missionaries of their several Boards, concerning the religious condition of the English speaking communities with which they are in contact, and should endeavor to ascertain the needs of such communities: (a) with regard to buildings for union churches; (b) with regard to men as pastors of such union churches.*

In closing its report, the Committee takes pleasure in acknowledging the testimony of many of its correspondents with regard to the admirable work being done in a number of points in the far East, through the International Committee of the Young Men's Christian Association. With the possible exception of the strong Associations at Shanghai and Manila, however, this work at the present time is done almost exclusively on behalf of the native populations. There are a number of points, such as Yokohama, Tokyo, Kobe and Hong Kong, where there seems to be need for work along Association lines among the English-speaking young men. Doubtless as time goes on, the International Committee will be able to take advantage of such openings. It must be borne in mind, however, that the work of the

Association, as its leaders would be the first to emphasize, is of a supplementary character. Whatever facilities for religious worship it may provide cannot take the place of the common worship of a definitely organized Christian congregation.

John W. Wood. Robert E. Speer. W. Henry Grant. **https://tinyurl.com/y6g68ro2**

The records of this meeting also contain a fascinating plea from the Rev. Edward Arthur Wicher, who was serving as pastor of the Union Church in Kobe, Japan. It illustrates the deep concern that church people had, not only in Asia but in the United States, for expatriates living abroad who, in the view of the pastors and denominational representatives, were in dire need of pastoral care to protect them from falling into sinful life patterns when outside of their own culture.

Discussion

Rev. Edward Arthur Wicher. (Pastor Union Church, Kobe, Japan.) What I will have to say this afternoon will be all too fragmentary. The moral condition of these places in the far East is almost inconceivable in many respects. I will speak now only of those that I know intimately.

We have in the City of Kobe, a population of some fifteen hundred white foreigners; four hundred of these are young men apart from their families. These communities, many of them, have been left through all these years of missionary enterprise without having anything whatsoever done for them. And naturally there is a gulf between the missionary and the resident. When I went to Kobe there was only one young man who professed to be allied to the church; after awhile there were forty. We found that not only could these men be brought into the church, but we found also that we could organize them for Christian work among the Japanese, they went to the Japanese Young Men's Christian Association, they came to me one night and the other nights they took turns in teaching the young Japanese and also teaching them the Bible. And this is one specimen of the work that can be done in the East.

Some of the noblest and purest men that I have ever known were in my congregation in Kobe. When a young man goes out there and passes through the fires he comes out with a different character from that with which he entered, he has been purified as by fire, and there is a certain strength in his character after that that there was not before he came.

Then these men are ready to support the church. I suppose that over half of my support came from men who did not belong to the church. But the problem of paying for the church will not be the greatest problem. More than we think subscribe towards idolatries. There are Japanese churches which have been partially built with money received from foreigners. Besides this they contribute to many institutions such as the Yokohama Orphanage, which is administered by missionaries of the American Board. These undertakings could be organized for positive aggressive work if they were brought back again into the Christian influence. We have here sons of the men who were trained in the pious Godly homes of Scotland, we have had the sons of the rector, we have had the sons that have come from the best homes of America, and we have seen them go to wreck, body and soul, because of the awful conditions that obtain in the far East. And this is in full view of an on-looking heathen world, and they know it. I have known Buddhist priests to rebuke the Godless Christian foreigner for his conduct.

Now what will be done? You are building up the Foreign Missionary activity with one hand and pulling it down with the other. In almost every case these foreigners in the East are opposed to missionaries.

These fifteen hundred foreigners in Kobe have thousands of Japanese in their employ. In every large commercial house there will only be three or four men at the head of the house, but there are thousands of Japanese in their employ; the bookkeepers are Japanese, the typewriters are Japanese, all the clerks and subordinates are Japanese. Sometimes they will have a thousand employees in a single foreign house and only three or four foreigners at the head of that house. Those young men will even tie their neckties as their foreign superior does. The Japanese are very anxious just now to be foreigners; they will imitate them in every way, and you will find that those in the foreign community who go to church on the Sabbath are having a very wide influence on the Japanese employees.

The larger number of foreigners living in the East have not been brought up in the Anglican Church, they are attached to their own and they will never be at home in any other. And besides that we have some four thousand tourists passing through Japan every year. The missionary is already overburdened. Our Eastern men do not want missionaries. You may send them chaplains, but if you send them out to them and call them missionaries, immediately there is a gulf that divides. We may help to support chaplains, but we will have to leave them there with that title, and perhaps labor along with our support for two or three years before the community itself can support them.

Now it is from America that the work must be done. I would suggest something, if possible, that would be modeled upon the work that is done by the Continental Committee of the Church of Scotland in the cities of Europe.

I believe that that model, modified to suit the varying conditions, will best accomplish the work that is needed in the far East. And there will be some twelve or fourteen chaplains needed in time. These reports call for the ones that are needed most now. Very largely the key of the missionary enterprise will be found in the Eastern ports, and if you have the foreigners banded together in the bonds of love and faith and service they will provide for the native congregations constantly the models of prayer and service that are needed by congregations all about. I pray God that this work may not be allowed to drop, but that something may be accomplished.

Rev. Harlan P. Beach (Educational Secretary Student Volunteer Movement): I think that the first class of places referred to in the report are places which can be fairly easily managed; the second and third classes in other cities are the ones that cause difficulty. I had a long talk with a man, who probably now is the head of the Union Church in Yokahama—tho he was not at that time—with regard to the possibilities there. That was in the second class of places mentioned. There was this difficulty which was alluded to by the speaker. These young men are there without wives, without families, there is no restraint placed upon them at all. The church can do something for them that the Association cannot do. The problem is better met by the Association than by the church in some cases, but the difficulty of the Association is that it does not furnish any home life. As others have talked to me on the same question it seems to me as if that might be the solution for cities of the second class. I think, however, that we ought to remember that in every one of the cities, no matter what the class may be, if there happens to be an Association in the city it will meet one need of the young man; it brings him into connection with young men of his class in a most efficient way. I do not know what other travelers have to say of the Association, but I am sure of this in my own case, I was profoundly impressed by the work of the Young Men's Christian Association. Now it seems to me that one thing which Boards and Secretaries could do is to provide aids for the second class of places. Take Tokio, for example; Tokio is without a proper Union Hall; Mr. Wood said rightly that one reason why the Anglican churches were more desirable than any others, even for non-conformists, was that they looked more like churches; the others were halls. We must remember that our work is being undone; that cannot be emphasized enough; our work is being undone simply because of a lack of these places.

In response to very urgent appeals from the missionaries, work has been started not only at the points stated but at

Hong Kong; there is a building valued at nearly one hundred thousand dollars at Calcutta; and such work is being done at Bombay and other places. In South America one of the strongest Young Men's Christian Associations is at Buenos Ayres, with a membership of between five and six hundred. The same is true also of the City of Mexico, where the railroad companies are co-operating with the citizens of the foreign community in maintaining a Young Men's Christian Association for the American and English young men. The appeal for the extension of this work from the residents is very strong, and it is justified in the light of the results. It is the policy of the Foreign Department to respond, as far as their resources will permit.

Mr. Robert E. Speer (Presbyterian Church, U. S. A.): The situation is perhaps most acute in those communities where there are not enough European young men to furnish the constituency for the Young Men's Christian Association. In the cities where there is a sufficiently large number to give ground for the work of the Young Men's Christian Association there are also strong churches, as in Shanghai and Mexico and Hong Kong and Manila. There are a large number of cities, however, as Mr. Beach suggested and as was pointed out in the report, where the number of young men is not sufficient as yet to warrant the establishment of Associations and where there are no strong churches, union churches, or Anglican churches, or congregations of the American Episcopal Church. And indeed the need is very great.

If nothing more can be secured here in this Conference than the increase of our interest in the spiritual needs of our own country in these communities a great deal will have been done. And if only the members of this Conference could take the time to read over this large volume of replies, on the basis of which Mr. Wood has presented this report, there would be no doubt about the increase and the permanence and the depth of the interest in those organizations.

One impression made on me in reading them was the numerical smallness of the English-speaking people; I supposed there were many more Europeans in many of these communities than there are. There were only three or four places where there were over four or five thousand. On the other hand the reports very much increased my comprehension at least of the importance of these communities from the point of view of our interests. As Mr. Wicher said there are two regards in which they are' exerting a terribly damaging influence on our interests. They are damaging them by misrepresenting our gospel and by furnishing a standing example of the apparent lack of power of our gospel to redeem character. It would be an easy thing for almost everyone here today, I suppose, to cite instances of this. I remember an illustration told me by one of our missionaries in the interior of Central China, of having been preaching once to a crowd of Chinese in the interior with reference to the superiority of the Western religion and its influence on the lives of the men; and he was very much startled when a Chinaman stopped him and said, "I have been through street in Shanghai;" a street to which foreigners resorted, and that was a complete refutation of what the missionary had been saying.

It is a hard thing for missionaries to commend Christianity when it is so plainly condemned by so many of these representatives of Christian lands, between whom and the missionaries the people may not make discrimination. It has been said that a large majority of these people disbelieve in the missionary enterprise. Some of the papers published in these ports directly antagonize missionary movements. Tourists meet such people in the clubs and in the hotels and they get from them an antagonistic view of missionary activity. And these are the people who come home and whose testimony is accepted. These men and women live out in the mission field, they claim to know all about the mission work; you cannot condemn their testimony as the testimony of the globe trotters, who have not lived for years there, and yet they testify against the missionary enterprise.

And the power on the other hand of good men in these communities on the foreign field, in their influence among the heathen, and their power as witnesses for the missionary enterprise when they come home, shows us how much we could gain for our cause if we could in any way curb these things. There is another consideration that ought to impress on us an interest in these places; we are losing in some of these lands almost as many Americans as we are gaining heathen. I suppose down in Mexico City there have been years when more Americans have gone to ruin than we have brought Mexicans into the Christian Church. It is rather a losing work to send our own flesh and blood down there to be lost, laying ourselves out to win the Mexicans and not succeeding in winning as many of them as we are losing of our own flesh and blood. These communities are going to increase greatly in the coming five or ten years; we shall see more than these three or four or five thousand Europeans in many places before ten years have passed away, and now is the time to take hold of these communities and determine their character. There are sections of our own country that show to this day the evil effects of the neglect of their religious life. These European communities will show the effect of that neglect in the future, and on the other hand they will show the influence of positive Christian institutions and activities established among them now in their early days.

Rev. Wm. M. Bell, D.D.: I feel prompted to just speak briefly as a result of some opportunities of meeting those settlements in heathen countries. I think as representatives of the Missionary Societies we have been derelict in regard to our duty as to these white-faced people that live in the ports. I think we have not adequately met their spiritual needs, and therefore we are in some sense blameworthy. We have gone on the supposition that when these people go into these heathen countries they will be all right; we feel largely from our own spiritual environment that they will stand the gale, but experience shows that they will not unless they have a little better bracing than they get at home. You have heard of the man who had a great temptation who said in apology that the outside pressure was so great he could not resist it. His friend said, "Where was your inside bracing?"

We are at fault. I feel that we ought to face our sin this day; I think that the churches that are backing up these Mission Boards have not followed these white-faced men as they ought to; the Young Men's Christian Association is not a church, it will never do the work that its pastors ought to do. I think we ought to find a practicable settlement of this problem, and my solution of it is that we unite or co-operate in some practical way and give some of the best pastors that we have under the American flag to some of these Foreign Boards for the maintenance of the Christian standards of life for these men that go out there and fight the battle, which often is a losing one because they are not properly supported. You and I will never know how much we owe to our environment, on account of our surroundings. Many a man struts around here in our cities at home with a pompous sense of his own high character who could not stand the pressure for two years in a heathen land. I think we have failed to follow these men with the most potent ministry for which united Christendom can stand today. I think it is a shame and a sin that so many of these white-faced men are renegade in these Foreign Boards; they should have the best pastors that the world affords. After meeting these men as I have met them, some of them reeling drunk, some of them blueing the air with their profanity and giving the most complete lie to all that Christianity stands for, it is appalling to the heart— the Lord help us and guide us and let this thing stick in our hearts until we do something adequate to meet the needs. **https://tinyurl.com/y3kdtl6t**

From that sterling call of 1902, many of the U.S.-based traditional denominations did begin to send out pastors specifically designated to serve the expatriate population (which, at that time, consisted primarily of White, U.S., British, Canadian, Australian and New Zealand business people, educators, diplomats and missionaries). Several reports from the multi-denominational board in subsequent years reported on the growth and change among these congregations.

1917

The work at Yokohama is summarized in the following brief extracts from the annual report of the pastor, the Rev. William Martin, M.A., who made a short visit to America, generously provided by the Church, to have necessary treatment for his eyes:

"In the truest sense, the pastor of a church like ours, 'preaches to a procession.' It is true there is a strong and most consecrated nucleus, non-missionary as well as missionary, who stand to their guns most loyally, and because of whose loyalty and devotion we have been able, with God's blessing, to accomplish much this past year. We do not forget, however, that it is in large part to minister to these birds of passage that our church has been established, and such ministry, if it lack the joy of seeing the building up of a congregation such as one might expect in more settled communities, has nevertheless a charm of its own. The voice of its pulpit may literally be said to travel to the end of the world. Its regular worshippers include Americans, Canadians, British (from all corners of the Empire), Dutch, Danes, Syrians, etc., and most of these after a longer or shorter sojourn with us, return to their own lands, carrying back with them, we believe, some lessons of faith and life that they have learned here. In addition to these, we have almost every Sunday some tourists from the ends of the earth, and some missionaries on their way to or from their mission fields. This last is one of the most delightful features in the work of the church. We have had as many as 45 missionaries at a single session, and their presence has been an inspiration to us, as, we were assured by them, our fellowship was a joy to them. In a single

year we greet more veterans of the Cross from the mission fields, men and women whose praise is in all the churches, than the average home pastor meets in a lifetime. "The congregations at the Sabbath service are well maintained, and the attendances will bear most favorable comparison with those of any churches in the home land. Our prayer meeting has a fair attendance. The Sunday-school has maintained its high standard of efficiency, with an average attendance of about one hundred. During the winter of 1915-16, the pastor conducted a class of young men in the study of the Evidences of Christianity. There was an excellent attendance throughout the entire course. He also conducted an afternoon class for ladies in the study of the life of Christ. The Ladies' Auxiliary has been of the greatest service, not only to the church itself, but through the work it has done for war relief. We have consecrated men and women who have the interest of the church profoundly at heart, and, though the difficulties are many and great, we are confident that our labor will not be in vain in the Lord."

Here is a report on the broad scope of international church work in 1917. Certainly, it reflects a growth in the number of full-time pastors designated solely for work with international (Union) churches:

Last year your Committee assisted or had other direct relation with the following Union Churches:

Manila: Rev. Bruce S. Wright is the pastor. There is an English-speaking population of 4,000, of whom 3,000 are Americans. The Union Church has 345 members: 53 were added during the year. The average attendance mornings is over 200, evenings is over 100, and at Sunday-school is 170. The Women's Auxiliary, Boy Scouts, Camp Fire Girls and large Adult Bible Class are active organizations. The Budget of $6,000, including benevolences, was secured through an every-member canvass by eighteen teams. "The Endowment Fund Society" bought a $500 Liberty Bond for the Church Endowment Fund. In three *years, the Church has had identified with its work members of twenty-two denominations and of sixteen white nations. The pastor's three-year term of eminently useful service expires in April, 1918, and the Committee is asked to nominate a successor.*

Hankow: Rev. Arnold Foster is the pastor. The Union Church here is vigorous and self-supporting. It has asked the Committee to assist with the building fund: the Committee has been able to secure $500 for this purpose during the year and may be able to raise a like amount next year if Hankow still needs this assistance.

Peking: Rev/ Charles F. Hubbard, D.D., serve the Church helpfully for a term of three years and a half and recently returned to America. Although the pulpit is being well supplied, a new pastor should go as soon as possible; Dr. Hubbard's full, interesting field report contains the following: "The outstanding feature of this work is the diversity of the social, national, and denominational elements. The opportunity for reaching the English-speaking educated Chinese and Japanese is important and hopeful. Among Catholics, both of the Roman and the Greek churches, we find, too, occasional opportunity of helpful ministry. During this past year there have been added to the population more than a hundred souls through new American enterprises. After the great war is over there may be expected a considerable influx of foreigners. The Union Church needs a 'local habitation' of its own, a new church building, with associated parish house for Sunday school, prayer-meeting, and social gatherings, and with library and reading-room and young men's club facilities. All the great nationalities of the world are included in our fellowship, and from twenty-five to thirty different denominations, a genuine unity of spirit is secured by emphasizing the great common essentials of Christian faith."

Yokohama: Rev. William Martin is the pastor. The English-speaking population of 2,250 includes 400 Americans and 1,100 British. The Church has 103 members, of whom fourteen wee added during the year. The average attendance at morning service is 100, and 105 at Sunday-school. The Pastor's Aid Committee calls on newcomers, and tourists are invited through the hotels. The work has been well maintained during the year in spite of rather severe losses through the war, removals and Deaths.

Kobe: Rev. Willis E. Parsons, D.D., is serving as pastor for a short term succeeding the Rev. Stanley F. Gutelius who returned to America last spring. The membership is fifty-four, nine being added during the year. The morning attendance averages about 90, with about half that number at night. The Sunday-school has six classes with sixty in attendance. The Church serves many tourists en route to other ports. A new, permanent pastor will probably be needed next fall.

Tokyo: Rev. Doremus Scudder, D.D., has served most successfully in his first year as pastor of this new organization. Two hundred and seventeen members have been received. The average attendance at church is over 150 and about 70 at Sunday-school. The School and Women's Society help in the support of local charities. Services are held in the Ginza Methodist Church (Japanese; the usefulness of the Church would be greatly increased by a plant of its own, toward which more than $8,000 has already been raised. The Church appeals to friends for $35,000 for site and building.

Mexico City: Rev. George C. Lenington, formerly pastor of the Dutch Reformed Church in Tompkinsville, Staten Island, N.Y., entered this pastorate last February. Through an extremely difficult year, the Church has faithfully served the Kingdom in that distracted capital. The English-speaking population now numbers about 1,800, of whom over 1,000 are Americans. The Church membership is ninety-six, 30 being added this year; twenty-five of the total are missionaries. The average attendance at church is fifty-five, and at Sunday-school is seventy-six, with two adult Bible classes. There have been practically no tourists in Mexico during the year. New features are mid-week meeting for Bible study and prayer, a Sunday evening service and a Communion Class for young people.

Panama Canal Zone: The Union Church is a collegiate organization with congregations at several points. Balboa Heights reports a year of progress with the Rev. Sidney S. Conger as pastor. Of the 5,000 English-speaking residents, 225 are members of the Church, 61 being added last year. The morning and evening attendances average 175 and 80, respectively, and Sunday school 300 with 100 in the Sunday-school at Ancon. An active Christian Endeavor Society, a Teachers' Training Class and prayer meeting at both Balboa and Ancon are helpful features. A first-class ground floor of what is planned to be a large, well-equipped plant has just been completed by a building fund of $30,000, two-thirds of which the pastor solicited in the States last winter. Mission work is done among the Chinese and other races on the Zone and financial aid is sent abroad. At Christobal, Rev. John C. Abels,, pastor, 81 have been united with the Church in the past fifteen months, but the many losses leave the membership only 100. As Deaconess of the Church and as principal of the Chinese Day School, Miss Lucy Bittinger, formerly of India, is serving. The Chinese in the Zone have no religion and it is hoped that the day school and Sunday-school for them may make the next generation Christian. Gatun is the headquarters of the Rev. Raymond E. Marshall, who went there after graduation at Drew Seminary last spring. The Rev. George A. Miller of the Methodist Mission in Panama gives part time to the work of the Union Church. The low ebb of religious life makes fishing for men difficult and discouraging, but the workers are not disheartened.

Rio de Janiero: Rev. Isaac B. Harper, formerly pastor of the First Methodist Episcopal Church of Terre Haut, Indiana, reached the field last April and has been leading the congregation forward in a very commendable way. Of the 3,000

English-speaking people in Rio, only 500 are American, the rest being British. The Church has 130 members, of whom 37 were added during eight months of last year. The average morning attendance is 50; occasionally there is a second service on Sunday. The Ladies' Guild is a recent and active organization, the work of which included a circulating library.

Special effort is made by the pastor and the Guild to secure the interest and co-operation of new arrivals. The monthly church paper, "The Community Outlook," is very popular and helpful. The congregation worships in the Brazilian Methodist Church and is greatly in need of a building of its own.

San Juan, Porto Rico: The Presbyterian and Methodist congregations are now holding joint services; a Union Church is proposed. Our Committee, at their request, nominated as pastor a competent Methodist to whom a call was extended; circumstances arose which led the nominee to decline and the congregation has now called another pastor. The combined membership of the two churches is about 100, with a constituency of about four times as many among an English-speaking population of from 1,500 to 2,000.

Havana, a year ago, seemed ready for a happy co-ordination of its three congregations into a Union Church and a local committee was formed to this end. Various circumstances, however, have made the step inexpedient, but we trust it will not be too long delayed as there seems to be a growing need for a strong, united leadership for the foreign colony in that increasingly important city.

Santiago, Chile: Rev. W.H. Lester, D.D., is the pastor. The Committee has been asked informally if it might be able to assist this Church if occasion arose, and we replied that the Committee stood ready to try to help in any appropriate way. The membership of the Union Church is about sixty, and the average attendance between 100 and 125. The Church owns a good, centrally located building with an attractive club room. For the recurrent vacancies in these important pastorates abroad, your Committee will warmly welcome suggestions of suitable, available men.

Tourist Directories. The edition of the Latin American Guide is exhausted, but should probably not be reprinted at present. The Asia Directory continues to be supplied to tourist steamers and centers abroad....

Discussion

Dr. Wolf: We ought not to pass a report of this character without reference to the splendid character of the work which is being done. I speak advisedly, because I have attended a number of these union churches during my time in the East and I want to say this: that it is one place where because of circumstances, whether we want to unite in Christian work or not, we must unite for the great purpose of serving those who go abroad and who need the ministrations of just such churches as this Committee has been supplying in the great centres of the East as well as here on this western side of the world. The plea that has been made ought to be heeded by all the Boards. It is of the first importance that American who go to the East do not permit their religion to remain in cold storage, but that they link themselves up, if they go to any of these great busy cities, with one of those churches, and do what they can to further the interests of the religious life of our brothers and friends that go to the east, and who if they do not keep alive the spirit of Christ in them there will not be any credit either to Christianity or to the church of Jesus Christ. **https://tinyurl.com/y28y2qwz**

It should be mentioned here that decisions made by traditional denominations to divide geographical regions among various denominations in the late 1800s and early 1900s had a secondary effect on the development of new international or Union churches.

Comity agreements reached at the Congress on Christian Work in Latin America, held by North American denominational mission boards in Panama in 1916, for example, divided Mexico into several regions with the Presbyterians having responsibility for one area while the Methodists assumed work in other regions. Similar divisions were made within Brazil and by country in the rest of Latin America. Similar "comity agreements" were reached earlier in other regions of the globe such as the Philippines and India.

While many of these plans were generally perceived to be unworkable by national church leaders who ignored the agreements, the effect on the planting and growth of Union churches was noticeable. If, for example, Presbyterians were responsible for a particular country the international church there would have been established primarily through the efforts of those missionaries on the field, and thus would reflect that particular group's style, doctrine and pastoral leadership.

Not that they wouldn't have been multi-denominational in their makeup and outreach—almost all international churches no matter their roots are—but their pastors, Sunday school and form of government would likely have carried that influence for many decades.

Moving along a few years to 1940, we find these reports from the annual "Foreign Mission's Conference."

RIO DE JANEIRO, BRAZIL

Rev. Herbert S. Harr is Pastor. The pastor, on completing the fifth year of his ministry to this church and people, looks back with mingled feelings of appreciation, of joy and also of regret. He says: "Union Church has felt keenly the shock of powerful world forces and its pastor has lamented the disaffection loss of interest and indifference of many friends whose home background gave hope of better things, and laments the fact that the church's ministry has not been able to command and hold to a greater degree their interest and personal support. Financial support, yes, but not that active participation in the church's life and work so essential to both the church and to the professing Christian.

"Union Church, being undenominational, is in the vanguard of an interchurch movement which is destined to break down the barriers that have divided Christ's followers into so many different and often agnostic camps. The community churches in our homelands and the chain of Union Churches in various important port cities and world capitals, of which Union Church at Rio is one, are forerunners of a movement certain to spread and prevail over the disintegrating forces that have so greatly hindered the Church's progress. "Our church seems to sense a turning of the tide. The records for the year show a period of average activity, with a slight increase in church attendance and a revival of interest.

Foreign Missions Conference of North America, **https://tinyurl.com/y32kbol8**

As will be pointed out later, war, economics, natural disasters and stark political changes can radically alter the course of an international church, from altering its nature to even closure as local conditions may eliminate the expat community or make the operation of such a church impossible.

What follows are excerpts from the 1918 and 1921 reports on *Religious Needs of Anglo-American Communities on the Mission Field* as reported to the Foreign Missions Conference of North America that reflect some of those challenges:

1918

The general effect of the war on these union churches abroad has been adverse in some particulars and favorable in others; it has compensations there as well as at home....

Special mention perhaps should be made of the Tokyo church and the splendid way in which it has worked under Dr. Doremus Scudder, who went to Tokyo a little over a year ago from Honolulu. The new Union Church is a power for Christianity. Special mention should be made also of the great trial which the Mexico City church has been undergoing, as we may well believe. Rev. George Lenington, formerly of the Dutch Reformed Church of Statin Island, started his ministry early in the year and is serving with great acceptance in Mexico City.

Three churches speak of the special need for buildings. In Peking they meet on a noisy street corner, in the auditorium of the Princeton Y.M.C.A. building. In Tokyo they meet in a native Methodist church. They need their own building, and they are starting to collect funds for it. And, in Rio de Janeiro they meet in the Southern Methodist native church. We can easily imagine the conflict of yours and the little frictions which may arise in these places in trying to have two quite different organizations occupy the same building. And the young men, who constitute such a large proportion of the English speaking element in these cities, need certain institutional features in an American building, to be attracted to the religious worship and religious life we would like to have them hold to when they go abroad.

The pastor of one of the churches in the Canal Zone was in the country less than a year ago, and your committee helped him in financing the building at Balboa Heights. About twenty-three thousand dollars was raised, and the church has now built a basement, and later they hope to get funds to complete the building, which will seat six or eight hundred, and hold a Sunday school, as they have at present, of six hundred scholars.

Your committee on two or three occasions has been asked to call pastors. The policy has been only to nominate, and let the church call the pastor. Your committee would like still to adhere to that policy in spite of the recurring requests from abroad that the committee call pastors.

1921

Anglo-American Communities THE RELIGIOUS NEEDS OF ANGLO-AMERICAN COMMUNITIES ON THE MISSION FIELDS The post-war period is witnessing a marked increase in the size of the English-speaking Colonies in the large cities of Latin America and Asia; probably this increase is relatively greater in the number of Americans than of Britishers, for commercial and financial concerns of the United States and Canada are rapidly developing closer relations with lands across the sea. The Union Churches are becoming more deeply rooted in the lives of their communities where their growing moral and spiritual influences are a recognized and welcome power. A number of returned travelers have written the Committee in enthusiastic appreciation of the Churches they attended while abroad. In view of their larger potentialities, several Churches are feeling more than ever the urgency of buildings of their own, suited to their tasks. From various Union Congregations with which your Committee sustains a more or less direct connection, the following brief items are printed for permanent record:

Mexico City: Rev. O. W. E. Cook, Pastor. An encouraging growth in membership has occurred during the year, there now being 100 full members and 50 affiliated. The average attendance at Morning Service is 70 and at Sunday School 85.

With more settled conditions, a vesper service has been resumed monthly. The Chapel has been attractively equipped and redecorated at an expense of $3,000, which was raised locally. The missionary interest of the Sunday School and the assistance rendered by a good choir are worthy of note. The pastor has just resigned.

Tampico: Further letters have come, telling of the need for a Union Church in this growing center, where the foreign residents number 2,500 or more. A Sunday School of more than 100 members is successfully conducted. Suitable land and a Church building would be fairly expensive but a considerable portion of the funds would be secured on the Field.

Panama Canal Zone: The Union Church is a vigorous, well-managed organization with Congregations at four or five points along the Canal. Funds are needed from the States for the building program.

(1) Balboa and Ancon: Rev. Benjamin B. Knapp, Pastor. This is the largest Congregation, with a membership of 274, of whom 86 were added during the past year. Average attendance at Church service is 150 and 75, and at the flourishing Sunday School, 695. The Church has a Men's brotherhood, a Ladies' Society, and 3 Christian Endeavor Organizations: it supports a missionary in the Republic of Panama. Only the basement of the Church has been constructed; the main building is greatly needed; the Sunday School meets in various buildings and a real Church center is a necessity to a larger life for the Congregation.

(2) Cristobal: Rev. Harry Owen, D.D., Pastor. This City is growing fast, and also the Church and Sunday School. A Parsonage has been erected during the year. The Pastor is in the States busily engaged in a campaign for funds for all the Church buildings in the Zone. Your Committee has sought to cooperate with him in his estimable endeavor.

(3) Pedro Miguel: Rev. Edwin M. Oliver, Pastor. Over 600 Americans reside here, 50 of whom, on the average, attend Church and100 attend Sunday School. The Pastor, who took up this work during the year; writes: "This is a Lock-City; and the majority of the men work some part of Sunday."[5]

(4) Gatun: Rev. Charles B. Mitchell, recently of Pittsburg, Penna., became Pastor of this Church in the Fall of

---

[5] Author's note---a "lock city" refers to a town site along the Panama Canal

> *1920. The report for the next year will be awaited with interest. It has been proposed to the Federal Council of Churches that it furnish a home-base for these Churches which are under American flag in the Canal Zone.*

Rio de Janeiro: Rev. Isaac B. Harper, Pastor, was home on furlough during the year. The Church has 89 full members and 123 Voting members, with 34 additions. The Sunday services are held at an inconvenient hour in a Brazilian Church—a building is a pressing need. Boy Scouts and Camp Fire Girls are means of influencing the younger generations. "The work of the Union Church is steadily gaining a larger grip upon the life of the Community, the American section of which is rapidly growing."

Santiago, Chile: Rev. James H. MacLean, Pastor. Under progressive leadership the Church is extending its beneficent circles of influence, which, after 36 years of organized effort, reach far and deep. The membership is 36, with 8 additions during the year; average attendance is 120. Various auxiliaries are underbuilding the work, and a mid-week service has been instituted. "There has been a gratifying improvement in Church attendance, a noteworthy and commendable increase in our financial support, and a healthy activity, in the Sunday School, the Young Men's Club and the Ladies' Guild and the Choir.

Rio de Janeiro: Rev. Isaac B. Harper, Pastor, was home on furlough during the year. The Church has 89 full members and 123 Voting members, with 34 additions. The Sunday services are held at an inconvenient hour in a Brazilian Church-a building is a pressing need. Boy Scouts and Camp Fire girls are means of influencing the younger generations. "The work of the Union Church is steadily gaining a larger grip upon the life of the Community," the American section of which is rapidly growing.

---

where there is a set of locks which raise and lower the ships on their canal transit.

San Juan, Porto Rico: Rev. F. E. McGuire, M.A., Pastor. This Union of former Methodist and Presbyterian Churches is entirely self-supporting and maintains eight local charities besides contributing regularly to relief work abroad. There have been additions to membership at every Communion Service since the organization of the Church, the whole number now being 152, with 150 others as adherents. The Church provides the Pastor with an automobile. "The Protestant forces of San Juan will never go back to denominational work. The Union Church has demonstrated its worth."

Havana: The above report from San Juan might be helpful to the brethren in Havana that conduct small, denominational English services in four or five different centers every Sunday without seeming to feel that advantage would result from uniting their efforts.

The Committee understands that many members of various denominations greatly desire a unified body in order better to present the cause of righteousness in this unfortunately all-too-popular resort.

Yokohama: The Rev. William Martin, M. A., died on February 26, 1920, after a most helpful ministry of five and a half years as Pastor; the Congregation and community deeply mourn the loss of this beloved leader. The Committee has placed among its records copies of the printed In Memoriam and Memorial Resolutions issued by the Church. The Church desires as successor a Pastor with both British and American relationships (which Mr. Martin possessed), "preferably a Canadian." The Committee nominated a suitable man, but when the call arrived from the Church, unforeseen conditions transpired which led the nominee to withdraw. The various Departments of the Church's activities have functioned regularly during the year, the Sunday School of eighty members being especially successful.

Tokyo: Since the resignation of the Rev. Dr. Doremus Scudder, the pulpit has been supplied by various missionaries and visitors.

For six months of the past year the Rev. Dr. C. J. L. Bates served very acceptably as Acting Pastor. Although services must be held at a very inconvenient hour (the building is that of a Japanese congregation), attendance is very encouraging. A Church school of about 70 students is taught by the new missionaries of the Language School. Tokyo earnestly hopes that its great need for a Church plant will be supplied; the foreign community is also striving to secure a school for foreign children.

Kobe: Rev. Clarence H. Benson, Pastor. The English-speaking population has largely increased during the year. Twenty-eight joined the Church, making the full membership 84 and affiliated 49. The average attendance at the services of social worship on Sunday is 105 and 35, respectively, with 80 at Sunday School.

Prayer services are held in homes on Tuesday evening, and in the Church on Thursdays. Record should be made of the great loss sustained by the Church in the death of Peter Fraser, Esq., so long the Treasurer, and a strong, supporting friend of the congregation. An aggressive campaign is carried on to secure attendance of services by tourists.

Seoul: Rev. A. F. De Camp, Pastor. This Church has 116 attending members; mostly affiliated, and 30 absentee members. The principal service is held Sunday afternoon, in warm weather on the lawn of the U. S. Consulate General, with an average attendance of 80; Sunday School averages 50. The pulpit is generally occupied by others than the Pastor, who serves as "a superintendent" without salary. The offerings help support a Leper Home and a Deaf and Blind Home in other cities.

Peking: Rev. Robert W. Beers, Pastor: the membership of the Church has arisen to 397, with 146 added during the year: the service of worship is held at five-thirty P.M. in the Y.M.C.A. Auditorium, and the average attendance is 350, of whom about 30 are tourists. The Sunday School attendance is 100. A service for the U.S. Marines is held in their Barracks. The church is seeking to secure a greatly needed home for itself; its appeal to the U.S. Government, endorsed by the Acting American Minister; the American Chamber of Commerce of Peking, the Federal Council of Churches, the Committee of Reference and Counsel, and by this Committee, for the lease of a portion of unoccupied land on the old American Legation grounds was refused by the State Department.

Shanghai: Rev. Luther Freeman, D.D., Acting Pastor. The American Colony in Shanghai has grown to such an extent as to justify the consideration of developing the American Song Service into a Community Church. To cooperate in discovering and appraising the various factors in the situation, the Rev. Dr. Luther Freeman, recently Pastor of the Emory Methodist Church of Pittsburg, Penna., has gone to Shanghai. The Committee understands that the entire religious situation of the city will be carefully surveyed, so that any new organized effort may promote the common program to the fullest extent.

Hankow: The Rev. J. Wallace Wilson, of the London Mission, serves as Pastor. The Church desires a full-time minister and has asked for an unmarried man, "preferably a Canadian." The Committee has diligently cultivated several suitable "prospects," but without success: a strong man is needed in this tremendous city in the heart of China. The Church owns a centrally located property with two fine, substantial buildings.

Manila: Rev. Louis O. Richmond, Pastor. This vigorous, self-supporting Union Church has many successful activities and largely attended services, helpfully touching the life of the city at innumerable points. The full membership is now 145; affiliated, 196; added during the year, 113. "A flourishing Sunday School is the only roof-garden S. S. known." The annual budget for 1921 was oversubscribed through an every-member canvass; benevolences about $600. There is a splendid spirit of cooperation. The Church has been redecorated, baptistry added, and an electric blower added for pipe organ.

Tourist Directories: The editions of the Tourist Directory for Christian Work in the Far East and India, and of a similar guide for Latin America, were exhausted two years ago. Your committee has assembled material for a revised issue of the former, and, if funds are assured, proposes to print it, confining its scope to the Far East and making it as compact as possible.

We call attention to the estimable Guide to Missions in China recently prepared by the China Continuation Committee; it is very thorough and comprehensive for its size, and is fully illustrated. Each mission land visited by many tourists might well publish and distribute its own small handbook for tourists.

Needs:

1. *Houses of Worship. The most urgent requirement in seven or eight cities is for Houses of Worship; the long continued use of inconvenient buildings of other congregations is a depressing obstacle to life and progress. The Committee laid this need before the various Mission Boards asking each to enter its fair proportion of the total need of $960,000 in its denominational budget in connection with the campaign for increased funds; a number of Boards responded very sympathetically, several accepted their proportion as objectives, but we believe only one Foreign Board, the Methodist Episcopal, has been enabled thus far to assist financially in this building program, making a generous capital gran to the Canal Zone Union Church. Someway should be found of helping these Churches to secure property funds in the home-lands.*
2. *Pulpit Vacancies: Just now nominations of Pastors are called for by Yokohama and Hankow; Tokyo Church is also vacant. Before the end of 1920 the terms of service of the pastors at Peking, Manila, and Balboa Heights, C. Z., will have expired. The Committee finds it difficult to*

secure for these important posts suitable men as soon as they are needed, and bespeaks your active cooperation in this matter.

3. *Current Grants-in-Aid will be needed in 1921 by seven, possibly by eight, Churches, and the expenses for travel by pastors to and from the Field will be especially heavy this year, making the new budget a little larger than that of 1920. Therefore your Committee requests the continuance of the fully appreciated financial support upon which it is entirely dependent and for which it is deeply grateful.*

Recommendations to the Conference: The Committee has voted to refer to this Conference with recommendation for favorable action the two following important matters:

1. *The provision by the proper authority for religious services on Sundays on vessels owned, operated or controlled by the United States Shipping Board.*
2. *The transfer of the functions of this Committee to the Committee of Reference and Counsel, placing them in the hands of a subcommittee. In accordance with the Constitutional requirements of the Conference, the Committee, on December 14, 1920, sent to the Constituent bodies notice of this proposed change. It is, of course, expected that if this change is made the special contributions for Union Churches will be continued. The term of service of two members of the Committee, Dr. Chester and Mr. Home, expires with this Conference. Respectfully submitted, Stephen Baker; R.P. Mackay, S.H. Chester, George T. Scott, Frank A. Horne, James M. Speers.*

Discussion

Mr. Scott: You who know the world situation so well appreciate what a flood of life is going into Eastern Asia and

Latin-America from the United States and Canada. In Shanghai a year ago they said that twenty American firms were opening new offices in that city every month. These union, English speaking churches, located in the midst of these growing colonies, are therefore increasingly important. One who has not visited those cities, who has not conferred with the typical American or Canadian college man who goes over there to represent financial, manufacturing or commercial interests, cannot realize the down-pull of the life of those great cities upon these young Americans and Canadians. I wish you might see these churches functioning in the midst of these growing Anglo-American communities. Many of you know the Union Church in Honolulu; you have been at morning or evening service in that beautiful little church upon the bluff in Yokohama; you may have been in the Ginza church in Tokio, in the Union Church at Kobe; over in Seoul, if it were in the summer time, you met for vesper service under the American flag on the lawn of the Consul General. In the Y. M. C. A. Building on that busy, noisy corner in Peking, from two to four hundred Americans and British gather at five o'clock on Sunday evening—these Union Churches are perhaps the greatest focal point of the English speaking groups of those cities. You drop down to Nanking and see them in the chapel of the Union Preparatory School, up to Hankow, in those attractive brick buildings, that tremendous triple city where I think of the tremendous population and opportunity of the future. Down at Shanghai are two or three English speaking churches, one at Canton, and then at Manila, with a wonderful open-air Sunday School up on the roof—they say in the report this year that it is the only open roof-garden Sunday School in the world.

The same way we might picture these Union Churches all through Latin America and the four that are working along the Canal Zone.

The report continues concerning pulpit vacancies: *Strong men are needed. Not many outstanding men are willing to dissociate themselves from home life and work abroad. A number of men well along in years and about ready to retire, are ready to go out for a short term, before they finally retire. Most of these churches desire men a little younger than that, who can get into touch with the young life in their communities, for these pastors can be a great influence among the young Americans attached to great financial and commercial organizations. We need the help of every one that can aid in securing good pastors for this work. You will be interested in knowing that several churches lately have asked for an American with British relationships, "preferably a Canadian," who perhaps without divided loyalty, would class as about fifty-fifty in the groups of British and Americans that compose the English-speaking colonies.*

In addition, the committee addressed: *a layman sent a copy of a letter, which he wrote to the United States Shipping Board: "I am an American citizen and sailed from New York, September 15th, 1920, by the steamer "Huron." My object in this communication is to inquire if there is not some way that your board could enforce the holding of some religious service on the Sabbath day on all vessels owned, operated or controlled by your board. "It seems to me, in the absence of a chaplain, minister or religious worker, that some one could always be found among the officers or crew or passengers, if there are any, that could at least conduct a religious service. I am not a religious crank, but a professed progressive Christian man, and as I have concern for the future progress and welfare of our nation, I believe, as our government deem it desirable to foster religious worship on land and provide for it in the army and navy, that they should also unquestionably do so on the vessels they control at sea; therefore, I respectfully request your attention and interest in the matter." He has not informed us of any reply which he received from the Shipping Board.*

Mr. Herbert K. Caskey: I have a good many thoughts on the subject. I was at Yokohama the first Sunday I was in Japan, spoke morning and evening in the church, to between forty and fifty people. I felt that the man at Yokohama was only influencing from Sunday to Sunday a very small group of men. I talked to Mr. Scott about it and he said it was impossible to get the men at Tokio in the university to volunteer for that service.

I was in Manila; then I was in Peking for five weeks and, to be very frank about the service in Peking, Mr. Scott says three or four or five hundred people there go Sunday after Sunday. The enrollment at the language school when I was there was 180. Of course, there were some of those people that belong to the legation. Of course, they would not have to go to church. All the missionaries and candidates ought to go.

One missionary said to me, "Mr. Caskey, all we need out here is somebody that could bring a message like the one heard at Silver Bay, or at Northfield." Well is seems to me the man at the Union Church is the man to bring that message, to all our missionaries that can attend the service, to all our young missionaries there studying the language, to the legation and to the young men who have been in the universities. Peking is the center of the renaissance movement. Peking is the great educational center of China and for the next five years, I think we have no conception of the advance that is coming to Peking as a great center; and the man who can render the greatest possible service ought to be forced into the work at Peking, if possible to get him there. I know there is no bigger job on the face of the earth.

Bishop W. R. Lambuth: I desire to say that Dr. Freeman has just taken charge of the work at Shanghai. I was at the service in Shanghai about four weeks ago and every seat was occupied in Masonic Hall where they are holding their service. Their service has helped to uphold the moral atmosphere, and the fact that you have an American woman's club in Shanghai with a membership of five hundred would indicate the wonderful field there is there.

But I spoke of the very fine attendance and the admirable work which is being done already and will be done by Dr. Freeman whom you have sent. I wonder why, in the budget proposed for 1921, the five hundred dollars was not repeated.

Mr. Scott: In the expenditure for this year, five hundred dollars was towards the outgo of travel. The Shanghai Church hopes to be self-supporting locally for the current expense and simply asked us to bear the expense out.

Bishop Lambuth: I desire to add that the work in Kobe and Shanghai ought to be continued. [The question was put and the motion to refer the recommendations to the Business Committee was carried.]

At the Foreign Missions Conference of North America 1922 meeting—report for 1921, we read:

Dr. Garland Evans Hopkins, Washington, D.C., executive secretary of the Fellowship of English-Speaking Union Churches Overseas, announced a campaign to raise $300,000 for more than 60 churches (attended by British and American residents of various denominations) located in port cities, diplomatic and trade centers throughout the world. The Fellowship aims to strengthen the Union Churches, underwrite their budgets, bring them into closer relationship, and help them affect the native life of their communities, and it seeks funds from churches, business firms and individuals in the United States and foreign port cities. **https://tinyurl.com/y637p6cu**

Interrupted by war 1940-1945

Given that the majority of English-language, international congregations have historically been identified as ex-pat churches in that they have primarily served expatriates living in foreign lands, it is to be expected that political conflict, economic disruption, changing political perspective and especially war, would have a detrimental effect on the ministry or even the existence of these congregations.

In particular, World War I (1914-1918) and World War II (1939-1945) not only made the presence of non-military expatriates in war-torn countries just about impossible, but forced many of the churches to close and saw some churches damaged or destroyed with many records lost.

The picture of these interruptions is best illustrated by excerpts from the ecumenical oversight organization's minutes and from various historical accounts.

Committee on foreign missions, 1917

The disturbed state of affairs throughout the world continues to affect the organized religious life of the English-speaking colonies in the large cities on the foreign mission field. This effect is unfortunate in many of the union congregations in the loss in numbers and in local income, but is favorable in the deepened experience and devotion of those members that remain. Young men from some of these churches have fallen on the battle field and the willing sacrifice of Europe is an object lesson not unheeded by any foreign community in these far-distant lands. The opportunity for religious work by and among these our fellow citizens was never more obvious, while the need in perennially urgent.

RELIGIOUS NEEDS OF ANGLO-AMERICAN COMMUNITIES ON THE MISSION FIELD Presented by Dr. Robert E. Speer, Chairman of the Committee Wednesday Afternoon, ... Dr. Speer: I think it may be doubted whether there are any communities in the world where one could study the ideas and ultimate results of the war better than in these Anglo-American communities. They represent the outposts of our Western life, and things were seen and felt there quickly and accurately at the beginning that we saw and felt only slowly and less accurately. There was one of them in which the entire official Board of the Union Church was swept away. Four of them lost their pastors. And I have not seen any more affecting rolls of honor than the lists of the little boys, as one thinks of them, who grew up in many of these communities, like Yokohama and Shanghai, and many of the others, some of whom may never have seen before the lands which they fought for, but who joyfully gave themselves for what they knew to be the cause of mankind.

Just one last word with regard to what is sure to be the increasing importance of this work in these communities. We can be absolutely certain that in the new days into which we are coming these communities will rapidly increase. More English-speaking people than ever will be pressing out into these lands, and it will be more indispensable than ever that these groups of English-speaking people should represent our Christian character and conviction, that the missionary enterprise may not need to counteract any anti-Christian testimony borne by life or action in any of these communities.

We can thank God that there has been so much assistance given to the missionary enterprise by these communities through their clean lives and honorable dealing, but there is still more that might be done to make the influence of those communities all that it ought to be. And now the day is coming when a large number of men will press out in trade and commercial relationships from Great Britain and the United States. The day has come when more earnestly still we must see that the religious traditions out of which our countrymen go shall be carried with them, that their real

We can thank God that there has been so much assistance given to the missionary enterprise by these communities through their clean lives and honorable dealing, but there is still more that might be done to make the influence of those communities all that it ought to be. And now the day is coming when a large number of men will press out in trade and commercial relationships from Great Britain and the United States. The day has come when more earnestly still we must see that the religious traditions out of which our countrymen go shall be carried with them, that their religion shall not break down when it is transported to other latitudes and other longitudes, and that the full missionary possibilities of these Anglo-American communities are utilized, for the sake of the missionary undertaking, for the sake of the larger missionary influence of Christendom on the non-Christian world.

Union Church, being undenominational, is in the vanguard of an interchurch movement which is destined to break down the barriers that have divided Christ's followers into so many different and often antagonistic camps. The community churches in our homelands and the chain of Union Churches in various important port cities and world capitals, of which Union Church at Rio is one, are forerunners of a movement certain to spread and to prevail over the disintegrating forces that have so greatly hindered the Church's progress. Our church seems to sense a turning of the tide. The records for the year show a period of average activity, with a slight increase.

While many international churches in Europe were affected by either world wars, several churches in Asia found themselves disrupted by two of them plus the Korean Conflict. This report comes from the Union Church of Seoul.

Though the church was not able to settle permanently in one location for many years, Seoul Union Church held regular Sunday meetings for foreigners until 1940. However, war was brewing and American and British consular officials were advising their citizens to leave the Orient. On November 16, 1940, 216 missionary men, women, and children sailed from Inchon on the S.S. Mariposa. The dwindling congregation continued to meet until December 7, 1941. On December 8, World War II had begun. The dozen or so men of the congregation were escorted to the Methodist Seminary where a classroom became their home until repatriation six months later.

After World War II, by the summer of 1947, some 50 or more missionaries were living in Seoul. The need was recognized once again for a foreigner's afternoon church service so as to not conflict with missionary involvement in Sunday morning Korean church services. Seoul Union Church services were organized once more. The next step was to elect a pastor. Dr. William E. Scott was named, and he consented on the condition that either he or an associate pastor would conduct the service. Prior to that, the pastor had organized and coordinated the speakers, usually preparing a list for 3 months at a time. Except when out-of-town speakers were present, the speaker of the day conducted the entire service. Though this offered great variety, both in speaker and message, electing a pastor brought with it a consistent thread of message, vision, and purpose. The congregational unity continued to grow.

With the "red invasion" on Sunday, June 25, 1950, missionaries once again evacuated Seoul. The communists withdrew after Gen. MacArthur's landing at Inchon, and in September of 1950, some missionaries returned to Seoul. Seoul Union Church services were held in the Adams home, but the Chinese Red army made it necessary to evacuate Seoul once more. By Christmas 1950, Seoul was a ghost town. Late in 1951, Rev. L. P. Anderson returned to Chung Dong, Seoul, but it was another year before there were enough missionaries to hold separate services. According to the diary of William E. Shaw, services were resumed in the Adams home on September 14, 1952 and continued to meet in various homes for about a year. In 1954 the TaiWha Center became available for use. Seoul Union Church continued to meet there until 1979.

The Union church in Tokyo suffered a similar experience during World War 2:

During World War II, Tokyo Union Church entrusted the church to a Japanese pastor, Ugo Nakada, a member of the congregation who struggled throughout the war to keep the church from being taken over for secular purposes. On May 25, 1945, during a fierce bombing raid, Tokyo Union Church was hit by a firebomb that completely gutted the building. By 1947, however, worship services had begun again for the TUC congregation at

Aoyama Gakuin, and in November 1951, the rebuilt church, restored to the Bergamini design, was rededicated.

After the war, the composition and character of the TUC congregation changed as the foreign community gradually expanded; the congregation began to include more business and professional people and fewer missionaries. Up to this point, ordained pastors from among the missionary community had always volunteered to lead worship services. In 1952, however, the church decided to call the first full-time pastor for the congregation.

Then there was the interruption of services at the Kowloon Union Church in Hong Kong:

During the period from December 1941 to October 16th, 1947 the Church ceased to function on account of the capture of Hong Kong in World War II.

When Hong Kong was occupied by the Japanese, the Church property was left unprotected and suffered severe looting and damage. All Church and manse furniture and fixtures, and the roof of the school hall disappeared. The church hall was an empty shell used for the stabling of Japanese horses.

When residents began to return to the Colony, efforts were made under the leadership of Mr. A.W. Ingram to reconstitute the Committee of Management and the Trustees. Repairs were undertaken and furniture purchased. This included two of the old pews, found in a second hand shop. The Church was again opened for public worship with a rededication service held on October 19th, 1947.

The main problem facing the Church in 1947 was how to obtain a permanent minister. For a few years, missionaries, visiting preachers, and...chaplains made a wonderful contribution, and the Church was indeed blessed by their ministry. In August 1949, The Rev. A.E. Small of the London Missionary Society arrived in the Colony hoping that he might be able to get back into China. While waiting, he was invited to serve as acting Pastor, and his first service was held on the last Sunday of August, 1949.

European churches, of course, also suffered the interruption of two world wars.

The (American Church in Berlin) was a lively center of religious and civic life until the outbreak of World War I, when it was closed in 1916. Reopened in 1921 and in spite of very unsteady times, the congregation resumed a prominent role in the American community. The church was closed again with Germany's declaration of war on America in 1941, and the building was destroyed during bombing raids in 1944. With the help of the American and Foreign Christian Union, the congregation continued from 1945 by sharing facilities with various congregations in Berlin-Zehlendorf and from 1964 was housed in the Alte Dorfkirche of the Paulus Gemeinde. **https://tinyurl.com/y4afof6f**

Postwar Expansion 1945-1991

Numerous factors following the end of World War II and the brief Korean conflict led to a sharp increase in the number of international congregations in the 1950s and 1960s. These factors included:

1. Enhanced travel made possible by the development of expanded and faster airline service to many previously inaccessible areas of the world.
2. The growth of international business including the needs of redeveloping war-torn Europe and Asia. Known as the "the post war economic expansion", it was a period of strong economic growth beginning after the war and ending with the 1973–75 recession. The United States, Soviet Union, Western European and East Asian countries in particular experienced unusually high and sustained growth, together with full employment. Contrary to early predictions, this expansion also included many

countries that had been devastated by the war. **https://tinyurl.com/yxw6e3ao**)

3. The passion of many who served in war-torn nations to return and be involved in the redevelopment of those societies. These ideals led to the establishment of Christian relief groups such as World Vision in response to the needs observed by many military people during the various conflicts.

In 1947 Rev. Robert Pierce met Tena Hoelkeboer, a teacher, while on a trip to China. She introduced him to a battered and abandoned child named White Jade. Unable to care for the child herself, she asked, "What are you going to do about her?" Rev. Pierce gave the woman his last five dollars and agreed to send the same amount each month to help the woman care for the girl.

This encounter was a turning point for Rev. Pierce. He began building an organization dedicated to helping the world's children, and in 1950 World Vision was born. The first child sponsorship program began three years later in response to the needs of hundreds of thousands of orphans at the end of the Korean War." **https://tinyurl.com/y65rhfns**

In 1970, after having left World Vision, Pierce founded Samaritan's Purse, a Christian relief and development organization currently headed by Dr. Franklin Graham, the son of famed evangelist Dr. Billy Graham.

4. The threat of communism and the resulting motivation to present a Christian way of life and belief to those affected. That led to an additional *"way that veterans influenced postwar religious developments in the area of Christian foreign missionary enterprises. The war took a generation of young men, as well as a significant number of young women, far beyond their hometowns and exposed them to distant lands and foreign peoples. At the same*

> *time, the experience of war motivated some veterans to invest themselves in work that they found meaningful. For evangelical Christians, no work had more meaning than sharing the Gospel with those who seemed to live in apparent isolation of its message. In the midst of battle, no small number of men pledged their service to God in exchange for survival—some remembered their promises. Others simply sought to make their lives meaningful as they sought to reconcile their own improbable survival with the deaths of friends whom they considered to be more worthy. Historian Joel Carpenter concluded that the war "had an enormous impact on the North American missionary impulse."*

In the mid-twentieth century, American Christian missions abroad changed significantly. Even before the war, the pressures of modernism led denominations to begin questioning the goals and legitimacy of foreign missions. After the war, the pressures of decolonization led many to view foreign missions as a form of cultural imperialism and support from mainline Christians continued to erode. Overall, however, the number of American missionaries abroad continued to grow, buoyed by an influx of evangelicals. From 1925 to 1960, the number of North American Protestant missionaries more than doubled, yet the number associated with mainline bodies stagnated. Similarly, after World War II the Roman Catholic Church and the LDS Church sent record numbers of missionaries abroad. At Wheaton College, a bastion of evangelicalism, thirty-one percent of the class of 1950 became missionaries. David Howard, a 1949 Wheaton graduate, recalled that returning veterans ushered in a "golden age of missions." He lauded, "The vision originally received by these men and women while overseas in the military and then stimulated and cultivated while at Wheaton College has borne fruit for half a century in missionary outreach."

Even before they left the service, some soldiers and sailors set their minds toward mission work. Some formed connections with already established missions overseas. In the Philippines, US troops connected with Ed and Marion Bomm, American missionaries who had been imprisoned by the Japanese. With the Bomms, a group of service people spearheaded evangelistic projects that eventually developed into the missionary organization Far Eastern Gospel Crusade. In addition, military service provided some veterans with skills that proved quite valuable in mission work such as experience in aviation. In a 1944 letter, marine Lyman Mason reported that he intended to use his skills as an aviation mechanic as a missionary in South America. Similarly, Elizabeth Greene, a Women's Air Service Pilot, wrote that she was "eagerly awaiting the time when God will use my flying to take the glorious gospel to those who are 'without Christ—having no hope." After the war, Greene and several other military aviators established the Christian Airmen's Missionary Fellowship for the purpose of supporting overseas missions. Such programs also benefited from cheap surplus supplies and equipment from the military following the war." Beyond the Battle: Religion and American Troops in World War II, Kevin L. Walters, the University of Kentucky. **https://tinyurl.com/y6n2v78c**

Each of those factors led to a rapid increase in expatriate populations as diplomats, business people, relief workers, educators, students and missionaries struck out internationally with a resulting increase in the growth of existing international congregations and the establishment of dozens more in the 1950, 60s and 70s. **Used by permission**

Union Church of the Canal Zone

The establishment of a network of Union Churches in the Panama Canal Zone was most unusual in how it came about, raising as it does the question of whether, since it was established by the United States Congress, it was, in fact, unconstitutional.

(The **Panama Canal Zone** was an unincorporated territory of the United States from 1903 to 1979, centered on the Panama Canal and surrounded by the Republic of Panama. The zone consisted of the canal and an area generally extending five miles on each side of the centerline, excluding Panama City and Colón, which otherwise would have been partly within the limits of the Zone.... When reservoirs were created to assure a steady supply of water for the locks, those lakes were included within the Zone.

In 1904, the Isthmian Canal Convention was proclaimed. In it, the Republic of Panama granted to the United States in perpetuity the use, occupation, and control of a zone...for the construction, maintenance, operation, sanitation, and protection of the canal. From 1903 to 1979, the territory was controlled by the United States, which had purchased the land from the private and public owners, built the canal and financed its construction. The Canal Zone was abolished in 1979, as a term of the Torrijos–Carter Treaties two years earlier; the canal itself was later under joint U.S.–Panamanian control until it was fully turned over to Panama in 1999. (Adapted from Wikipedia)

There are those who would argue that the establishment of the Union Churches in the Panama Canal zone violates the First Amendment which states: *"Congress shall make no law respecting an establishment of religion, or prohibiting the free exercise thereof..."*

However, in providing for moral and religious safeguards the Congress and Canal Zone authorities early on provided government-paid chaplains. That provision ended with the completion of the construction of the canal.

From there, under the leadership of a group of laymen, the Union Church of the Canal Zone was organized in February, 1914. All Protestant denominations except two (Southern Baptist and

Episcopal/Anglican) cooperated with this piece of ecclesiastical statesmanship. A centralized organization maintained work in all the civilian "gold" towns (those populated by Caucasians) along the Canal, employing four pastors, who had to be ordained men of American, Protestant churches. This Union Church did not regard itself as a denomination but as a federation for Christian service. No attempt was made to establish a doctrinal position, and members were not asked to sever their relations with their home churches. (Adapted from *Prowling About Panama*, by Bishop George. A. Miller, Abingdon Press, 1918)

A further step, the one that called into question the constitutionality of what happened, occurred on December 31, 1941 when the U.S. congress passed this act:

AN ACT

To incorporate the Union Church of the Canal Zone.

Whereas the Union Church of the Canal Zone is an unincorporated evangelical religious organization which has established and maintained union churches at various points in the Canal Zone since its organization in 1914, succeeding in that year separate union churches which had been maintained for a number of years previously; and

Whereas it has parsonages and church buildings at the following points, to wit: Balboa, Pedro Miguel, Gatun, and Colon; and

Whereas the Federal Council of Churches of Christ in America, a corporation of the State of New York, and the boards of various cooperating churches in the United States desiring to make provision for worship by the adherents of their respective denominations who from time to time reside temporarily on the Isthmus of Panama and who do not desire to sever their denominational ties in the United States have contributed toward the establish-

ment of the Union Church of the Canal Zone; and

Whereas the said Union Church of the Canal Zone is not related to any of such denominations in the way of ecclesiastical subordination or subjection thereto; and

Whereas it is desired to insure the continuance of the work in which the said Union Church of the Canal Zone has been engaged Therefore

Be it enacted by the Senate and House of Representatives of the United States of America in Congress assembled,

CORPORATION CREATED

In *Christian Cooperation at the World's Crossroads*, author Robert H. Rolofson wrote that "This is probably the only church incorporated by the Federal Government."

In an interview granted in 2010, the Rev. Clarence Payne, a former pastor of the Balboa Union Church, explained, *The Canal was built by the US from 1904 to 1914. During that early period, many of the American workers came from the American South. They were mostly white and mostly Protestant. There was a desire, a need to continue spiritual life; so here in the Canal Zone, they ran Sunday schools in the YMCAs and other informal recreational buildings such as the clubhouses.... In the early years, the Panama Canal Company provided chaplains to conduct services in these places for the workforce.*

As time went on, as more workers began to bring in their families and permanent communities were created, they perceived the need to have their own churches.

Towards that end, they did some intelligent thinking: Let's not replicate what we have in the US with various denominations of churches at four corners of an intersection. Let's combine the denominations into a union church. The Episcopal church couldn't support that, and they established their own churches. The Baptists did the same. But among other denominations, there was an effort to establish interdenominational churches, union churches. The National Council of Churches took this on, and inside their offices at 475 Riverside Drive in New York City they opened an office of Union Churches in the National Council of Churches. The National Council of Churches had no authority over the Union Churches, but they offered support, in any case. So the Union Churches of the Canal Zone came to be, prior to the opening of the Canal....

In any case, the union church movement caught fire. There were between seven and nine union churches in the Canal, each with its own building. Balboa Union Church, Gamboa, Pedro Miguel, Gatun, Margarita, Cristobal (a beautiful stone building) and one on the West Bank, whose name I don't remember. Every one of them brought pastors down from the States. They chose a joint mission statement, and they called themselves the overarching title, "Union Church of the Canal Zone."

INTERVIEWER: Why did the US Congress do that? Do you have the sense that they were trying to push a certain doctrinal theology into the Canal Zone and Panama?

REV. PAYNE: I don't know. Except, of course, that the Canal Zone was a territory by treaty of the United States Government. Certainly, in the early 1900s the US was a Protestant, Christian country. Protestantism ruled. There were Catholic immigrants, but the dominant religious movement was Protestant....

Meanwhile, during this period, the Canal Zone, churches thrived. They were very active centers of religious and community life. I might add that in those early days, community life was centered around the churches and the Masonic movement.
https://tinyurl.com/y37otlra

Over the years, seven Union churches were formed in the Canal Zone. As time passed, some such as the Cristobal Union Church closed as territory was returned to Panama. In all, seven churches were organized in these Canal Zone communities. As of 2019, only two remain operating under their original name and as expat churches: Balboa and Gamboa. Some of the original buildings were torn down, others are occupied by other Spanish-language churches.

With the transfer of the Canal Zone property to Panama under the 1988 treaty, the Union Church of the Canal Zone, unconstitutional or not, went out of existence. Ministry with an expat congregation continues in the two Union Churches that remain plus other congregations in Panama City, including Crossroads Bible Church which formed independently of the old Union Church system, LifeBridge International Church which was planted more recently by the International Baptist Convention and other traditional, international churches which existed also outside of the Union Church system and are related to Anglican, Lutheran and other bodies.

Ecumenical organization

As seen in previous minutes, the Foreign Missions Conference of North America was a voluntary cooperative association of the foreign mission boards of the United States and Canada. The Conference provided the boards "with a medium for consultation with other boards working in the same fields or lines of work; for cooperation in planning and united action when needed; for the administration of joint projects when boards desired this service; for cooperation with other nationwide interdenominational organizations in the United States; and for cooperation with twenty-five similar groups in other lands which, with the Foreign Missions Conference, constituted the International Missionary Council."

The Conference held annual meetings of representatives of its constituent boards "to confer on issues, determine policies, detect overlapping, and initiate advance projects…." The activities of the Conference were primarily carried out through area representative committees and functional representative committees. The former were concerned with geographic areas; the latter with matters such as literacy, Christian literature, rural missions, and medical missions. There were also a number of standing, special, and inter-agency committees. The area representative committees included Africa, China, Europe, India, Japan, Korea, Near East, Southeast Asia, and the Committee on Cooperation in Latin America. The functional representative committees included the Associated Mission Medical Office; the Christian Medical Council for Overseas Work; Christian Religious Education; radio, Visual Education, and Mass Communication; Rural Missions Cooperating Committee; Treasurers Committee; and the Committee on World Literacy and Christian Literature. The Standing committees included Arrangements for the Annual Meeting, English-Speaking Union Churches Overseas, Executive, Executive Staff, Finance and Headquarters, Interchange of Christian Leadership, Missionary Personnel, Nominating, Public Relations, Research, and Special Programs and Funds. (Adapted from *Guide to the Foreign Missions Conference of North America Records of the Presbyterian Historical Society*. Available at: **https://tinyurl.com/y5m2mr65**

In general, these support systems were funded and directed by the various denominational mission boards and served primarily as a conduit for funds but also as a matching point for churches seeking pastors and vice versa.

Eventually, the denominations saw that they needed a more active relationship with the churches to help place pastors and provide other supportive services. Thus, they moved to establish an office which could handle some of those pastoral tasks as well as to help promote the visibility of the Union churches through the participating denominations.

In 1950 the Foreign Missions Conference of North America joined the National Council of Churches where its activities were assumed by the Division of Foreign Missions.

Here is a report for 1950 that was presented in early 1951, the year that the Department of Churchmen Overseas was formed and housed in the National Council of Churches of Christ.

English-Speaking Union Churches Overseas

We are witnessing the phenomenon of the world's most powerful nation being one in which the Free Churches are the dominant religious group. In former times it was comparatively easy for tax supported State Churches to follow their nationals as they went abroad to represent their countries in diplomacy or business. All over the world one finds Roman Catholic, Anglican, and Church of Scotland institutions built and staffed to serve these groups. Today, as new thousands of American diplomats and businessmen, merchant marine personnel and tourists, go abroad, they find in most places no adequate ministry to their religious needs. Such churches as exist are doing good jobs but, by and large, Americans abroad have reason to feel that the churches back home take little interest in them.

Our committee is in correspondence with approximately sixty churches, or groups considering the organization of a church. Some are entirely self-supporting; others will soon be. There are those, however, which must have assistance for many years. No small amount of money is involved.

The postwar period offers a psychological time for new emphasis upon the mission of churches for our fellow citizens in foreign services of business and government. We must no longer be content with providing them some small service after enough Christians in the foreign community have organized themselves into a church. We must initiate such churches and continue to assist them in every way. There are many countries where missionary endeavor is not permitted where the Christian witness could effectively be heard through the medium of such church groups.

In the last annual report it was stated that a Fellowship of English Speaking Union Churches Overseas had been organized. This organization includes any English-speaking church in a foreign country, whether independent or under denominational auspices, which desires to become a member. It encourages contacts among pastors, officers, and members of union churches across the world and serves as a clearing house for the exchange of information. Its president is Dr. Henry Sloane Coffin; its first vice-president, Dr. Daniel Poling. Your chairman serves as executive secretary.

A campaign for enlarged support for English-Speaking Union Churches Overseas has been conducted under the leadership of the Rev. Cecil L. Morgan, formerly pastor of the Cristobal Union Church. The campaign will continue into 1950, and it is hoped will secure a sufficient increase in support to make possible the large program envisioned. During the year, your chairman visited English-speaking union churches in Beirut, Cairo, Berlin and Paris. Conferences were held with groups interested in initiating union churches in Lisbon, Madrid, Addis Ababa, Athens, Rome, Prague, Brussels, Copenhagen, Helsinki, Stockholm, Oslo and Kleflavik.

Garland Evans Hopkins, Executive Chairman

The Department of Churchmen Overseas began in 1951 as the Joint Department of American Communities Overseas. The joint department was created within the NCC by the merger of the Committee on English Speaking Union Churches Overseas of the Foreign Missions Conference and the Committee on Religious Work on the Canal Zone of the Federal Council of Churches. In 1958 the word, "Joint," was dropped from the title as the department became a regular part of the Division of Foreign Missions. In the next year it became the Department of Overseas Union Churches. Then in 1962 it became the Department of Churchmen Overseas. When the Division of Foreign Missions became the

Division of Overseas Ministries in 1965, the Department became the Churchmen Overseas Program under the Department of Specialized Ministries. It remained as such until the NCC reorganization of 1972 when it became the Ministry to Service Personnel/ Overseas Union Churches and the Committee on American Laymen Overseas within the Overseas Strategy and Program Department of the Division of Overseas Ministries.

From its beginning, the Department's purposes were "to encourage the growth of ecumenical fellowship among these union churches across the world" and "to strengthen the Christian impact of English speaking communities abroad." Its functions were:

1. *Building up a fellowship of union churches and extending the outreach of each church.*
2. *Developing a system for relating church members from North America to these union churches.*
3. *Establishing and maintaining contacts with business, labor, and other groups with a view to strengthening the Christian witness through the personnel of union churches outside the continental United States.*
4. *Consulting with government as needs require.*
5. *Rendering assistance in the establishment and maintenance of union churches as needs require.*
6. *Representing member communions and boards in other types of ministry to these communities as may be authorized by the General Board.*

J. Quinter Miller was acting executive secretary of the Department in 1951 and 1952. Robbins W. Barstow was executive director of the Department from 1952 to 1959. From 1960 to 1972 Raymond A. Gray served as director.

Guide to the National Council of the Churches of Christ in the United States of America Division of Overseas Ministries Records **https://tinyurl.com/y6an7k3k**

In its formative years, the office was supported annually by the following denominations:

American Baptist Churches
Baptist Union and Missionary Society of New Zealand
Christian Church (Disciples of Christ)
Church of Scotland
Cumberland Presbyterian Church
Episcopal Church (USA)
Evangelical Lutheran Church in America
Evangelical Lutheran Church in Canada
Presbyterian Church in Canada
Presbyterian Church in Aotearoa, New Zealand
Presbyterian Church (USA)
Reformed Church in America
United Church of Christ
United Methodist Church
United Reformed Church in the U.K.
Uniting Church in Australia

As this article implies, the name of the New York office changed frequently, often with the nomination of a new director, the changing of the oversight board, or a change in the philosophy of what the group was to do.

It is a bit difficult to trace the further name development after the above change in 1972 to Ministry to Service Personnel/Overseas Union Churches and the Committee on American Laymen Overseas within the Overseas Strategy and Program Department of the Division of Overseas Ministries.

In time, however, it became known as International Congregations and Lay Ministries under the Rev. J.R. "Jack" Collins who assumed the position in the early 70s. Prior to ICLM, Dr. Collins had served in Hong Kong with "The Laymen Abroad Program of the East Asia Christian Conference." He explained the purpose of that program as "an expression of concern for the laymen abroad on the part of Churches of East Asia.... The program concerns include participation of laymen abroad in local churches in Asia, pastoral ministry to these laymen; enabling churchmen abroad to appreciate Asian cultures; and new forms of association that overcome the barriers to constructive relationships of Asian laymen and laymen from abroad religiously, culturally and socially.

"...These challenging and imaginative activities of laymen abroad that have been evolving are programs of intentional Christian laymen abroad who are projecting a responsible Christian life in which they approach their occupational pursuits with a missionary intention.... This is a significant part of what we mean by the church in mission because laymen in the sense of *laos* are the church." (*Ministry to Laymen Abroad in Asia*, Published by (among others) Churchmen Overseas, National Council of Churches of Christ in the USA, 1969)

When Dr. Collins assumed the role of director of ICLM, he merged the coordination of Union Churches with the expanding role of developing significant ministries among Christian laity while serving outside of their original country.[6]

At this point in time, long before email, cellphones, the Internet, easy international phone calls and other modern communication systems, correspondence between churches and United States denominations or potential pastoral candidates in the United States or elsewhere was done primarily by mail, a process that could take weeks. In addition, the expense and time

---

[6] It should be noted that inclusive language was not on the consciousness of people at the time these historic documents were written as it has become in our more modern age. While most expatriate workers were male, there were females involved in significant employment as well. That should be considered when reading the use of the term "laymen" to cover both male and female employment. As mentioned in the introduction to this book, we have transcribed all historic documents using their original spelling, terminology and phrasing

involved to bring a pastoral candidate for an interview was often prohibitive. That was especially true for churches in Asia, Europe or Africa which were looking for a new pastor.

Thus, the ICLM office in New York City (housed in the Interdenominational Center at 475 Riverside Drive) served as a clearinghouse for both potential candidates and churches in the search process.

ICLM maintained a regular vacancy list which was made available to denominational placement offices and interested candidates. Churches would notify the office of their vacancy and their particular requirements for a new pastor. The office, in turn, would publicize the vacancies in their own list as well as denominational magazines and placement offices.

In response, interested pastors would file their résumés with the office for circulation to churches that requested a recommendation. From there, churches would review potential candidates, perhaps request a church member on leave to visit the person, and eventually call a pastor mostly sight-unseen. Only on rare occasions where the distance was short or the church had sufficient funds would they invite a candidate to visit.

In addition, the ICLM office organized a conference for international pastors each year, one each in Europe and the Middle East, Latin America and Asia. These week-long events were a time of inspiration and renewal for pastors as well as fellowship among those with similar ministries.

The office also provided emergency services. Should the pastor and church fall into a serious conflict, the director would, if all possible, fly out to the church for several days to investigate and help both pastor and congregation to make a decision about whether the relationship would continue.

Under ICLM leadership, a significant regional organization was formed in Europe and the Middle East. Called the Association of International Churches in Europe and the Middle East (AICEME), its purpose was to provide contact, congregational support and pastoral support to English speaking Christian congregations in Europe and the Middle East.

The Association of International Churches in Europe and the Middle East traces its origins to an annual gathering of pastors and their spouses serving English-speaking international churches in Europe and the Middle East. Concerned about isolation experienced by English-speaking churches in Europe in the 1950s and 1960s, the Foreign Language Office of the European Conference of Churches, the International Congregations and Lay Ministry Office of the National Council of Churches in Christ USA, and Presbyterian missionary Ray Teeuwissen organized a conference in Geneva in 1967 for pastors and their spouses serving English-speaking international churches in Europe and the Middle East. The annual meeting continues to this day.

At the pastors' conference in 1974 in Antwerp, Belgium, the pastors attending resolved "that there should be a more formal structure than the present Annual Conference of Pastors and Wives Serving English Speaking Churches in Europe and the Middle East" and "that the name of the new organization be 'The Association of International Churches (Ecumenical - English Speaking - Europe and the Middle East)'".

By the conference in Athens in May 1975, nine pastors reported their churches agreed to the formation of an association of churches. The pastors voted and established the new association. A special committee was appointed and articles of association were drawn up. Invitations to join the emerging association were sent to English-speaking churches around Europe and the Middle East. By the close of the Association's first meeting in Paris on 1 May 1976, nine churches were charter members: the American Protestant Church in Bonn, the International Protestant Church in Brussels, the American Church in London, the International Church in Copenhagen, the American Church in Paris, the American Protestant Church in The Hague,

International Church of Stockholm, Vienna Community Church, and the English Language Church of Tehran.

In April 1981 the Association changed its name to the 'Association of International Churches in Europe and the Middle East'.

Today the Association includes over 30 churches in 20 countries across Europe and the Middle East. http://aiceme.net/history/

It should be noted that what in these years was known as ICLM underwent further name and responsibility adjustments under new leadership. Among the subsequent names were International Congregations and Christians Abroad and The Network of International Congregations which exists as this book is written solely as a website with links to churches, listings of pastoral vacancies and some historical information.

Following the term of service of Dr. Collins, the several directors headed up the office as it transitioned from a full-time presence in New York City to a part-time voluntary ministry with no institutional support or formal relationship. As such, it was housed in the office or home of the incumbent and primarily involved the website found at www.internationalcongregations.net.

The various people who assumed responsibility, either on a paid-staff basis in an office or as a volunteer working out of their own office or home included Russell Spry Williams, Rev. Arthur O.F. Bauer (under whose leadership it became known as International Congregations and Christians Abroad), Karl Reko, Scott Campbell, Rev. James A. Dwyer and, at the time of the publishing of this book, Bob Rollins, pastor of the Sampa Church in Rio de Janiero, Brazil

Union to International

Amidst the fellowship and shared activities of AICEME there developed in the late 1970s and early 1980s a fresh exploration of what international congregations were, how they should be viewed and identified.

Historically, American churches and denominations identified these unique congregations as "Union churches." Such churches were those which fully represented a multitude of denominations. In other words, they might bring together Presbyterian, Methodist, Congregational and perhaps other denominational churches into one congregation.

Within the United States these types of churches most frequently were found in small towns or rural areas where, simply put, there weren't enough Presbyterians to form an independent congregation, nor were there enough Methodists, Lutherans, Congregationalists, etc. Thus, the most expedient practice was to gather all Protestants together in one congregation large enough to call a full-time pastor and provide the variety of educational, worship and fellowship activities that members desired.

Outside of the United States a similar process was followed in national capitals where there, again, were not enough people from any one denomination to form a specific denominational church, let alone a multitude of denominational bodies each large enough to function on its own.

Thus, the international churches which were founded in large cities around the world used the common name of Union to identify their nature and attract Protestants of a variety of denominations.

(It might be noted that a few of the early Union Churches were named "The American Church." Examples of these still exist today in Paris, France, (both a multi denominational church and an Episcopal congregation), Berlin and Bonn in Germany, The Hague, The Netherlands, Oslo, Norway, Geneva, Switzerland (Episcopal), and London, England.)

With the expansion of international business and education as well as ease of travel, a wider variety of members from countries outside of the United States (and England, Canada, Australia, etc.) began to appear and participate in these union congregations. Leaders began to experience a different distinction than just multiple denominations. Instead they were noting participants from a variety of countries on all inhabited continents. Thus, they came to identify these churches more as international rather than as multi-denominational. Thus, from the 1980s they were, more and more, referred to as "international congregations."

In more modern times, Union churches refer primarily to those churches which still maintain that title in their names. Otherwise they are better identified as multinational, multidenominational congregations.

Part of this transition grew out of a concept introduced by Dr. John R. Collins of the office of International Congregations and Lay Ministries who told a gathering of Union Church pastors in Bogotá in 1975 that "as international, interracial, intercultural, inter-denominational congregations (Union Churches) are a prototype of the church of the future," ...both overseas and in home countries. ("Union Churches in Latin America", *The Christian Century*, April 28, 1976."

The Baptist and other sub-streams

As with the broader Protestant spectrum, tracing the actual first international Baptist church is just about impossible.

Herbert Stout and his identical twin brother, Herman, first went to Germany as U.S. military members just after World War II. While in Wiesbaden, Germany, they joined other Christian soldiers who ministered to German children, many left homeless after the war. The Stout brothers were eventually reassigned, but both felt a call from the Lord to return to Germany one day to plant English-language churches.

Herman returned in 1957 and Herbert in 1958, along with their families, to start churches in Wiesbaden and Frankfurt. These two churches cooperated in starting 30 new churches and missions in the next six years. The Stout brothers described this work: "God led all the way, and He blessed beyond the wildest dreams that the Stouts ever had." These churches were the genesis of the IBC.

The International Baptist Convention, an umbrella organization for international English-language churches, has its roots in the Association of Baptists in Continental Europe (ABCE) and mission work by the Southern Baptist Convention (SBC). Following the faithful work of the Stout brothers, two Baptist churches in Germany—Immanuel Baptist Church in Wiesbaden and Bethel International Baptist Church in Frankfurt—formed the ABCE circa 1959. The Stout brothers were pastors of the two churches in Wiesbaden and Frankfurt. Together these two churches started ABCE while the two brothers were still serving as pastors in the churches.

Beginning in 1961, the Foreign Mission Board of the Southern Baptist Convention in the United States sent a missionary couple to work with these churches. Some churches from England joined the ABCE in 1964, and the name was changed to the European Baptist Convention (EBC). The first EBC churches were started to minister to United States military personnel stationed in Europe. The name was changed to International Baptist Convention after the body expanded outside of the region.

Those who wish to read a more detailed description of the work of the Stout brothers and the beginning and growth of international Baptist churches in Europe will want to see their book, *Appointed By Christ Exclusively*.

But, other congregations were formed earlier. Capital City Baptist Church began in 1954 as an English-speaking service in the Mexico First Baptist Church. There were several English-speaking families who wanted to study God's Word and worship in English. In 1958 this group was organized into a church and began to meet in various locations around the city. In 1967 the church was donated some land by Mr. S Boling

Wright in memory of his wife, Mary Conger Wright. The cornerstone ceremony was observed on July 2, 1972 and the first building was completed in November 1972 on the property with it now stands.

The church was originally founded to reach the English-speaking community of Mexico City in particularly the ex-pat community. Things have changed over the years. A Spanish-speaking congregation was started in 2003 and there have been other congregations to begin in the church's facility. Currently a Korean group meets regularly on Sunday afternoons.

In other parts of the world Baptist churches began largely through the efforts of Southern Baptist missionaries who served such congregations on a part-time basis.

For many years pastors for these churches were supplied by the mission board of the Southern Baptist Convention in the United States—known as the Foreign Mission Board and later as the International Mission Board. However, in the mid-1990s the board decided to cease the recruitment of pastors and support of these churches, preferring instead to focus on unreached people groups around the world. They did not consider English-language international churches to be key in this new direction.

The exit strategy was, at least in the EBC (now IBC) to provide a final IMB couple to help the churches move from full support of missionaries to self-support by the churches. In addition, the EBC/IBC office, which was staffed by IMB missionaries and volunteers including the General Secretary of the IBC, was transitioned to a much-reduced staff supported by the EBC/IBC. John Merritt, who served as the EBC GS since 1972, was an appointed FMB/IMB missionary. He retired in 1996 and was replaced by James Heflin, a preaching professor from Southwestern Seminary. James Heflin was fully funded by the EBC. The IMB continued to provide a few interim pastors but phased out this provision over time. By 2005 or so, no IBC churches had IMB personnel as pastors. language, Baptist churches including a small congregation in Quito, Ecuador known as First (later International) Baptist Church.

With that change, an independent organization, International Baptist Church Ministries was formed in 1997. IBCM was formed by a group of interested person who wanted to support English language churches in Europe and others areas overseas. Most of the pastors had served as pastors or laypersons in churches affiliated with the European Baptist Convention (EBC). With the IMB of the SBC revising its strategy for English-language ministries, the founders created a tax-exempt organization though which financial support could be sent to the English-language churches.

IBCM's purpose is "to present the Gospel to all persons with the goal of bringing them to a saving knowledge of Jesus Christ and to form local congregations for the Christian nurture of those who respond." Through the financial contributions of members and other mission-minded individuals, IBCM is able to support these churches and thus continue the teaching of all who are willing to learn about Christ's redeeming love. (http://ibcmworld.com/about-us/history/)

Its primary goal was to provide financial support to English-speaking Baptist churches affiliated with the European Baptist Convention (now the International Baptist Convention). In the later years, IBCM's support expanded to churches in Latin America and Asia. IBCM's purpose is to present the Gospel and to form local congregations.

The number of churches IBCM supports has grown each year and the organization has been instrumental in helping to plant local international Baptist churches, provide funding, identify pastors to serve in those churches and hold regular retreats for international Baptist church pastors.

Around 2015, the Hawaii Pacific Baptist Convention allowed Baptist churches in places like Bangkok and Tokyo to join their convention, effectively meaning that the Southern Baptist Convention now has churches outside of the USA. This is bringing the International Mission Board back into the IC world as many of these churches have IMB personnel at them. *(From David Fresch, Executive Director of MICN-Missional International Church Network).*

As we will see later, among the traditional denominations the Baptists continue to be very active in planting new churches in various international cities.

Baptist ICs in Latin America have come together in recent years under the Latin American LEAD Team:

In 2004, with the guidance of Dr. Tom Hill, a retired missionary who had also served in Frankfurt, Germany, as pastor in the early 1990s and later as interim pastor at IBC San Jose, Costa Rica, we hosted a fellowship for pastors and leaders of English-speaking, international churches in Latin America. We had about 15 people attend representing 5 or 6 countries. This was the beginning of what would eventually be called the Fellowship of International Churches in Latin America. (FICLA) Our purpose was to try once a year to have a conference for pastors of international churches from Mexico, Central America, Latin America and the Caribbean. We called ourselves baptistic in theology but we were open to churches from different denominations. As I recall, IBC, Costa Rica hosted this conference one more time in 2005.

Then in 2006 we branched out. We actually had two gatherings, one in Bogota and the other in Buenos Aires. It was at these conferences that Jimmy Martin (Executive Director of the International Baptist Convention) first joined us I think, though he may have come to CR the previous year. Because of Jimmy's presence and because the IBC convention was now expanding, a number of churches from Latin America formally joined the convention. We continued to have annual meetings. One year was in Panama. This was when we were moving close to planting a church in Panama. We met twice in São Paulo and once in

Mexico City. At the same time, some of us were also traveling to Europe for IBC convention meetings.

Around 2011, we made a transition. The convention was focusing on church planting. As a part of this, they were forming regional LEAD teams. (Leading, Encouraging, Achieving, Dreaming). So we began to have meetings that were still for training and fellowship but also to strategize about church planting. FICLA sort of ceased to exist and was replaced by the Latin American LEAD team. We have now planted two churches in Central America with a number of other cities in Latin America where we are wanting to plant churches. We have met and done feasibility studies in Lima and Rio de Janeiro. There are now six churches in our region that are formally connected to the convention.

For more information, contact Rev. Paul Dreesen at paul_dina@hotmail.com.

(Dr. Jimmy Martin, General Secretary of the International Baptist Convention and David Fresch Executive Director of Missional International Church Network (MICN) contributed material to this account.)

Other Denominational International churches

It should be pointed out that while most of the Union/International churches were established as multi-denominational, several denominations in addition to the Southern Baptists also established international congregations during this period. In particular, it should be noted that United Methodists planted a number of churches in Europe as did several U.S.-based Lutheran groups. Many of those congregations exist today and exhibit many of the characteristics of the broader multi-denominational bodies.

Among those whose churches remain active at the publication of this book are congregations started by various Lutheran bodies, the United Methodist Church and the Christian and

Missionary Alliance denomination in Canada. Information on some of those follows:

Lutheran bodies

One scanning the lists of ICs in Europe and Asia will find several Lutheran churches. While there does not appear to be any central office dealing with these, many refer to an affiliation with the Lutheran Church in America.

More information may be found at: **https://tinyurl.com/yxa8ol6k**

C&MA (Christian and Missionary Alliance)

When Alliance founder A. B. Simpson left a lucrative pastorate in New York City, he had a call from God to reach the lost masses both in New York and around the world.

Prostitutes, longshoremen, and the homeless received the reconciliation message that all people are eligible for Christ's amazing grace.

He set up the Missionary Training Institute (MTI) to provide training and resources for men and women God was calling to take the gospel to the world. During that time, Simpson's group sent out the first team of missionaries to the Congo in 1884.

Since then, thousands of people have followed God's call to serve through The Alliance in the United States and abroad. In 1974, The Christian and Missionary (C&MA) officially became a denomination, but it still had at its core a heart for overseas missions. Past Alliance president Dr. L. L. King said of the C&MA that it "was not established as a mission divorced from the normal activity of a church, but a church which had within it the life and function of a mission.... The mission came first and the church grew out of a mission."

Today, the C&MA focuses on planting churches in the United States and overseas. Alliance international workers minister among the least reached peoples planting churches and training national church leaders, providing relief and development assistance, medical and dental care, and microenterprise projects. More than 2,000 churches in the U.S. minister Christ's love to their communities and cities. **https://tinyurl.com/y4tk8wxs**

While the Christian and Missionary Alliance churches (C&MA) have long been noted for their church planting efforts around the world, their entry into international, English-language churches has been a recent development and has largely come from their Canadian organization.

Brem Frentz, who now serves as Vice President of Global Ministries for the Canadian branch of the C&MA, reports that while the C&MA has historically planted churches, it was only in recent decades that efforts to establish English language churches specifically targeted at expatriate communities has begun.

Those efforts began in the 1990s and involved locations such as Hanoi in Vietnam, Indonesia and other locations. "We see these as Kingdom churches, not just congregations of the C&MA," Rev. Frentz explained.

He further explained that the denomination targets three general audiences in forming such churches. These include (a) Local national members such as professors and students who have studied abroad and returned to their home country with experience among third-culture people and a desire to continue in an international community; (b) Local expatriates who are affiliated with Non-Government Organizations (NGOs), and (c) Internationals in general, including entrepreneurs from other nations, embassy staffs, military members serving outside of their own country, and influential business, political and educational people who have third culture experience.

In 1999, a delegation of C&MA personnel meeting in Szepalma issued a declaration outlining basic principles for their work in forming new international churches:

Szepalma Declaration On International Churches

The Role of International Churches in world mission is to be a catalyst for global missions mobilization ...

- *By reaching influencers living in the host nation*
- *By assisting in the development of churches within and outside the host culture*
- *By equipping expatriates returning to their home nations*
- *By providing strategic care, training and resources for Christian workers*
- *By preaching and modelling the unity that the gospel provides within the ethnic and theological diversities of the community*

The Operational Values of an organization committed to the ministry of the International Churches

Demonstrates kingdom values through a willingness to live beyond denominational lines, relinquishing the need for credit or ownership

- *Views this ministry from a global impact perspective as opposed to a geographically based view*
- *Negotiates involvement with International Churches based on each unique context and not on a 'one-size-fits-all' policy*
- *Seeks to reduce its administrative involvement to only what is necessary to maintain alignment with its purpose*
- *Decentralizes administration and accountability to the region*
- *Builds partnerships:*
  - a. *for forming pastoral teams*
  - b. *with existing International Churches and related agencies (e.g. CAI) of like-minded message, mission, purpose and passion*
  - c. *by establishing national/regional networks*

- *Trains and deploys personnel specifically for International Churches*
- *Encourages the self-support of International Churches*
- *Creates funding options to support the placement of personnel*

The Christian and Missionary Alliance in Canada June 1999

New Evangelical denominations and "pop-up" churches: Reaching a new generation as globalization explodes; The third stream 1990-

Just as some in the traditional protestant denominations thought that they had carried out their responsibilities to establish international churches and minister completely to the world-wide expat community, world and church events turned the global scene upside down and pushed the planting and growth of international congregations into an entirely new paradigm.

The first event was **the fall of the Soviet Union**.

The Soviet Union, officially the Union of Soviet Socialist Republics (USSR), was a socialist state in Eurasia that existed from December 1922 to December 1991.

Its government and economy were highly centralized. The country was a one-party state, governed by the Communist Party with Moscow as its capital in its largest republic, the Russian Soviet Federative Socialist Republic (Russian SFSR). Extending across the entirety of Northern Asia and much of Eastern Europe, the Soviet Union spanned eleven time zones.

The Soviet Union had its roots in the October Revolution of 1917, when the Bolsheviks led by Vladimir Lenin overthrew the Russian Provisional Government which had replaced Tsar Nicholas II during World War I. In 1922, the Soviet Union was formed by the Treaty on the Creation of the USSR which legalized the unification of the Russian, Ukrainian, Transcaucasian and Byelorussian republics that had occurred from 1918.

Following Lenin's death in 1924 and a brief power struggle, Joseph Stalin came to power in the mid-1920s. Stalin committed the state's ideology to Marxism-Leninism (which he created) and constructed a command economy which led to a period of rapid industrialization and collectivization. During this period of totalitarian rule, political paranoia fermented and the late-1930s Great Purge removed Stalin's opponents within and outside of the party via arbitrary arrests and persecutions of many people, resulting in over 600,00 deaths.

Suppression of political critics and forced labor were carried out by Stalin's government. In 1933, a major famine that became known as the Holodomor in Soviet Ukraine struck multiple Soviet grain-growing regions, causing the deaths of some 3 to7 million people.

On August 23, 1939, days before the start of World War II, the Soviets signed the Molotov-Ribbentrop Pact agreeing to non-aggression with Germany, after which the USSR invaded Poland on 17 September, 1939.In June 1941, the pact collapsed as Germany turned to attack the Soviet Union, opening the largest and bloodiest theatre of war in history.

The territories overtaken by the Red Army became satellite states of the Soviet Union and the postwar division of Europe into capitalist and communist halves would lead to increased tensions with the West, led by the United States of America.

The Cold War emerged in 1947as the Eastern Bloc, united under the Warsaw Pact in 1955, confronted the Western Bloc, united under NATO in 1949.

In the mid-1980s, the last Soviet premier, Mikhail Gorbachev, sought to reform and liberalize the economy through his policies of glasnost (openness) and perestroika (restructuring). Under Gorbachev, the role of the Communist Party in governing the state was removed from the constitution, causing a surge of severe political instability to set in. In 1989, Soviet satellite states in Eastern Europe overthrew their respective communist governments.

With the rise of strong nationalist and separatist movements inside the union republics, Gorbachev tried to avert a dissolution of the Soviet Union. A March 1991 referendum, boycotted by some republics, resulted in a majority of participating citizens voting in favor of preserving the union as a renewed federation. Gorbachev's power was greatly diminished after Russian President Boris Yeltsin played a high-profile role in facing down an abortive August 1991 coup d'état attempted by Communist Party hardliners. On 25 December 1991, Gorbachev resigned, and on 26 December 1991, the Supreme Soviet of the Soviet Union met and formally dissolved the Soviet Union, thereby ending the Cold War, and the remaining twelve constituent republics emerged as independent post-Soviet states. The Russian Federation—formerly the Russian SFSR—assumed the Soviet Union's rights and obligations and is recognized as the successor state of the Soviet Union.

In summing up the international ramifications of these events, Vladislav Zubok stated: "The collapse of the Soviet empire was an event of epochal geopolitical, military, ideological and economic significance".

Adapted from https://tinyurl.com/6ubun3j

Major characteristics of the Soviet era which affected churches were the strict repression of most religious practices, the refusal to admit missionaries, and strict regulation or prohibition of any foreign churches.

An exception was the Moscow Protestant Chaplaincy which began in the early 1960s and continues today as a shared ministry of The United Methodist Church, the Evangelical Lutheran Church in America, the Reformed Church in America, the American Baptist Churches USA, and the Presbyterian Church (USA). MPC was established by the National Council of Churches of Christ USA under the Roosevelt-Litvinoff Agreements of 1933 to provide Protestant ministry to the American community in Moscow.

The existence of an English-language, international church in Havana, Cuba during the Soviet era might also come as a surprise. The International Christian Community, which describes itself as "*An English speaking ecumenical church united in Christ*" has met for many years, serving members of the diplomatic community as well as others who have been permitted to reside in the country.

The church describes itself this way:

What Type of Church is ICC?

The International Christian Community (ICC) is a group of Christians from different countries, denominations and churches that confess their faith in God the Father, Son and Holy Spirit. They meet in an ecumenical spirit to show their faith in Jesus Christ through worship, studying the Bible, discussion and participating in Christian events. The Sunday service is held in English and is attended by foreigners and a large number of Cuban Christians.

Why Was The IC Started?

ICC was founded in 1990 to minister to English speaking people who are living in, or visiting Cuba, and has been an associate member of the Cuban Council of Churches since 2002. It aims to make its members feel that they are not just members of a church congregation, but of a wider Christian community during their time in Havana.

Reasons to Visit The ICC:

- *The International Christian Community offers the only English language service in Cuba. It is an international ecumenical congregation, thereby giving members the chance of belonging to a community of Christians from different countries, and from different Church traditions.*

Christian ministers and speakers from abroad who are known to the ICC are often invited to preach during visits to Cuba meaning that the congregation benefits from a wide range of excellent teaching.

- *ICC also provides a unique opportunity for foreigners living in Cuba to have fellowship and develop friendships with the local Cuban community. These relationships often provide foreigners with some of their most precious experiences whilst in the country.*
- *The church has a great worship team and choir that prepares a combination of modern and traditional songs and choruses for use during the service. It also incorporates Christian music from countries represented in the congregation.*
- *Children's Church is offered in English and Spanish and is both fun and educational. It is a great opportunity for expatriate and local children to come together to learn more about scripture and the Christian faith through discussion, art and crafts, drama and music. The teachers follow a British ecumenical program called ROOTS that is designed specifically for children and young people.*

For many years the congregation gathered at a Cuban Methodist church, but as of the writing of this book it meets at an Episcopal cathedral at Calle 6, entre 11 y 13, Vedado in Havana. https://tinyurl.com/y448u533

The fall of the Soviet Union ushered in a period of openness to foreign religious expression, including the establishment of numerous international congregations, particularly in countries that are now more or less independent while previously under Kremlin control.

The result was an initial influx of missionaries into those nations, the expansion of business investment which brought numerous expatriate residents to these previously closed countries, an explosion of students wanting to study in previously-forbidden nations, the introduction of Peace Corps workers and others in relief and development programs and the development of new churches to serve those English-speaking foreigners.

From Central Asia where new international churches popped up to Eastern Europe in countries such as the Czech Republic, new churches were formed to meet the spiritual needs of foreign business people, diplomats, students and others.

The second development was **the rise of globalization:**

Globalization means the interconnection of national economies across the world on issues such as trade, investment, labor, banking and the movement of people, goods and services. That seems like a mouthful, but it basically boils down to governments increasingly allowing their citizens do business across borders.

Still, it's a pretty wide-ranging concept.

Globalization is not a precise term. It can mean any way that nations have become interconnected. Although far from a new phenomenon, the term "globalization" gained popularity in the 1990s. The fall of the Soviet Union created the idea of a newly interconnected world, one not divided into the Cold War's armed camps, giving rise to globalization in the popular consciousness. The most common form of globalization, certainly the most high profile, is foreign trade.

But trade isn't all that globalization involves. Broadly, it also encompasses wider contacts between nations and their people, expanded educational exchanges involving both students and professors, increased cross-border trade involving the establishment of manufacturing plants, the international increase in demand and supply, communication and contact, and an immense increase in the number of people working and living abroad. https://tinyurl.com/y2mvr7kc

According Laurence E. Rothenberg, a fellow at the Center for Strategic and International Studies in Washington, D.C, globalization is the acceleration and intensification of interaction and integration among the people, companies and governments of different nations.

Globalization has resulted not just in goods and services travelling across borders. It has also resulted in people moving across borders. The effects of globalization have resulted in the number of expatriates rising in the developing countries as well. **https://tinyurl.com/y4tnk8od**

The implications for international churches are obvious. As educational, business, religious, cultural relations open up and expand between various nations, it is a natural conclusion that people—whether those in business or education or religious entities-will find it easier and profitable to relocate to where the action is and business can be conducted.

In 2012, an article in the Bangkok newspaper, *The Nation,* reported, *"Over 43 percent of companies across Asia project an increase in cross-border traditional expatriate assignments in the next two years... And, 85 percent of them expect to send their staff to posts in neighboring Asian nations. Globally, 45 percent of all international companies expect to send an increasing number of employees abroad to all parts of the world."*

Those statistics offer an expanding opportunity for outreach by international churches, but also present a challenge in formulating ministries to meet the unique needs of third-culture members.

A strong economy at the time portended an increase in expatriate business people with the accompanying opportunity for international churches to reach out and expand their ministries.

Yet, just four years later, in 2016, we learned that Brexit, the plan of Great Britain to leave the European Union, might lead to a diminishing number or shifting population of expats in Europe. (See *Brexit Offers Opportunity for International Congregations in Europe* on page 349).

And, that same year saw a surge in nationalism among many Western countries, led by the election of U.S. President Donald J. Trump, which foretold a withdrawal from international contracts and business and the potential decline in the number of expats in many categories.

The third development was **the diminishing of traditional Protestant denominations and the rise of independent, evangelical churches:**

Dr. L Thomas Smith, Jr, President and Professor of History and Theology at Johnson University in Knoxville, Tennessee described this most succinctly as: "The disintegration of the denominational structures of the American church…along with the expansion of "non-denominational" (mostly evangelical) church networks." (*Above Every Other Desire, The History of Johnson University*, 1893-2018 by Dr. L. Thomas Smith Jr., published by Xulon Press, 2018. Page 153)

Rev. David Packer who has served as the pastor of several international Baptist churches including in Singapore and Stuttgart, Germany carries on that description:

WHAT HAPPENED? When I started my ministry in the 1970s, it was assumed that a church would be associated in a responsible relationship with other churches of similar faith. A non-denominational church was looked at skeptically, as though they were unpredictable and even a bit proud – seeming to be better than others. A denomination brought responsible doctrine, accountable relationships, and meaningful partners in the Gospel.

But somewhere in the 1990s things began to change for churches in the U.S. From somewhere there arose an anti-denomination way of thinking. Non-denominational churches grew at the expense of denominational churches. Part of this is due largely to an anti-institutional trend as a whole across the U.S. Americans are suspicious of institutions, having felt betrayed more than once by them. Another factor is that many denominations formed when transportation and communication between nations and states was difficult, and now many of the things that used to separate us are removed. Almost all denominations across the world have some geographic and ethnic issues behind their history, and once these are removed are they still relevant? Also, the Jesus Movement Revival of the 1960s and 70s led to influential churches and movements that emphasized "just being Christian is enough." Denominations were viewed as too narrow and divisive. Some denominational leaders were liberal also and took stands that seemed like a betrayal of trust of the common people who were much more conservative. Yet, when the grass roots rose up in complaint, they were viewed by some as being too negative, too controlling, and even of some unchristian behavior. And toss in a moral failing or two, a doctrinal scandal, or some financial mess and it developed into a perfect storm. So rather than trying to fix things, people felt powerless and denominations seemed increasingly irrelevant. Highlights, International Baptist Convention, August 2018 https://tinyurl.com/y47kr54m

With the drastic decline in traditional, mainline denominations and their churches, a resulting leap in the planting of independent, non-denominational evangelical churches has occurred. While some of them are affiliated with denominational bodies but don't identify as such, the majority are "pop-up" churches. These worshipping bodies coalesce around the personality of a leader/pastor, seminary trained or not, who leads a group to open up a worship center in a high school auditorium, an abandoned super market, a shopping center, an old warehouse or some other re-purposed facility.

As these congregations have stabilized, grown and developed their own identity, they have reached out to new communities and planted new churches. And, some have looked to establish international congregations as a part of their evangelistic outreach.

Several of those outreach efforts have developed within more traditional entities. Take the International Baptist Convention. We saw in the previous chapter that numerous IBC-related churches span the globe. Some are tied to the Southern Baptist Convention in the United States while others are the result of outreach of IBC.

The current IBC church-planting effort is explained this way:

People from every nation under heaven are gathering in cities around the globe seeking business, education or social opportunities. As this population shift takes place, another shift is occurring. Those international populations increasingly speak English as a common language. When a Chinese student attends university in Germany – the language he speaks with his roommate from Argentina is English! In international business, sports, education and social networking, even among air traffic controllers in the skies, English is the common language of the world.

As the international English-speaking population grows, the opportunities for the spread of the gospel grow. International Churches are English-speaking congregations where people from around the globe gather to worship, and learn about life in Christ. For many, it is their first opportunity to hear the gospel and worship without fear of persecution. Here they find community, support one another, grow in faith, and reach out to their family and friends with the gospel.

International Church Planting is an exciting way to "go into all the world" by reaching population centers where the nations have gathered!

Our Mission: We exist to mobilize and multiply disciple-making churches.

Our Vision: We envision a movement of global-minded churches that are reproducing healthy disciples, leaders, and congregations.

We dream of...

- *stimulating churches toward mission advancement.*
- *helping churches to keep their focus on making and multiplying disciples.*
- *developing pastors and leaders in essential ministry skills.*
- *becoming a catalyst for strategic church-planting.*
- *nurturing a spirit of love that bridges cultures, nationalities, ethnicities, generations, politics, privilege, position, and religious backgrounds.*
- *fostering fellowship and connections among pastors and churches.*
- *supporting churches in times of need and transition.*

Our Core Values

Partnership *We believe that working together with other churches to reach common goals enriches churches. Every church has something to offer. We also believe in connecting with other Christ following groups. We can achieve more in this way than working independently of one another. We believe that cooperation is a gift of God. (Phil. 1:3-11, Eccl. 4:9)*

Healthy Churches *Because we believe that the local church is God's primary means of presenting the Gospel and establishing His kingdom, we will seek to help churches achieve their unique, disciple making mission in relevant and effective ways. (Acts 2:42-47, 1 Thess. 1:2-10)*

Church Planting *We believe that every church should be involved in some way in helping to start new congregations. We desire to expand our reach to strategic places around the world where the Gospel is needed. (Acts 1:8, Matt. 28:18-20)*

Unity *The unity of the Spirit among our churches exhibits the oneness of all believers in Christ. We will seek to work out differences that may arise because we believe the power of the Gospel to unite us is stronger than the power of our enemy to divide us. (John 17:20-23, Eph. 2:19-22)*

Diversity *Since Jesus commanded us to make disciples of all nations, we celebrate that people from many nations and cultures come together in our churches. We believe that our diversity expresses the creativity and eternal plan of God. (Gen. 12:3, Rev. 7:9-10)*

Fellowship *We believe that community among Christ followers facilitates encouragement, prayer, edification, and accountability. We believe that Christian friendships develop when we take the time and effort to share our joys, sorrows, and challenges. (1 Thess. 5:14, Gal. 6:2)*

IBC efforts are focusing on several dozen cities where international Baptist churches do not exist. At the publication date of this book, those cities included: Helsinki, Finland, Tallin and Tartu, Estonia, Tartu, Estonia, Riga, Latvia, Malmo, Sweden, Rotterdam Netherlands, Oslo, Norway, Stockholm, Sweden, Florence, Italy, Catania, Italy, Athens, Greece, Istanbul, Turkey, Barcelona, Spain, Valletta, Malta, Lisbon, Portugal, Grafenwoehr/Vilseck, Germany, Mannheim, Germany, Heidelberg, Germany, Munich, Germany, Frankfurt, Germany, Strasbourg, France, Paris, France, Rio de Janeiro, Brazil, Curitiba, Brazil, Bogotá, Colombia, Quito, Ecuador, San Miguel Allende, Mexico and Lima, Peru.

It should be interesting to note that at least two of those cities previously hosted international Baptist churches which later closed. Those are Quito, Ecuador and Bogotá, Colombia, where an existing English-language Baptist church eventually merged with the Union Church of Bogotá. The Bogotá church made the move during the intense activity of guerrilla groups, especially the FARC (The Revolutionary Armed Forces of Colombia—People's Army [Spanish: Fuerzas Armadas Revolucionarias de Colombia—Ejército del Pueblo.]) During that period many expatriates fled the country because of safety concerns. Today the major international church there is known as the United Church of Bogotá.

The old Union Church in the Colombian capital traced its roots back to 1867 when the first English language worship services were conducted by Protestant missionaries. In the late 1960s or early 1970s it merged with the local English-language Anglican/Episcopalian church, and then with the Baptist church during the violence of the 1990s.

One church of this new Baptist effort is already off the ground. *LifeBridge was launched just over 5 years ago* (approximately 2014) *with the vision of providing the community with an English speaking Church, for the international community living in Panama City, Panama.*

After Panama City saw a boom of expatriates it was clear that an English-speaking church was a necessity. It was at that time that Glenn Herschberger and his wife came to Panama City to plant and lead LifeBridge, with the help of a key leadership team. LifeBridge saw growth and it became even more evident the need and desire for this unique community. In 2013, Glenn and Susan were called back to the States to serve in a different role.... LifeBridge *continued to be a light in Panama because of the incredible leadership team that continued to faithfully meet and serve. In 2017, Nate and Jendi Korpi moved to Panama and have taken on the lead Pastor role.*

LifeBridge sees over 20+ nations represented on a Sunday and provides a community for Christ-followers for those who find Panama City home, whether it be for 2 weeks, 2 months, 2 years or a lifetime. https://tinyurl.com/y3qj423x

Another of the newer churches is located in Germany: *Multination Church is an International church located in the heart of Frankfurt am Main Germany with a second location in London, England. We intentionally have services in English as we have a goal to plant international, English speaking churches all over the world! Join us for worship every Sunday at 11:00 in one of our two locations: Frankfurt and London.* http://multination.org (Multination Church is the name of the former Bethel International Church in Frankfurt, one of the two founding churches of what is now the IBC).

Assemblies of God

In this third stream of international church planting exists a new sub stream, that of the Assemblies of God. These efforts have been less organized compared to other denominations. As Cathy Ketcher of the Assemblies of God World Ministries Research and Archives office explains:

Efforts to organize the planting of English-language churches overseas have taken place only during the last several years. Before that, English-language churches came into being as a matter of necessity to reach expatriates or provide them with a place to worship, but a definitive list of them was never created. (Personal email to the author, June 21, 2019)

In the August, 2016 issue of the AOG denominational magazine *WorldView,* Greg Mundis, the executive director of AOG missions, tells of one denominational program initiated to plant such churches:

Around the world about 100 strategically located international churches share the gospel and disciple believers from every continent. AGWM has launched the Momentum initiative with a goal to plant 100 new international churches in the next few years....

From the earliest beginnings of international churches—today one of the most effective ministry strategies in key cities around the world—missionaries were led of the spirit to minister in a specific need in a particular place....

Today, around the world, about 100 Assemblies of God international churches are sharing the gospel with and discipling new believers among the growing multitudes who travel to and through strategic cities on every continent....

The newly launched Assemblies of God World Missions Momentum initiative is coordinating with missionary teams and local church leaders to plant another 100 international churches.

When I served as AGWM regional director for Europe, I had a strong conviction—thanks to the clear growth of the international church movement even then—that the continent was on the threshold of a new initiative of the Spirit. New ministries and possibilities awaited development for evangelism and church planting among an array of immigrant groups. Out of these church plants, there was enormous potential to train workers to be sent back to their home cultures (many of which do not allow traditional Christian ministry by any Western groups) and to work in their cultures in European cities. As I continue to interact with our AGWM international church pastors, I see this trend continuing to grow....

The growth trajectory of the international church movement now includes individual congregations that number in the multiple thousands, some with 50 or 60 nations represented....

When Larry Henderson, (then senior pastor of Vienna Christian Center) ...describes the heart of international church outreach, he voices a deeply held belief shared by missionary pastors of Assemblies of God international churches around the world.

"What's unique about the international church," Larry insists, "is that is has an effect both locally and globally. As a network, we're working in the countries where God has called each church to be planted. We're not removed from the national church. We're helping the national church in significant ways to teach nationals as well as the internationals they're trying to reach. But the reach of the international church goes far beyond the local setting into literally all the world."

"Like the apostle Paul before us, we are living in a globalized world," says Richard Dunn, Momentum coordinator. "The cities of our world offer us an opportunity to reach many foreign-born

people who are searching for answers to life's problems. They come from around the world to live and work and study. Some are escaping oppression, war or poverty in their home countries. Among these world citizens are also believers who want a place to serve and grow in their faith."

Joe Szabo who pastors another AOG church in Europe said, "If I could sum up in three words what an international church is supposed to be, it is to be a lighthouse, it is to be an oasis, it is to be a launching pad."

(Adapted from *WorldView* magazine, August 2016)

Other AOG efforts are reflected in the descriptions of regional umbrella organizations which follow.

Global, regional umbrella organizations

With an explosion of new international churches being established by individual congregations during this era of expanded freedom and business, numerous umbrella groups have also been organized to help provide resources and coordination. Several of them are reviewed here.

Asia Pacific International Churches

This is a loose network of churches in Asia Pacific that relate to the World Assemblies of God Fellowship (WAGF). The group meets about every 18 months and the meetings largely consist of sharing ideas and best practices.

The coordinator of the group is the Key Ministry Advocate for International Churches in the Assemblies of God USA World missions department. Currently that is me. The group also includes some of the churches in China where leadership relates to the USA AGWM.

Most of the churches have USA AGWM missionaries as lead pastor, though not all of them.

Contact: David Kenney at dave@iesjakarta.org

FEIC Fellowship of European International Churches

(FEIC) is a relational network related to the Assemblies of God and comprised of congregations that minister to the unique opportunities, needs and challenges of international communities in European cities. The network offers supportive relationships, resources, strategic church renewal and leadership development opportunities.

Our network churches are a tapestry of cultures and traditions, races and people groups, languages and nationalities. FEIC churches are committed to planting new churches, positioning existing churches for strategic development, and partnering with national churches to do international ministry and accelerate the work of the Gospel among Europe's diverse international population.

FEIC is led by Larry Henderson, senior pastor of Vienna Christian Center, and Tony Ibarra, founder of Jesus

For All People Ministries. www.feic.org

Larry Henderson: larryhenderson@me.com,

Global International Church Network (GICN) *is a relational connection for a global network of international churches and is related to the Assemblies of God. Its intentional desire is to establish visibility, encourage vision and enhance the vitality of its churches.*

The idea for Global ICN was birthed during a time of worship and prayer at Summit 2011 of the Fellowship of European International Churches (FEIC). Several members commented on friends of international churches outside of Europe who sought to have the same relational community that is enjoyed in Europe. Several pastors and leaders of international churches from outside of Europe were already attending Summit events, with others connected through online correspondence. The need for a global relational connection resurfaced throughout the conference. Clearly, God was speaking.

Coming away from the 2011 Summit, FEIC Founder Terry Hoggard felt that God was leading to invest in creating a global network to connect international churches relationally. Since then, joining with the Assemblies of God World Mission, a development team has worked to establish the foundation and functionality of GICN. https://www.globalicn.com/

Asia Baptist Network

The Hawaii Pacific Baptist Convention (HPBC) is a network of 155 churches and is related to the Southern Baptist Convention. This includes 121 churches in the Hawaiian Islands (81 churches on O'ahu and 40 churches on "The Neighbor Isles" of Hawai'i, Maui, Moloka'i, Lana'i, and Kaua'i) as well as 13 churches of the South Pacific Baptist Association (American Samoa & Samoa), 10 churches of the Baptist Association of Micronesia (Guam & Saipan), and 9 churches which are a part of the Asia Baptist Network (Okinawa, Mainland Japan, South Korea, Thailand, and Philippines). Their network of international churches is called the Asia Baptist Network and Friends.

Today, Hawaii is a mix of cultures and races. Strategically situated at the crossroads of the Pacific where East and West meet every day, Hawaii has been called the "Melting Pot" of the world. Baptists in Hawaii have a great heritage and reputation and must demonstrate the radiance of a living Christ to the mission field of the pacific. https://www.hpbaptist.net/history/

International Christian Community

THE MISSION OF ICC is to establish and partner with English-speaking, internationally diverse, gospel centered churches in all the principal cities of Europe, and beyond. Our vision is for every church to become a radiating center of light in a secularized environment, offering the *hope of the gospel of Jesus Christ* to all people regardless of background, nationality, or economic status, then to *equip and send believers "to the ends of the earth"* with the good news.

ICC seeks to provide resources, community, and encouragement for individuals, pastors and churches.

ICC often functions as a church planting organization, establishing new English-speaking congregations in cities where gospel-centered churches are desperately needed.

In some cases ICC also partners with existing churches that align with the mission. We are always overjoyed to discover other English-speaking congregations that we can come alongside as they spread the gospel and enrich their people and their cities.

The ICC organizational infrastructure helps provide funding and development resources for new and struggling congregations in a uniquely challenging mission field. ICC offers the support of a cross-continental network of like-minded believers and gospel-focused churches. http://icceurasia.com/

International Churches Net

A global resource network for English-speaking international churches. This is strictly a website that provides a resource for individuals and churches to identify, connect and network with others who share similar passions for global evangelism and ministry. It is primarily a listing of many such churches around the world. http://www.internationalchurches.net/

Missional International Church Network,

The Missional International Church Network is focused on Starting and Strengthening International Churches. It can be said that we are a multi-, inter-, non-denominational network of churches, missions organization, and church networks.

In order to accomplish our mission, we have defined the following Impact Initiatives:

- ***Conferences*** - Our first initiative is hosting Compelling Conferences that give lift to IC's and create opportunities for partnership and soul care for leaders
- ***ICXchange*** - International Church Exchange is an initiative to support International Churches (IC's) who would like to host a multi-IC event (i.e. conference, forum, roundtable) tailored to their context, so that the strengthening we are providing is as relevant as possible
- ***Church Starting*** – We envision IC's multiplying through the cooperation of mission agencies, denominations, church planters, and existing IC's all working together! We facilitate these partnerships and give guidance to steer and catalyze the work
- ***Equipping*** – IC's and their leaders experience great isolation and often lack the resources needed to carry out all God has called them to do. MICN endeavors to equip leaders and churches to be healthy and effective through mentoring, coaching, training, and caring for leaders along with making effective partners and resources available to IC's all over the world.

Guiding us in this process are our six Core Values:

Collegial Collaboration

A relational network of IC leaders, we highly value the comradery and community among peers across the globe, because together we can have greater kingdom impact.

Biblical Holism

Anticipating the return of Christ and the transformation of all things, we are a visionary movement of missionally engaged international churches and Christians.

Lead Followers

Recognizing that great leaders are first great followers, we value humility and integrity in leadership and provide care and encouragement for leaders to thrive.

Insatiable Learners

Pursuing wisdom, knowledge, and understanding, we constantly evaluate and innovate to stay relevant and sensitive to the ever-changing context and culture.

Multi-cultural Voices

Considering the diversity in context and cultural complexity, we provide an open platform where everyone has a voice so all can gain an international perspective.

Spirit-led Prayer

God-size movements need God-size prayer, for our vision & network, our initiatives & strategies, and our partners & members, anticipating God to inspire the prayers He will answer.

The Missional International Church Network was founded in 2004 by Warren Reeve. He was pastoring at an international church in Indonesia and bringing people from various backgrounds and missions agencies together to work in unity toward reaching people in their community. That effort grew into a movement that still sees over 300 Muslims baptized every month. As other IC leaders heard of the fruit being seen through Warren's IC, they wanted to know how they might get their churches to be on mission, or missional, in the same way, and the first MICN conference was born.

Over the years we have seen a lot of fruit come out of bringing IC leaders together to talk about how their churches can work for the good of the city, country, and world that we live in. One

IC has seen over 4,000 Vietnamese come to Christ as the result of its pastor being inspired through MICN. Another has seen their own missions endeavors expanded further through the connections MICN has provided. An IC plant recently had funding granted by MICN, so it could rent a space to meet weekly for a full year and have time to build up its giving.

And it is clear pastors are finding it helpful, as the network has grown beyond Southeast Asia. It first expanded into the Middle East when Warren became the pastor of an IC there. Over the years churches from all over the world have become affiliated with us, but we had focused most of our efforts within the 10/40 window. But in 2016 MICN was part of hosting an event in Hong Kong where pastors from IC's from all over the world and various networks were in attendance. David Fresch, who pastors an IC in Norway and is a leader in the International Baptist Convention, was in attendance, and Warren asked David to join the MICN International Leadership Team after meeting him. David now serves as the Executive Director of MICN, and there are a growing number of other pastors in Europe and Africa asking for MICN to be more active in their part of the world, which will be the next step in MICN's organic growth.

You can learn more about the Missional International Church Network at https://micn.org or by emailing *admin@micn.no.*

Network for International Congregations

This website with a listing of many international churches and several related articles is the successor to the long line of international church offices established by the traditional U.S. denominations and housed for many years in the office building of the National Council of Churches at 475 Riverside Drive in New York City. Over time, as traditional denominations reduced and eliminated their support for the office, it reduced to a part-time position and eventually relocated outside of New York to the residence of whoever was directing it.

This organization along with its extensive list of churches and pastoral openings can be accessed at www.internationalcongregations.com. The current director is Bob Robbins, the pastor of the Sampa Church in Sao Paulo, Brazil. He succeeded Dr. James Dwyer of California who operated the website for many years after serving international churches in Europe.

http://www.internationalcongregations.com/
internationalcongregations@gmail.com

AICEME, Association of International Churches in Europe and the Middle East.

This organization was described earlier. While reported to be still active, as of this writing its website has been severely garbled and efforts to repair it have not been successful.

CIF

The China International Fellowship is a relational network of international fellowships and the leaders of those fellowships in China. It is related to the Assemblies of God. We gather to support, encourage and to pray for each other. We meet annually for an event called the Gathering. For more information, write: cif@scfenglish.com or cif@bicf.org

While many of these groups maintain a list of international churches, other listings can be found online. Two additional resources are:

https://www.internationalchurches.eu/
http://www.internationalchurches.net/

What's Next?

As one can see by reading through the historic documents and church histories in this book, the nature of international congregations has long been debated and has changed due to historic and ecclesiastical developments over the centuries.

Even within a few years, the projected trajectory of these churches can change rapidly due to global economic, social and political trends.

As we have pointed out, the establishment and expansion of international churches has occurred during periods of peace and prosperity. The end of global conflicts such as World Wars I and II led to a growth of the number of expats and thus an increase in international churches. Without a doubt, the development of the phenomenon of globalization exponentially expanded the number of expatriates in fields such as business, education and Christian ministry. These and other factors led to a surge of evangelical missionary work, including the foundation of independent, international churches in many localities as thousands of a new generation of expats sought Christian fellowship in English in their new locations.

In an article from 2012, found later in this book, I speculated that anticipated growth among Asian businesses would lead to an increase in the number of international churches in that region.

Again, in 2016 I wrote about the effect on European ICs of a possible exit from the European Union by the United Kingdom (Brexit). I said, *"In a constantly changing world, economic and geo-political changes are an often-overlooked dynamic that can affect churches in terms of the ebb and flow of participants and the development of programming to meet new dynamics....*

A new report from the Wall Street Journal highlights a similar opportunity throughout Europe due to Brexit, the recent vote by British citizens mandating that their country leave the European Union within the next few years. That change will result in numerous business executives and their families leaving the United Kingdom to settle in European cities, according to the newspaper. This projected change has brought concern to Englishlanguage expatriate schools across the continent as they attempt to gear up for the influx....

While International Congregations may not have... overflow concerns, the impending wave of English-speaking expats to scattered European churches can be a unique opportunity for the ICs to expand their ministries, find new ways of service and grow their congregations. As has been done in other locations, ICs which link with English-language schools can use that relationship to provide relocation and orientation services to newly arrived residents, offer counseling and family support as people make the transition, and advertise the availability of their church for worship, fellowship, Christian education and other services.

As this book is written, many nations find themselves in another changing political climate as more isolationist leaders assume power and attempt to withdraw their countries from much of the broader scene offered by globalization.

As a result, the development of worldwide business models and the large flow of expats to new opportunities outside of their homeland may be declining. Thus, in the short term, international churches can expect to see a decrease in participants and longevity of members in their flock. Even the establishment of new churches might slow as long as those isolationist politics play out. (The two articles mentioned here may be found in a later chapter titled *Previously published articles by the author.)*

Ultimately, these more narrowly focused values will recede as a new generation sees the world though different eyes and grasps the grand opportunities of a globalized world and the blessings of these unique multicultural gatherings.

When the author first entered the field of ministry in Union Churches, the debate at congregational council meetings and annual gathering of pastors concerned the nature of the organizations, in particular, whether they were islands or bridges.

Island:

Those who argued for their identity as an island saw them as a social and theological refuge from the stress and struggle of living in a foreign country amidst cultural, economic, health and language differences, let alone the insecurity of being a Christian in a non-Christian atmosphere.

Union churches, it was argued, were to be seen as a place of refuge where one could worship in a Christian atmosphere among people who shared a common language and very similar cultural background. It was there that children could be raised and taught, youth could find compatible friends and activities and people in general could experience familiar food, language, friendship and encouragement from others going through similar experiences.

Bridge:

On the other hand, there were those who argued that ICs should be more interactive with the culture and society in which they were located and offer opportunities for outreach, evangelism and service. Thus, many developed their own means of reaching out or joined hands with missionaries and others who were already working on a local level to address perceived needs and offer an opportunity for cross-cultural experiences and service.

For some churches, the bridge concept is easily understood in that the bulk of their membership consists of people such as missionaries, teachers, development workers and others who are already in the country for service reasons. One such church in the author's experience was the International Church of Bishkek which involved very few diplomats or business people but many missionaries, teachers, social workers and others who were there specifically to be of service.

A recent statement from that church illustrates how they have incorporated the outreach/cross cultural model in their congregation:

Philosophy of Ministry

While the Bible gives many images of the church, there are specific images that are helpful to keep in mind when one thinks of the International Church of Bishkek:

- *A Watering Hole – In desert places, watering holes are important. Those who come to such a watering hole are often thirsty, and are looking to be refreshed; they also plan to go from the watering hole to their next destination. It is essential that ICB is a watering hole that satisfies the weary and provides for all those who come what is needed to face the challenges they will certainly face. Many foreigners and locals have active ministries outside ICB and therefore tend to focus on them rather than a lot of involvement in the activities of ICB; they too come seeking refreshment.*
- *A Wedding Banquet – Many who come to the church come from backgrounds where the pastor is viewed as more important than all others; some who come have a magical view of the role of the pastor related to prayer. It is essential for ICB to model the biblical image of the wedding banquet, which God the Father prepares for his Son, to which we are all invited. Each of us sits as equals at this banqueting table, clothed in Christ's righteousness. Each of us offers our gifts like loaves and fishes to Jesus for him to multiply and use for his glory.*
- *A Discipleship Community – Some who come, even if they have been Christians for many years, have never learned how to help another to grow in Christ. Many who come are new to the Christian faith and are just learning to*

> *take ownership of their own growth in Christ. ICB takes seriously the call to form people in Christ through the Scriptures such that they feel able to help others to grow.*

This trend in IC life has been highlighted in Sadir Joy Tira and Tetsunao Yamamori's book *Scattered and Gathered: A Global Compendium of Diaspora Missiology:*

"Historically ICs tended to be more insular and operated in maintenance mode. In 1987, International Congregations Christians Abroad Director, Art Bauer, attempted to capture the evolution of the IC from colonialism in six single descriptive phrase(s): American Union, International, English, Context, Missional, and Evangelical (Art Bauer, Being in Mission, (New York: Friendship Press, 1987), 12-13). Bauer said, "The English-speaking International Congregation is a multi-cultured, multi-denominational, local fellowship of expatriate people who are united in Christian belief and who share an identity as foreigners with English as a common language," Since then, ICs are intentionally moving toward a more aggressive model of Kingdom expansion as compared to an ecumenical agenda. Now they are becoming missional. In the excellent unpublished article[7] entitled "Gateway to the Nations: The Strategic Value of the International Church in a Globalized Urban World" missiologists Michael Crane and Scott Carter wrote in 2014: "ICs around the world are making an invaluable contribution to the church's mission to make disciples of every nation. Around the world God has used IC's as instrumental in sowing seeds of the gospel of Jesus Christ on the frontiers of lostness." The most encouraging and exciting characteristic trend of the IC is utilizing IC expatriates for outreach. Where local governments and cultural contexts allow for it, ICs are initiating various service ministries. Pastor

[7] Since that book was published the article has been posted online at https://tinyurl.com/y598kv5b

Jacob Bloemberg of the Hanoi International Fellowship (HIC) in communist Vietnam has developed and implemented a strategy called "Love Hanoi: Engaging City Leadership through Christ-Centered Civic renewal." His doctoral dissertation, written for Bakke Graduate University, has received several impacting responses. The Hanoi City Chief of Police invited HIC to the newly built theater at police headquarters to present Love Hanoi. "The official government security website praised the protestant churches campaign to "Love Hanoi" in their online report of the event.

Sadir Joy Tira and Tetsunao Yamamori, S*cattered and Gathered: A Global Compendium of Diaspora Missiology,* Wipf and Stock Publishers, Eugene OR, 2016.

Through the efforts of MICN, numerous international churches are developing a more holistic model of operation. One such congregation, as mentioned above, is the Hanoi International Fellowship in Vietnam. Opening doors to city officers in an officially atheistic country such as Vietnam was uncertain at first. Dr. Jacob Bloemberg, the church's pastor, describes their approach:

Our first meeting was with a Colonel from the Protestant office of the religious department of Hanoi's security police. When that went well, he came to visit our worship service...and was impressed by our casual way of worship compared to Catholic services. Next came an invitation to meet the Colonel's boss, a General, at the city police headquarters....

When I was invited to state my request, I answered, How can we as foreign Christians love Hanoi?...The General was speechless, as he would have expected me to ask for permits for our church, for our rights as foreigners to worship freely....

Our posture and our actions to love the city and contribute to society through our Love Hanoi campaign had built bridges with local and national government.

(Dr. G. Jacob Bloemberg, *Love [Your City], 5 Steps To City-wide Movements.* Forthcoming)

Those of us who have approached government officials in semi-closed countries with hat in hand might have done much better to have gone with a plan to engage the community with service.

The predominant characteristic of the third stream of international churches since 1990 has been that they come out of the growing evangelical stream of Christianity, especially in North America. In comparison, the second stream represented the traditional "mainstream" American denominations such as the Presbyterians, Methodists, Lutherans, Disciples of Christ and others.

One of their major contributions to IC ministries was the concept of cooperative work among those denominational groups and the inclusive fellowship that their churches represented. Thus, a "Union" church or "International" congregation would represent people from a wide variety of denominational backgrounds, varying governmental structures, and diverse nationalities and ethnic groups.

As I mentioned in the first chapter of this book, those who served during the era of "Union Churches" held out pluralism as a value that might one day become the practice in churches of the home countries. I quoted Dr. John R. "Jack" Collins who then served as director of the office of International Congregations and Lay Ministries saying: "as international, interracial, intercultural, inter-denominational congregations

(Union Churches) are a prototype of the church of the future,"... both overseas and in home countries.

While I rejoice that new churches are being established to provide ministry to third-culture people around the world, and many of the older churches have adapted to serve a newer, younger generation, I'm afraid that, perhaps, we are losing the dream Jack had.

Numerous competing churches are being established with little or no contact with each other or recognition that, indeed, there are other international churches in their own cities. I have heard pastors proclaim they serve the only international church in their city or they "are the only game in town" when, in fact, there are up to a dozen more such congregations where they serve.

I regret seeing a movement which brought different Christian churches together dissolve into a separation which can be harmful and divisive.

Multi-national, multi-ethnic, multi-denominational: some common characteristics, but often with a different twist

The main characteristic of the international congregations is that while they are multi-national, multi-ethnic and multi-denominational, each one is different depending on its history, the political-social context in which it exists, the church tradition of it leadership the extent of transition they experience and a host of other factors.

Among those characteristics that are common are their multi-denominational nature, a more rapid turnover of members than in homeland churches, their mix of expats and third culture local people and their mix of background ecclesiastical traditions.

Expats are, by nature of their work, more likely to be short term. Students, diplomats, business people are very apt to be in country for three to five years (or less for students) before they are moved on by their sponsoring entity (employer) or the completion of their project. Meanwhile local third-culture people who have worked or studied outside of their own country may return, desire to know and associate with an expat crowd, and will settle with an expat congregation.

With the decline of traditional denominations in home countries such as the United States, younger expats will search out a congregation that meets their spiritual and worship needs regardless of its name or denominational background. Thus, international Baptist churches will find their congregations populated by Presbyterians or Methodists or Anglicans while any number of Baptists may turn up in an Anglican or Assemblies of God international congregation. That dynamic can be a catalyst to new forms of worship, exploration of preaching styles or other activities that suit the needs of the expat population.

Those successful international churches are the ones which have learned to adapt to their diverse congregation without compromising their basic biblical understandings and theological convictions.

What is more likely to be modified is the style of governing, worship, activities and fellowship.

A final observation--unique dynamics

While many churches today, international or local, have added security to their weekly gatherings, others in unique situations must take other precautions, ranging from snow to storms to earthquakes and local political activity.

Perhaps the most unique local caution would be that of the Community Church in Hong Kong:

General Typhoon and Black Rain Weather Policy

When a Typhoon Warning Signal No. 8 or higher is hoisted or a Black Rainstorm Warning is in effect two hours prior to all scheduled church activities (worship services, Bible studies, Life Groups, youth activities, children's programs etc), these activities will be cancelled. Church activities will resume within 2 hours after the Typhoon Warning Signal No. 8 or Black Rainstorm Warning is lowered or cancelled.

Sunday Weather Policy

If in the circumstance that a Typhoon Warning Signal No. 8 or higher is in effect or expected to be hoisted on a Sunday, our Sunday Services are as follows:

9:30am service
If a T8 signal on Sunday morning is in effect at 7:30am or expected to be issued by 9:00am, our 9:30am service is cancelled.

11:30am service
If a T8 signal on Sunday morning is in effect at 9:30am or expected to be issued by 11:00am, our 11:30am service is cancelled.
(Community Church, Hong Kong)

History: Individual union and international congregations

We have spent much of this book outlining the broad history of the international church movement. This has involved focusing on denominational and agency support for planting and maintaining such churches. Minutes and publicity from these groups have highlighted the strong support among churches and denominations in countries such as the United States, Canada and the United Kingdom.

But, as we will now discover, the more detailed history of international congregations is written in the narrative of individual congregations, large and small, from those scattered over the face of the earth in almost every non-English speaking country. Those locations are where expatriates and third-culture people have found a place of worship and service and the Kingdom has grown.

Let us turn now to these churches and their unique stories. (Much of this material was adapted from church websites, books or third-party sources such as Wikipedia).

Europe

St. Andrew's Anglican Church in Moscow

St Andrew's Anglican Church in Moscow is the sole Anglican church there and one of only three in Russia (The church in St Petersburg was established 1723). It continues the tradition of Anglican worship in Moscow that started in 1553 when Tsar Ivan the Terrible first allowed the English merchants of the Russia Company to worship according to their own beliefs. The Russia Company, now operating mainly for charitable purposes, continues to financially support the Anglican Church in Moscow through the congregation of St Andrew's.

The first Anglican worship in that city may have been held in the Old English Yard, now on Varvarka Street, the center of the Russia Company in Moscow. The first English church building in Russia was probably built in Arkhangelsk in the 17th century, with its chaplain serving both Arkhangelsk and Moscow from 1705. In 1754, with most foreigners in Russia residing in the new capital, St. Petersburg, the Moscow congregation was served by the chaplain from St. Petersburg. Services were probably held in the Reformed Church in Moscow›s German Quarter.

1860 photograph of the British Chapel, established in 1828

Sometime after the city burned in 1812, services were held on Tverskaya Street in the palace of Princess Anne Aleksandrovna Golitsina. From 1817 to 1818 services were held in the home of the British Ambassador, Earl Cathcart. British, German, and French Protestants all attended the services about this time. In 1825, the Russia Company established an independent chaplaincy in Moscow, and Tsar Alexander I, in one of his last official acts, approved the establishment of a church on September 7. A chapel was

opened, or perhaps re-opened, on Tverskaya Street in November 1825 with 100 of 400 British residents attending. The Russia Company provided 200 pounds to renovate the building, which sat 200 people, with an additional 100 pounds promised annually. The annual expenses were estimated at 4,750 rubles. The Rev. Charles Barton (or Burlton) was appointed by the Russia Company as chaplain in 1825 and the British Chapel was built in 1828 on the current site of St. Andrew's, at 8 Voznesensky (Ascension) Lane. It was designed by Richard Knill Freeman, of Bolton, in the Victorian Neo-Gothic style.

At the time, the congregation was evenly divided between supporters of the Church of England and those who supported the Presbyterian Church of Scotland. As a compromise, the church was named after St. Andrew, the patron saint of Scotland, and the Anglican Book of Common Prayer was to be used. To further establish St. Andrew›s as a United Kingdom church, national symbols of Scotland (the thistle), England (the rose), Ireland (shamrock), and Wales (the leek) are incorporated into the church architecture.

Jonathan Holt Titcomb, the Bishop of London's coadjutor for North and Central Europe, consecrated the church on January 13, 1885.

Jane McGill paid for the building of the parsonage in 1894. In 1904 she founded St. Andrew's House for indigent governesses and other ladies, on nearby Tverskaya Street.

During the October Revolution, Bolsheviks mounted a machine gun post in the church tower to stop troops of the Provisional Government from advancing toward the Kremlin. The Bolsheviks were dislodged on October 29, 1917.

According to Herbert North, son of the chaplain "we spent nearly a week in the basement with no light and little food. On emerging from the house at the end of the fighting we found many spent cartridges in the courtyard and two large pools of blood."

The church was confiscated in 1920 and the Chaplain, the Rev. Frank North, was expelled from Russia to Helsinki. He served in Helsinki, officially as the Chaplain to Helsinki and Moscow. During the following 71 years, the Helsinki chaplain would occasionally give services at the British Embassy in Moscow.

The church and parsonage were used by the Soviets as a hostel for girls and to house diplomats from Finland and Estonia.

In 1964 Melodiya took over the church as a recording studio. Dmitry Shostakovich and Mstislav Rostropovich both recorded at Melodiya's St. Andrew's studio.

Following perestroika, on July 15, 1991, the Helsinki Chaplain, the Rev. Tyler Strand, celebrated the first Eucharist at St. Andrew's since 1920.

Queen Elizabeth II visited the church on October 19, 1994, and agreed with Russian President Boris Yeltsin that the church would be returned. Russian Prime Minister Viktor Chernomyrdin signed the order to return of the property religious use, though in Russia, all religious property is officially state owned, with the congregation only having the right to use the property. Chernomyrdin›s order was not immediately effective, with the property re-registered to the state only in January 2008 and Melodiya occupying parts of the property until about 2001.

Adapted from Wikipedia, the free encyclopedia

Cathedral Church of the Holy Trinity in Paris

The Cathedral Church of the Holy Trinity in Paris is a church in the Anglican tradition. It owes its more commonly used name, "The American Cathedral" to its original American expatriate community as well as its link to the Episcopal Church founded in the United States after independence was won in 1789

In the 1830s, services were first organized in the garden pavilion of the Hotel de Matignon, then the home of Colonel Herman Thorn and today the official residence of the French Prime Minister. A parish was formally established in 1859 and the first church building consecrated in 1864 on Rue Bayard.

A New Church Is Built

In the 1870s, Dr. John Brainerd Morgan (1843-1912), a cousin of J.P. Morgan, became the second rector of the parish and began a successful fundraising campaign to erect a new and larger church. The present site was purchased on Avenue George V, then known as Avenue d'Alma, from the Duc de Morny, a half-brother of Emperor Napoléon III.

The Cathedral was built between 1881 and 1886, following the plans of the great English architect George Edmund Street (1824-1881). First services were held in September 1886 and the church was consecrated on Thanksgiving Day, November 25, 1886 coinciding with the dedication of the Statue of Liberty in New York, thus reinforcing both our French and American alliances.

A Master Of Gothic Revival

G. E. Street, a leading practitioner of the Victorian Gothic Revival architecture movement, designed the current church in this style. The Cathedral is considered the unique and finest example of this movement on the European continent and is listed on the register of French historical monuments. Street's other works included the American Church in Rome and the Royal Courts of Justice on the Strand in London. Street died in December 1881 before the finalization of the plans; his son, Arthur E. Street and another prominent English architect of the day - Arthur Blomfield, then took over the work.

Construction of the church edifice was accomplished by Henry Lovatt of Wolverhampton with the tower and other works continuing for more than two decades following the 1886 consecration of the nave. The tower, dedicated on Easter Sunday in 1909, rises 276 feet (84m) and is among the tallest in Paris.

Stained-glass windows designed by James Bell of London glassmakers Bell & Beckham, were executed between 1883 and 1893 in the same Early decorated style of architecture as the church. They are the only stained glass of their kind in France.

In March 1923, Holy Trinity became a pro-cathedral, defined as such in that it continues as both a parish church and serves as the seat for the Bishop in Charge for the Convocation of Episcopal Churches in Europe. Then in 1925, the name became the American Cathedral of the Holy Trinity. **Used by permission**

The American Church in Paris

The American Church in Paris was the first American church established on foreign soil. It is an interdenominational, Protestant congregation with roots dating back to 1814.

Our beginnings may be traced to the needs of American Protestants living in France in 1814, who sought a place to worship God in their native English language.

The first worship service was held in the apartment of an American merchant, and in 1815 the French Reformed Church opened the doors of its church, the Oratoire du Louvre, to these Americans, providing a place for them to hold regular services. People of all nationalities and denominational backgrounds were welcome to worship.

In 1839, a new American missionary organization, the American and Foreign Christian Union (AFCU), (http://www.afcubridge.org) was formed when three separate mission agencies merged. Today the AFCU includes ACP alumni who volunteer their time and energy to serve as a board of trustees, to participate in the selection of the senior pastor, and to support the church through efforts to build the endowment.

In 1857, the AFCU asked Dr. Edwin Kirk, a Presbyterian minister, to go to Paris to help the congregation become officially organized and find a permanent home. That year, the congregation chartered the American Chapel in Paris and purchased a site for a church building to be built on rue de Berri.

In 1923, when Dr. Joseph W. Cochran came to Paris with his family as the new pastor, he found that the church building on rue de Berri was not only in desperate need of major repairs but was too cramped for the growing congregation. Through Dr. Cochran's vision, plans for construction of our present church on quai d'Orsay began. Read more about the history of the American Church in Dr. Joseph W. Cochran's book, *Friendly Adventures: A Chronicle of the American Church of Paris (1857-1931)*. It can be read online at: https://tinyurl.com/y55cffod

Since the end of World War II, the American community in Paris had become increasingly diverse, and the number of English-speaking people of other nationalities has significantly increased. Today, no more than half of the regular worshippers at the American Church are American, with the other half coming from some 40 different countries of origin. The number of denominational backgrounds is equally diverse, so that now, more than ever before in its history, the American Church is an international and interdenominational community of faith.

The American Church in Paris is deeply rooted in the history of this city. It has been a living community of faith through all the major events of the past two centuries. Many people have found a spiritual home here and have been deeply engaged with the larger community of Paris in a wide variety of ministries and services.

Architecture

The first church building was erected in 1857 for a cost of $46,000 at 21 rue de Berri, just off the Champs-Elysées. The construction of the sanctuary on Quai d'Orsay was begun 1 March 1926, and was dedicated 6 September 1931.

The sanctuary is divided into three parts: the narthex (entryway), the nave (with the pews) and the chancel (the front of the church). The design of the sanctuary is based on a 15th century Gothic plan, including the central aisle flanked by two cloister side aisles. The main level of the sanctuary can accommodate approximately 600 people, with additional seating for 100 in the balcony above the narthex.

DID YOU KNOW?

- Woodrow Wilson attended services regularly during the World War I peace conference
- Ulysses S. Grant, Teddy Roosevelt and Dwight D. Eisenhower worshipped at the ACP
- Dr. Martin Luther King, Jr. preached from the pulpit on 24 October 1965
- Father Daniel Berrigan, Joan Baez, Bob Dylan and James Baldwin attended student meetings at ACP in the 1960s
- The first American Boy Scout Troop in Europe was formed out of the ACP Sunday School
- ACP participated in the founding of the American High School and American College in Paris
- ACP celebrated the Commemoration Service in memory of the victims of September 11, 2001 and former President Jacques Chirac was in attendance.
- Rev. Jesse Jackson preached at the ACP in 2007 and 2009.

Used by permission

International Baptist Church of Zurich

In September, 1987 an English language worship service was being held regularly on Sunday evenings in the chapel of the International Baptist Theological Seminary in Rüschlikon. This service was led by two American missionary families who were associated with the seminary: Charles and Bobie Cottle and Wes and Jean Miller. At the same time, the German-speaking Rüschlikon Baptist Church was holding bilingual Sunday morning services in the seminary chapel. Noting the growing attendance at the Sunday evening services, the team believed the time had come to establish an English-speaking church. A place to meet was found in Wädenswil, at the Hotel Engel, and a small group began worshiping there on Sunday mornings.

On December 13, 1987 the Lake Zürich Baptist Church was established with 18 members. Ben Leslie, a student at the Rüschlikon seminary, served as pastor.

A highlight of 1988 was the church's January move into the Evangelical Methodist Church building, on Rosenbergstrasse in Wädenswil. The Methodist service concluded at 10 a.m., which gave several members of the English-speaking congregation an opportunity to meet for choir practice. For the next few years, the International Baptist Church became known for its special music program since among its congregation were many opera singers. The service began at 11 o'clock, followed by a Bible

Study for adults. This schedule was typical as long as the church met in Wädenswil.

In April of 1989 the church name was changed to the International Baptist Church of Wädenswil. (This was done to accommodate the other Swiss lakeside Baptist churches in Thalwil, Horgen and Rüschlikon,) Also in that same year, the church joined both the Swiss Baptist Union and the European Baptist Convention.

In 1995 when the Baptist Theological Seminary in Rüschlikon relocated to Prague, Czech Republic, the European Baptist Federation elected not to sell the chapel along with the other property. Instead, it was given to the Swiss Baptist Union for their use. They, in turn, offered it to the local Baptist churches for their use as a worship center. With the departure of the Seminary population, the bilingual Rüschlikon Congregation was decimated, the remaining families decided to merge with the existing Thalwil congregation. This congregation already had its own building and did not wish to relocate. The International Baptist Church of Wädenswil had been experiencing space problems for quite some time, and gladly accepted the invitation to rent the building as the sole tenants, seeing it as an answer to prayer. The chapel, however, was in great need of renovation. The European Baptist Federation allocated a sizable amount for replacement of the heating system and for structural repairs. Additional funds were needed to convert the basement into useable Sunday school space and a fellowship area. The Rüschlikon Baptist Church generously contributed a large sum, even though they were no longer going to be using the building regularly. The remaining balance was contributed by the congregation and interested individuals. Renovations were completed in February of 1996, and a Dedication Service with participants from both the Rüschlikon and Wadenwil congregations was held on March 3, 1996. In anticipation of the move and given the close proximity to Zürich, the church changed its name to the International Baptist Church of Zürich (IBCZ) in 1996.

In November 2016 IBCZ finished the extension of the Seminary Chapel. Parts of the terrasse has been changed into two new rooms that can be used for Sunday School.

Today IBCZ has primary use of the former Seminary Chapel in Rüschlikon. As has been true throughout the history of IBCZ, it is an ever-changing group of people. The congregation encompasses people from all walks of life, many countries, and from various denominational backgrounds. **Used by permission**

The American Church in Berlin

The beginnings of our church date back to about 1865, when American families met in private homes to worship. In the years after the founding of the Kaiserreich (1871), the church experienced rapid growth. In 1903 it was able to dedicate its own building near Nollendorfplatz. The church was a lively center of religious and civic life until the outbreak of World War I, when it was closed in 1916. Reopened in 1921 and in spite of very unsteady times, the congregation resumed a prominent role in the American community. The church was closed again with Germany's declaration of war on America in 1941, and the building was destroyed during bombing raids in 1944. With the help of the American and Foreign Christian Union, the congregation continued from 1945 by sharing facilities with various congregations in Berlin-Zehlendorf and from 1964 was housed in the Alte Dorfkirche of the Paulus Gemeinde. The congregation developed into an international community and kept growing even after the Berlin Wall fell and the American military left Berlin. In the Fall of 2002 the American Church in Berlin returned to Schöneberg to a new church home-the historic Luther-Kirche on Dennewitzplatz. The congregation is once again near to its original location in the heart of the city. To be a community reflecting the light of Jesus Christ is both exciting and challenging. We are committed to being an ecumenical home for people from diverse nations sharing God's love in Jesus Christ. **Used by permission**

The story behind Stimson Memorial Chapel, American Protestant Church

Allied High Commissions governed Germany following the military occupation at the end of World War II. On May 3, 1949 the Federal Republic of Germany was created from the three western occupation zones and the newly elected Parliament (Bundestag) decided in a close vote to establish the "provisional" seat of government in Bonn. The American High Commission for Germany (known as HICOG) was at the time located in Frankfurt. Due to a shortage of housing in the Bonn area the HICOG was required to construct new housing for approximately 400 American employees and 800 Germans with their families. An 80-acre (32 hectares) parcel of farmland and orchards was purchased from the von Carstanjen family in Bonn-Plittersdorf. This construction began in February 1951 and was completed in the summer of 1952. The housing area contains 440 apartments, a shopping center, movie theater, school, club, gymnasium with swimming pool and a chapel, which was built in the style of 18th century churches in colonial New England. The HICOG moved to Bonn in 1952 and High Commissioner John J. McCloy dedicated the chapel on 18 July 1952.

Mr. McCloy decided to dedicate the chapel to the memory of his World War II superior, Secretary of War Henry L. Stimson, who had died in 1950. Henry Stimson almost single-handedly opposed Morgenthau Plan and proposed instead in a 1944 memorandum to President Roosevelt that the defeated Germans be given an opportunity to reconstruct their country and develop democratic institutions. Henry Stimson was thus the forerunner of George Marshall, who in 1947 as Secretary of State proposed the now famous Marshall Plan through which the American government provided billions of dollars to assist Europe to recover from the devastation of the war. In the vestibule of the Chapel is a bronze bust of Henry L. Stimson donated by his widow.

In 1956 the Stimson Chapel became the official chapel of the American Embassy, which succeeded the American High Commission for Germany. The chapel served not only the Protestant and Catholic worshippers from the families of the American Embassy, but also opened its doors to all English-speaking worshipers residing in the Bonn area. This included nationals from the foreign embassies or residing in the area, as well as an increasing number of German citizens. They were attracted to the American style of worship and church community life, which includes a strong youth program, community outreach and support of Christian missionary activities in many parts of the world. This multi-national participation has continued to the present. Throughout the 50 years of its existence citizens of more than 40 nations have participated in the religious and community activities of Stimson Memorial Chapel.

The dramatic international developments of the fall of 1989 led to the reunification of Germany on October 1, 1990 after 45 years of division. On June 20, 1991 in a close vote (338-320) the German parliament decided to move the capital from Bonn to Berlin. This meant that the American Embassy also would move to Berlin. During the succeeding years the American Embassy sold the housing area in Bonn-Plittersdorf and all of its property in Bonn - except for the Stimson Memorial Chapel.

On June 20, 1999 while visiting Germany to attend an international G-8 Summit Meeting in Cologne, President William J. Clinton came to Bonn and officially turned over the keys to the Stimson Memorial Chapel to Bonn Lord Mayor Bärbel Dieckmann. The U.S. government had decided to give the chapel to the city of Bonn as a gift and symbol of post-war German-American friendship. After 47 years in Bonn the American Embassy officially moved to Berlin on July 1, 1999.

With the departure of the American Embassy a substantial number of active members of the Protestant and Catholic congregations remained in the Bonn area and were anxious to continue worshipping in the chapel. The two congregations therefore formed a "Förderverein Stimson Memorial Chapel e.V." (SMC) to foster continued use of the chapel after ownership was transferred to the city of Bonn. SMC is financially and organizationally in charge of the complete maintenance of the building.

Today, the building is used by five congregations: APC, a Korean and a Sri Lankan congregation, a Russian-Messianic congregation and a Spanish speaking congregation. The Catholic congregation, now part of the Archdiocese of Cologne, had to move out of the building in 2004 by order of the Archdiocese. The present religious programs of the congregations guarantee that the Stimson Memorial Chapel will continue for the foreseeable future to serve international worshippers from more than 30 nations through Sunday worship services, youth programs, music, bible study and other community activities.

An American Giant Redwood tree has been planted on the chapel grounds as a further symbol of American-German friendship. On August 14, 2000 the Historical Monument Office of the State of North Rhine-Westphalia officially registered the Stimson Memorial Chapel on the list of historical monuments of the City of Bonn.

The "Förderverein" signed a Usage Agreement with the city of Bonn, which designated the "Förderverein" as the responsible association for the management of the Stimson Memorial Chapel and surrounding property.

American Protestant Church of The Hague

From its beginning, the American Protestant Church of The Hague has been an international, interdenominational church – home away from home – for many people.

Its forerunner by half a century was the English-language church services held for summer tourist in The Hague. This was organised by the Dutch Reformed Church at the suggestion of a Dutch school teacher named Jacob Smelik.

The Reformed Church in America became interested and in 1903 it offered to supply ministers and to be co-sponsor of the services, which were held in a building on the Prinsestraat in the centre of The Hague. This tradition continued until 1940, with the exception of the years of World War I, 1914-1918.

At the end of World War II in 1945, the Dutch Reformed Church set up a committee to reinstate summer English-language services. In doing so, it worked closely with Rev. A.C.J. van der Poel, Chief of Chaplains of the Royal Netherlands Air Force, who served as a liaison with the Consultative Committee of Air Force Chaplains from the ten NATO countries. The outcome was that English-speaking church services were held on the first Sunday of the month during the tourist season in the historic Grote Kerk in the centre of The Hague. The services were conducted by U.S. Army and Air Force Chaplains from nearby military bases.

In the mid-1950's, a dedicated group of American military and embassy personnel started a Sunday School and Youth Fellowship for junior and senior high school young people that met in the American School, and soon had an enrolment of 175 children.

As time went on, more American businessmen and military and Embassy personnel came into The Hague area and the desire to have year-round regular church services grew. The U.S. Air Force Chaplains were asked to contact the Dutch church for help in finding an alternative place to meet as the Grote Kerk had no heating in the wintertime. The answer to prayers came from the Board of Deaconesses who ran Bronovo Hospital at that time with their offer to use the hospital chapel for monthly services. From that time until the congregation moved into its own church home, the hospital's Head Matron, Sister van Hardenbroek; her assistant, Sister Mooyart; Chaplain A.M. Nortier, the Chief of Staff; and all the nurses offered generous hospitality and did their utmost to meet the needs of their foreign guests, and came to hold a fond place in the hearts of the early church members.

By 1955, it was clear that the congregation of more than 100 worshippers was continuing to grow and that soon it could no longer fit into the hospital chapel. The monthly worship services were led by a young Air Force Chaplain, Richard B. Hayward, who was stationed at nearby Soesterberg Air Base. One day he was asked by some members of the congregation for help in starting a church with a pastor from the U.S.A. He agreed and wrote the National Council of Churches of Christ in New York City, which supervised 93 overseas churches, to advise what steps needed to be taken.

Just at that time, Rev. Gilbert Bremicker, a newly-retired Presbyterian pastor from Berwyn, Illinois, with 25 years of experience, wrote to the National Council of Churches stating that he and his wife, Emogene, wanted to help a church in Europe. Rev. Bremicker and the fledging congregation met and as a result he was called to be the first pastor of the new church.

On September 16. 1956, Rev. Gilbert T. Bremicker was installed as the first permanent minister of the American Protestant Church at Bronovo Hospital Chapel, The Hague.

Under the guidance of the new pastor, activities increased and a constitution was drawn up, and as the congregation was outgrowing Bronovo Chapel, a search began for a church building of their own. Through a talk given by Mrs. Catherine

Carp to the American Women's Club of The Hague it was learned that the Protestant Pavilion at the Brussels Exposition was for sale.

The inspiration for a Protestant Pavilion at the Brussels Expo came from Rev. Pieter Fagel, Pastor of the Netherlands Congregation in Brussels. He thought that since the Catholic Church was to have a big exhibition, the Protestant church (which was a small minority in Belgium) should have one as well.

The Pavilion, which cost almost one million Dutch guilders, was financed through the combined efforts of a committee in the U.S.A. and one in Europe. The churches in Germany, in particular, gave generously, as did visitors to the Pavilion.

Perhaps the most unusual help came from a strict Reformed Church in a small village on one of the Dutch Islands in Zeeland that had been damaged by a flood several years previously. The church was the receive an organ bought through flood relief funds, but instead of taking it at that time, the church loaned it to the Pavilion to be used during the six months the Expo was in operation.

The Pavilion was designed by a Swiss architect living in Brussels, Mr. Calame-Rosset. It had two levels, the upper level being devoted to an exhibition designed by Rev. Robert Kurtz of Zurich, Switzerland. It illustrated God's gifts and promises to man and the pioneering work of the church, such as German Kirchentag, industrial missions, and lay organisations. It also told about the World Council of Churches, displayed a Christian world map, gave information about Protestantism in Belgium, and described the work of the United Bible Societies.

One of its striking features was the mirror in the centre of the exhibition.

There was a literature section, with various brochures and religious magazines, a visitor's book in which comments could be written and a beautiful leather-bound witness roll sent from the churches of America.

During the week there were two short services daily, alternately in four languages, for which booklets were available. Pastors represented a host of nationalities and denominations. It was a truly ecumenical gathering with all praying and singing together in their own language. There were organ recitals and prayer services in one or more languages.

Rev. Fagel had wanted to use the Pavilion as an ecumenical centre and a new home for his congregation in Brussels. However, following the Expo there were still debts to be paid off, so the building had to be sold.

At the closing of the Expo, the Pavilion was dismantled, crated and stored, waiting for a buyer. This came in the persons of the American Protestant Church congregation who had been searching for a site. The City of The Hague proposed a property in the dunes not far from Scheveningen. The land and building were purchased and Dutch architect M.M. Immerzeel was asked to draw up a plan which include the chapel, a two-story recreational, cultural and social center to be connected with the church building by a gallery, an auditorium, a kitchen and banquet facilities, a library, a motion picture projection room, a snack bar, and various meeting rooms which would be available for the whole community. Thought was also given to a manse, separate from the church that could accommodate a family of five. In the end, the cost of such an extensive plan proved to be prohibitive, and only the church was erected.

Acting on faith, the congregation went ahead, bought the land and had the crated pavilion shipped by barge to The Hague. On May 14, 1961, the groundbreaking ceremony took place and building could begin. Pastor Bremicker, U.S. Ambassador John Rice and Mrs. Rice were the first to put shovels to the ground.

Construction work was carried out under the supervision of the original architect and his Dutch colleague. Soon it appeared that the steel work had not been properly marked in Brussels and the building superintendent in charge of this work did not know how to proceed. When the person who had supervised this work in Brussels was approached to help, he accepted with alacrity, and within three days of coming to The Hague he had solved the problem. Moreover, he stayed with the project until it was completed.

The sanctuary, with a seating capacity of 350, was basically left unchanged. However, the open passageway that had allowed visitors at the Brussels Expo to view the chapel's interior was converted into a glassed-in reception center, with the second story harmoniously combined with an adjoining two-story church school wing. Central heating and a pipe organ were added in the new design.

Finding sufficient funds to pay the workers to complete the building became a problem. It was suggested that a 125 guilder a plate dinner be held and that former U.S. Secretary of State, Dean Acheson, who was defending a client before the International Court, be asked to be the speaker.

An Episcopalian minister's son, Mr. Acheson said he understood their situation, and would gladly accept their invitation if the dinner could be held before he left in ten days' time. Arrangements were made, one hundred and twenty-five men attended the dinner and the payroll was ensured.

The Dedication Service of APCH took place on Palm Sunday, April 8, 1962, with the participation of so many who helped make the dream of an American church a reality.

In November 1985, the Fellowship Hall was renovated through a gift of the family of American Ambassador Philip Young (1957-1961) and is dedicated in loving memory of his wife, Faith Adams Young.

At the end of December 1963, after seven years of fruitful and faithful service, Rev. Dr. Bremicker and his wife Emogene left The Hague. Before their return to the U.S.A. a special dedication service was held around the church tower, so beloved by the pastor, and it was given his name in honour of untiring service.

In January 1964, his successor David P. Thompson arrived with his wife and three children to take over, and so began a succession of devoted pastors to minister to "the American church in the Dutch meadow." **Used by permission**

Scots International Church Rotterdam

We are an English language Protestant Church in the city centre of Rotterdam. The church was started for Scots people who had moved to The Netherlands in the seventeenth century but today we have a much wider relevance to people from all over the world. We have a special appeal for those seeking an English language ministry and several people have said that they learned the English-language while coming here!

Many who are preparing to go overseas or come to The Netherlands from other lands find us to be a like a spiritual bridge back to The Netherlands. We also appeal to those who seek spiritual relevance that is recognizably Reformed or Protestant but open to global and wider influences. Our City-centre church draws a diverse congregation from across the south and west of The Netherlands. Several descriptions come to mind for this English-speaking community... an old church with a new face... an historic church with a renewed relevance...

But most importantly as one of the hymns puts it: 'All are welcome in this place!'

About Our Church

Our congregation was originally formed in 1643 from the large Scottish community of merchants, seamen and soldiers then living in Rotterdam, hence the name. The church has now a truly international make up with people mainly from Europe, Africa, America and Asia.

We remain connected to the Church of Scotland through the Presbytery of Europe but we are also liaised to the Dutch Reformed Church (PKN).

We are based in the heart of the city, aiming to serve the needs of the people of many nationalities and different denominational backgrounds living in Rotterdam, Delft, The Hague and other towns in the south-west of The Netherlands, with many travelling a considerable distance to worship. **Permission to use requested**

Immanuel Baptist Church, Madrid, Spain

Immanuel Baptist Church was first the dream of US military personnel in Spain back in the 1950's and 60's, as they desired a more biblical church for expats to gather in and share their common witness. It finally became a reality on Oct. 22, 1961, organized with the help of the Foreign Mission Board of the Southern Baptist Convention (USA), to minister to the English-language community of Madrid. The mission board continued to pay the pastor's salary until 2002.

For the first four years, the church met in a rented building located at C/ Gregorio Benítez, 8 – a former car mechanics shop! The ones who helped start the church were FMB missionaries Charles and Indy Whitten, who served in the pastoral role from Oct. 1961 – July 1962. (Two of their children, David and Margaret, were baptized in the mechanics service pit converted into a baptistry!) FMB missionaries Dan and Frieda White followed, serving about a year. Under their leadership the church applied and was accepted for membership on Oct. 12, 1962, in Orleans, France, in the Association of Baptists in Continental Europe (later to be known as the International Baptist Convention).

James and Ruth Watson, also FMB missionaries, pastored IBC from 1963-73. In Oct. 1963, IBC hosted the annual meeting of the European Baptist Convention, and in the same month was accepted into the Spanish Baptist Convention, held that year in Alicante. In Feb. 1964 (the Franco era), IBC was granted permission to post the first sign on any evangelical church in Spain advertising services – partly because the sign was in English! This was the result of pressure from the U.S. government, which had thousands of troops stationed in Spain. The American ambassador at that time, Robert Woodward, visited the church for Easter services that year and shared that he had brought Dr. Martin Luther King, Jr., to see the church property and the sign, because having that legally posted sign on an evangelical church in Spain had definitely attracted international attention. Efforts to purchase the Gregorio Benítez property failed, but Pastor Watson saw a "for sale" sign on an old summer palace, used as a hunting lodge, on C/. Hernández de Tejada, which had belonged to the royal family of Alfonso XIII, grandfather of the current King Felipe VI. The property had 28,000 m^2, plus an existing building of 410 m^2 built in 1910. To purchase the lot and renovate the building, IBC borrowed $73,000 from the FMB of the SBC, money that was later paid back in monthly installments to the mission board and then re-invested in the Spanish Baptist Loan Fund, enabling Spanish Baptist churches to borrow money for purchasing and repairing buildings for new churches and mission points all over Spain. The first church service was held in the new facilities on March 20, 1966.

Soon additional Sunday School space was needed, as church attendance doubled in size. Plans that had originally been intended as a greenhouse and garages at the back of the property were altered to create an educational building used for Sunday School classes. Work was completed on that project and the building dedicated on April 2, 1967, though its full legalization would await the year 2014!

Following the Watsons, James and Sylvia Foster served IBC, 1973-77. Then Dan and Frieda White returned to pastor, serving from 1977-1991. Michael and Susie Hester served next, from 1991-1996, followed by Tim and Christina Smith, 1997-1999, and Victor and Sherry Coleman, 2000-2002. In 1998, a portion of the auditorium roof collapsed and it was no longer possible to hold services in the sanctuary building. The European Baptist Convention donated $40,000 toward the repair and renovation, and donations came from many other sources as well. It was decided that in addition to repairing the roof, some remodeling was also needed: the sanctuary area was enlarged by moving an interior wall, the bathrooms and kitchen were completely renovated and a handicap toilet added, and all new appliances and cabinets were put in the kitchen. New heating and air conditioning were installed and windows enlarged. For more than two years, the church held its services in the educational building at the back of the property until a building permit was granted for the use of the auditorium. The work had begun in Nov. 2000, and the first service in the renovated building was held on June 24, 2001.

During its first 25 years, IBC was church home to hundreds of mostly US military personnel, as well as international diplomats and businessmen. In the early 1990's, however, as the US turned over control of the Torrejón air base to the Spanish, the membership of the church began to change from a majority of North Americans to predominantly international. This trend became even more pronounced with the massive immigration to Spain that began in the late 1990's, continuing well into the new century, especially from Latin America, Eastern Europe, the Philippines, and Africa. Presently the church constituency hails from over 50 nations around the world. In 2002 IMB missionaries David and Susie Dixon came to IBC as interim pastor, but in the spring of 2003, their relationship with the mission board was severed and they accepted the call to continue as IBC's first pastor supported by the church.

Since the turn of the century, IBC has experienced phenomenal growth: Children's Ministry began to "burst at the seams," with a preschool playground installed in 2006; VBS ministry, begun in June 2004, became an annual outreach ministry, serving to plant seeds of the Gospel in hundreds of young lives, as well as to train many young people and interns; Youth and University Ministries were launched in 2004, with annual fall retreats and Christmas banquets becoming regular features, to challenge young people toward genuine discipleship. Spring fests and fall fests were another new outreach ministry that proved a perfect venue for cultural exchanges, making new friends, and expanding personal horizons. In Jan. 2008, after a year's study of IBC's needs by a "vision work group" convoked by Pastor Dixon, the church called Timothy Melton to join the staff as associate pastor, and that year IBC also began to experiment with two services. Starting in the fall of 2008, two morning services began to be a regular feature of IBC life.

Other ministries at IBC have continued to multiply, helping to connect people and stimulate them to grow in Christ and begin to serve others. The IBC Music and Worship Ministry expanded with the initiation of two services, involving two rotating teams and regularly including multiple instrumentalists; a full-fledged Audio-Visual Team was also added. The adult choir has grown in number and spirit, becoming an important instrument not only for stimulating worship, but also for social integration and witness, with a repertoire that varies from the classical Latin piece "*Ave Verum Corpus*" to anthems and ethnic pieces such as the Swahili "*O Sifuni Mungu*" ("Praise the Lord"). In the same way, children's choir has become a way of sowing the Word in the hearts of our children, regularly functioning in preparation for Christmas and Palm Sunday presentations in the worship service. The Hospitality Team also expanded its ministry with the two services, needing two teams for each Sunday to help organize the coffee times and cleanup. Another dimension of their ministry includes organizing occasional all-church lunches (especially on Dec. 6, Día de la Constitución), women's lunches (2-3 times a year), and brunches (especially on Easter Sunday), as well as special refreshment days at Christmas and Easter. A monthly men's prayer breakfast was started by Pastor Dixon in 2006 to help stimulate fellowship and discipleship among IBC's men. Women's ministry also grew, expanding beyond women's Bible studies to include Mom-2-Mom (for moms with children in the home), regional coffees held in homes around Madrid, mother-daughter gatherings, Advent workshops, and many other special events intended to promote cross-cultural fellowship, training, and encouragement in Christ among women. The Ushers and Greeters team has also grown in its ministry as the church moved to two services.

The Finance Team has been one of the longest functioning groups, working in close conjunction with the administrative assistant to oversee the church's budget and keep the church informed with quarterly reports. Bheng Belo, who has served as administrative assistant since 1999, also helps coordinate the use of the building by the different ministry teams and Bible studies, as well as wider use by other entities (for baptisms, weddings, mission gatherings, etc.). Another team of increasing importance has been the Publicity and Website Team. Since the IBC website was formed (about 2005), more people find the church through Internet than from any other source, and Sunday sermons are published there in both written and audio formats. The Translation Team, a more recent addition, then translates the written summary of Sunday sermons into Spanish, also posted on the IBC website.

The Social Ministries Team has grown with the economic crisis in Spain (since 2008), caring for the needy in our midst by organizing work skills workshops, computer training, monthly food distribution, a services directory, the "Blessing Board" (for anonymous donations), and Christmas gift boxes for needy families. Occasionally the team has helped with surgical operations for persons related to the IBC family. A similar initiative among IBC youth and university students resulted in the ministry of IMPACTO, originally an effort to reach out to homeless people of Madrid with sandwiches, hot drinks, blankets, coats, and gloves. This ministry has evolved to include occasional service projects to local soup kitchens and daycare centers for senior citizens. Other active ministries include the Decoration Team, bringing floral arrangements for Sunday services as well as helping to create a stimulating ambience at multiple special events; Bible teaching groups (Lifeway, Precept, Beth Moore, John McArthur, etc.); and the Deacon Ministry (2016: Rubén Borrás [chm], Andrew Blamo, Johnson Hughes, Eric Peters, Albert Calla, Manuel Zamudio).

Ethnic fellowships have always been a feature of IBC life, with different nationalities meeting in their mother tongue to promote fellowship and outreach among their own ethnicity. Originally there were only Filipinos meeting on a monthly basis and an Ethiopian-Eritrean group meeting weekly (a French-speaking group separated to form their own congregation, and a German-speaking Bible study has met for years, often including people from other churches). A pan-African fellowship has existed off and on, occasionally sponsoring luncheons or helping one of their number with family funeral expenses, and sometimes inviting African churches to join IBC's group for a special worship event. In 2005, with the arrival of several Indonesian families at IBC, an Indonesian Bible study fellowship was formed. In 2008 a Japanese ministry group began to meet at IBC (outgrowth of a home group), and in 2013, Korean and Chinese groups began to meet. All of these ethnic fellowships have served as arms of outreach to their people groups, and also as instruments of integration into the IBC fellowship.

While IBC has always had a strong interest in evangelism, providing many free Bibles and Scripture portions for distribution, an initiative of some IBC Filipinos has resulted in a Street Evangelism Team. Some Filipino women began gathering two Saturdays a month to make sandwiches and take them to "street people," also speaking to them about hope in Christ and offering them Christian literature (in several languages). Soon other IBC'ers became interested in this work and joined in the effort, including Latin Americans, Romanians, Indonesians, Chinese and Koreans, among them musicians who added their gifts to the effort to announce the Gospel.

In the spring of 2010, IBC celebrated its first bilingual services on Sunday evening as an outreach effort to Spanish-speaking friends, and the following year, in Dec. 2011, the Torrejón mission point was launched in Spanish under the leadership of Venezuelan missionaries Lucas and Betzabé Colmenares, meeting in a downtown hotel (known as Iglesia Bautista Emanuel de Torrejón). The IBC Missions Team has sponsored occasional mission trips to various destinations, including Morocco, Bilbao, and Lorca (May 2012 and May 2013). The Missions Team has also overseen the incorporation of several IBC'ers in prison ministry and hospital chaplaincy. Also a special VBS project was carried out in Spanish in conjunction with Iglesia Bautista Pueblo Nuevo at their location (July, 2013). In 2014, Iglesia Bautista Emanuel, Madrid, was established as a Spanish-speaking mission of IBC, pastored by seminary professor Fernando Méndez and his wife Elena Porras, with the collaboration of Houston's First Baptist Church.

In 2007, as IBC's growth began to outdistance the available meeting space, a vision work group was convoked to talk about IBC's future. Not only did the group discuss the need for another pastoral staff member, but also the need for more meeting space for small groups. Children's classes were having to meet in the kitchen, in the library, and in the pastors' office. Many options were considered, especially the idea of portable buildings for classroom space. The project grew in seriousness and weight to the point that a team of people was called together to consider the details of what was needed and to investigate the possible building contractors and architects. Finally it was decided that using traditional construction, IBC would gain in space and quality, and the costs would not be much more than for portable modules. The bidding process was slow and cumbersome as the project took shape, but finally the architectural firm of Aliarq was chosen, working with Jaime Legido and Marta Romera, and construction company Ankarsa, with a projected cost of about 420,000€. Most of the money had been collected by the time the work began, lacking only about 100,000€, which was borrowed from the International Baptist Convention fund in the fall of 2013 (total costs reaching about 530,000€). Ground-breaking was done during the last week of June, 2013, and the work was officially finished by April, 2014, though the final inspection from city hall did not happen until Oct. 9, 2014. The dedication of the new building took place on Dec. 6, 2014 (Día de la Constitución in Spain), with a potluck luncheon, and a program that included a time of worship, testimonies regarding God's provision, special prayers in several languages, and finally, a "human chain" all the way around the IBC buildings, with everyone singing the Doxology together and then "How Great Thou Art."

Today IBC serves as church home for people from over 50 nations who enjoy worshiping in English in a very international church with fellow Christians from other continents and denominations, with different ethnic backgrounds and a vast variety of personal and professional experience. The church relates to both the International Baptist Convention and the Spanish Baptist Convention (UEBE), cooperating for the purposes of missions and Christian education. Our goal continues to be to know Christ, to learn to be His Body together, and to make Him known, among internationals, among Spaniards, and among the nations. **Permission to use requested**

Warsaw International Church

HISTORY PREFACE

In October 2004, Warsaw International Church celebrated twenty years of ministry. We have taken the challenging step to achieve full financial independence and continue to be a spirit-filled place where Christians live out their faith while living in Warsaw. At this stage of WIC's journey, it seemed right that we should document some of this development, to assist in the growing of understanding and the appreciation for what God has been doing in this place.

In June of 1999 Pastor Bill Anderson documented the following WIC history:

Introduction

"One of the most memorable worship experiences for me was the Pentecost service about two or maybe three years ago. For the reading of the Gospel, then Pastor Bill Anderson had recruited ten or eleven readers who all read the same passage-but in their native languages. It was an amazing experience because it gave you a real perspective of the "speaking in tongues" of Pentecost, that is, of the diversity and unity of the church of Christ. I loved it." (Excerpt from the testimony of one longtime WIC participant.)

The Warsaw International Church has grown up to be a model and exemplary church for the new millennium: A quintessential celebration of diversity of language and culture, an inter-denominational, spiritual oasis representing every continent and so many countries, a weekly respite for foreigners and Poles who enjoy worshipping in the English language. WIC is not about nationalism, competing theologies or liturgies. Like many of the international churches that have sprung up in recent years, its message is simple and inclusive-that people of very different backgrounds can worship together in harmony.

The overwhelming obstacles facing Warsaw International Church (WIC) at its onset were swiftly embraced and helped form its essential nature over time. Foreigners wanting to pray in English were, and still are, of diverse cultural and religious backgrounds. The pioneers who founded the church did not, and most often, could not stay and help it take root. The pace of turnover in expatriate worshippers has always been breathless. As one pastor put it, "It is like watching a colorful parade pass by." Still, these apparent weaknesses soon proved to be strengths.

In its short life the church has grown from several drops in a bucket to a steady stream in every way, from a handful of worshippers to 100-plus active participants, from visiting pastors to permanent pastors, and, perhaps most significantly, from being almost fully supported by U.S. churches to now, today, being fully self-sufficient. The church has a reputation in Warsaw for welcoming diverse people and helping them get established-whether they are British, American Mongolian or Nigerian, for instance-a spiritual home away from home. Recalls founder David Swartz: "A multi-cultural congregation from all kinds of political, economic, and geographic backgrounds gathered together week after week in complete harmony to worship the Lord God and to find fellowship with one another. All kinds of satellite groups sprang up: Sunday school, a choir, Bible study, dinner groups, and excursions. It was great! I'm sure it still is."

1984: An English-Language Church In Communist Poland

Warsaw in 1984 was a city on edge. The fact that Martial Law had been lifted the year before made little difference in daily life, which was still quite hard, an extremely controlled, censored life marked by surreally long lines for very small shops frequently bereft of edible food. Many dissident men and women lived then in daily fear of arrest under the strong-arm regime of General Jaruzelski.

Of course there were small joys and a vibrant life inside one's own four walls. As we know now, there was also a growing strength in the underground Solidarity movement. And the tragic murder of activist Father Popieluszko in October 1984, almost certainly by renegade security police, was to be the beginning of the end of communism in Poland.

It was against this tense and remarkable backdrop, and coincidentally the same month as Popieluszko's seminal martyrdom, that the Warsaw International Church had its embryonic beginnings. On October 28, 1984, about 25 expatriates interested in English-language Protestant services attended the first worship in the less than celestial surroundings of the U.S. Embassy cafeteria, and a church was born.

Early documents show that the nascent church was most notably the work of one man, U.S. Deputy Chief of Mission David Swartz. "One reason for founding WIC, clearly, was my own need for religious worship and fellowship," Swartz recalls now. "I spoke Polish fluently but nonetheless found attending services to be less than satisfying." Swartz's position at the American Embassy, and the cooperation of his supervisors, allowed several likeminded people to meet there. In his professional life, Swartz was causing "great heartburn for Gen. Jaruzelski and his team" by continuing to meet with the likes of Solidarity leader and now-former President Lech Walesa. So Swartz was delicate in his management of the new church: "You can imagine how careful we tried to be in organizing WIC and, especially, to limiting our contacts with the local Polish populace. My great friend Adam Kuczma of the Polish Methodist church showed great courage in agreeing to preach at our services approximately once a month." On those occasions, Swartz met Kuczma at his home and drove the minister to the embassy to prevent him from being harassed or detained by Polish security forces. "We made the conscious decision to discourage Poles from attending services, because we knew the regime could make problems for them and also for us," says Swartz, "particularly when we had to seek the Polish government's support for and approval of the posting of the first pastor to WIC in 1986." Fortunately, Swartz was on good terms with the chief of protocol at the Foreign Ministry at that time.

Growing Pains, Growing Glory

In the fall of 1985, WIC was at its first crossroads. "Either we were going to take a quantum leap by seeking to institutionalize ourselves, associate with the National Council of Churches, and get a full-time pastor, or we were going to stagnate," remembers Swartz. The church at that time had become overburdened with a constant flow of visiting pastors, who, though often inspiring and quite gracious, needed accommodations in homes week after week. Finding, recruiting, getting visas for, and housing and feeding the weekly visiting pastors from Western Europe had reached its saturation point, and the search for the first full-time pastor was on.

In part, WIC used the Moscow Chaplaincy as a guiding light. This international church was already thriving even under the Iron Curtain and its sustenance from American churches was used as a model for the lifeblood of WIC. Perhaps, as in the Moscow case, American churches would pay for their clergy to come to Warsaw if some of the expenses of maintaining a pastor-apartment rental and car, for instance-would be borne by the informal membership. At a congregational meeting in September 1985, the WIC participants voted to seek to obtain a resident pastor.

WIC's first pastor, The Rev. Greg Seeber of the United Church of Christ, arrived in 1986 straight from Istanbul and to much joy. In fact, the National Council of Churches approached a number of denominations and ultimately, with the Reformed Church, the Evangelical Lutheran Church as well as the UCC formed a consortium to jointly sponsor pastors for three-year terms. Pastor Seeber found housing to serve as the parsonage in a renovated attic of a two-story house in Mokotow, a modest dwelling that served the pastors until 1994. During his years, members donated much of the furniture for the parsonage as they left Warsaw. The overarching goal-even then-was for the church to ultimately become self-supporting, although with 20 weekly attendees, it seemed highly unlikely.

Pastor Seeber's tenure was within the context of huge historical shifts in Poland. By the middle of 1988, there were democratic rumblings from the underground. De-legalized but far from dead, Solidarity stirred restlessly as strikes rocked the country. In August 1988, Lech Walesa met with Gen. Czeslaw Kiszczak, and the now famed shipyard worker became instrumental in quelling the unrest.

On February 6, 1989, representatives of the communist government, the opposition and the Roman Catholic Church joined in the Round Table Talks, and the dismantling of Communism in Poland had begun. After an unprecedented two months of talks, the government agreed to open elections but called for an early vote to throw Solidarity off-balance. Still, opposition dissident forces swept all the races. The faces of WIC would change and diversify as a result.

In September 1989, The Rev. Richard E. Lake took over the pastoral duties at WIC, a church that was rapidly transforming as more expatriates arrived for the purposes of work and study as Poles tasted freedom for the first time since before World War II. His wife, Phyllis Lake, who taught at the American School of Warsaw, joined him. Pastor Lake remembers now that "people were meeting in the Assembly Hall of the American Embassy, a spot reached by entering through one guarded door of one building, out the back, down a flight of stairs, across the parking lot, up more stairs, through a Marine-guarded door, and down more stairs." He adds, "One had to be a dedicated Christian to endure these hurdles every Sunday."

Beginning in May of 1990, according to Pastor Lake, there were visitors in the congregation every Sunday, and the numbers grew from about 15 or 20 in 1989 to over 100 by his departure four years later. Most people remained in Warsaw for a two- or three-year assignment, others for two to six months. "Very few church members had been in Poland more than three years," Lake recalls, "which meant that the turnover of members were very high with people new to the city becoming part of the congregation every week."

By 1991, WIC worship had moved to its current location on Ulica Miodowa, in a building that is the headquarters of the Evangelical Church of the Augsburg Confession in Poland (affiliated with the Lutheran World Federation). That move alleviated the difficult access to the U.S. Embassy facilities and provided more space for the growth in attendance that occurred at the same time.

"We followed the Ecumenical Lectionary for the weekly lessons," he recalls. "We adopted a rather smorgasbord style of the sacrament of the Lord's Supper by providing a common cup with wine, a common cup with grape juice; individual glasses with wine and the same with grape juice. We used a common loaf of bread and wafers. A rather amusing annoyance was the selection of hymns for the services. Seldom did we select hymns that everyone knew. One Brit sort of kept score. If there were two that he knew, he was happy."

As democracy and Western-style capitalism hit Warsaw like a small tidal wave, WIC was also gaining resources, and a vision beyond itself. It was during this time that consistent charitable efforts to its host country became part of its mission, and its long-standing relationship with "The House of the Mother of the Good Shepherd," an orphanage in Piaseczno, began. Presently, there are about 50 girl-boarders between 6- and 18-years-of-age and 40 day-care children from the local village; they come from abusive or simply dysfunctional families unable to care for the children.

WIC makes regular visits to the orphanages, and plans events, especially at holiday time. The WIC connection with the orphanage came about through a personal friendship that developed in 1980 between Ruthie Wiewiora (a resident of Poland from 1980 to 1996 and a founding member of WIC) and Sister Ziuta. When Sister Ziuta (and others) were able to re-open the orphanage in Piaseczno in 1989, Ruthie was a major coordinator of WIC efforts to assist them. Dean Ruehle (WIC member 1994-1999, and Council President in 1997 and 1998) says: "To see the joy on the faces of the children from Piaseczno whenever we are together brings great joy into my life. It is important for WIC to be able to share our resources with these children and to contribute to a brighter future for them. We can never do enough to share God's love with them."

Pastor Jack Hustad and his wife Helen served from summer 1993 to the summer of 1994 at WIC. Jack's strong and humorous preaching, and Helen's gifts of music to the congregation strengthened the lives of many people. They were instrumental in significant improvements in housing and furnishing. Pastor Hustad was also the organizer for the first Inter-faith Thanksgiving Worship in Warsaw (a uniquely American holiday and worship focus).

WIC Reaches Adulthood-Fully Self Sufficient

Pastor Bill Anderson and Terry Anderson, who also taught at the American School here, arrived in the prospering self-invention called Warsaw, 1994. The posting was a natural for them: They had stayed in touch with Terry's Polish relatives, and visited in 1981 and 1983. They had an intimate interest in the quicksilver changes that were taking place, because of family, heritage and curiosity. During Pastor Anderson's tenure, the average size of Sunday worship fluctuated within a range of 90 to 120-with less in the summer of course. But beyond statistics, the congregation touched and affected many lives during these four years.

In "Pastor Bill's" words: "My ministry here has been very satisfying. The warmth and energy of the congregation have been very enriching to me personally." According to Pastor Anderson, ministering to any congregation of this size often challenges a pastor to be a jack-of-all trades-messenger, secretary, driver, and, of course, spiritual guide.

Substantial administrative and social outreach programs developed under Pastor Anderson as well, from the first church office on Willowa and an active online involvement with alumni of the church worldwide-Marcey Grigsby established "Alumni Connections" in May 1999-to social work with Habitat for Humanity, a soup kitchen and a Warsaw Women's Shelter.

The most significant "official" milestone during this time was the growing nature of WIC's status, both in the United States and Poland. WIC is today a not-for-profit corporation in the U.S., which gives the organization tax-exempt status as a recipient of charitable contributions. WIC can also issue charitable contribution statements which are accepted by the Internal Revenue Service. In addition, WIC is registered as a church in Poland.

During those early days, it seemed untenable that the transient, colorful body called WIC could support its own pastor. But one of the hallmarks of Pastor Bill Anderson's tenure was the feat of self-sufficiency. In 1996, The Church Council formally voted to move toward independence. In 1997, half of the cost of the pastor was reimbursed to the founding churches. In 1998, 75% of the pastor's cost was reimbursed. Now, WIC pays for its own pastor, and is no longer dependent on any other church for its economic survival.

One challenge that has not changed through the church's development is the hurdles participants and pastors must jump over to develop relationships with the ever-changing congregation. And then when so many leave so suddenly, to stay in contact with the families as they traverse new terrain.

Said Pastor Anderson: "Because people are here for a short time, I know that we are often slower than we should be to establish contact, encourage participation, and effectively incorporate them into our community of faith. On the reverse, that constant change is one of the greatest advantages, as it brings in an ever new flow of ideas, talents, and experiences to our congregation."

MORE RECENT HISTORY

On May 23, 1999, Pastor Mark Atkinson was called to serve as the fifth resident Pastor of Warsaw International Church. Prior to his arrival in September, Pastor Ralph Carlson and his wife, Helen Carlson, helped the church through its summer transition. The Carlsons blessed us with their calm style and formed a bridge to the September 19 arrival of Pastor Mark, his wife Lois Ann, and their three children. Pastor Mark was our first minister to have ordination standing with the Presbyterian Church USA.

Pastor Mark and Lois Ann, who is also ordained, brought vigorous pulpit teaching and uplifting adult Bible study to our congregation. After about one year, however, the Church Council discerned that we had overreached financially when calling our first minister to be fully funded by us. The larger family required a doubling of our housing allowance and significant increases in support costs for three children doing home schooling. In the late spring of 2000 it was mutually agreed that Pastor Mark would not serve the third year of his contract as the church could not guarantee the original financial terms and the Atkinson family could not accept the incertitude of the financial outlook. Pastor Mark resigned and went on to serve the Union Church in Lima, Peru.

On August 1, 2001 we received Pastor Gene Preston as our interim pastor for one year. Pastor Gene came to us after eight years of serving as a pastor in Hong Kong. During their year with us, Pastor Gene and his wife, Nancy, were active in initiating groups and studies outside of Sunday worship. Our women's group, WOW, evolved from our first women's retreat, a project nurtured by Nancy

Pastor Kerry Purselle arrived in Warsaw on August 1, 2002. She and her husband, Dick, arrived from Brevard, North Carolina. Pastor Kerry is ordained in the United Methodist Church. She is our first female pastor, and she is also the first ordained female pastor in Poland to undertake full pastoral duties. Pastor Kerry brings joy and enthusiasm to the worship services. She loves music with the children and occasionally brings a puppet for the children's message. Dick is a great cook, and together they enjoy feeding both body and soul at gatherings in their home.

CONCLUSION

This quote from one of our pastors summarizes the ongoing spirit of our community of faith: "My memory is that we (the participants from all over the world and almost every theological persuasion) made it work. We prayed and sang and served mission together. There was a most profound respect and appreciation for the very diverse backgrounds and traditions, and a willingness to put one's personal demands for a specific liturgy or hymn or style aside for the sake of an ecumenical and international expression of Christian fellowship and mission." - Pastor Lake **Used by permission**

The Middle East

The Union Church of Istanbul--A Historical Sketch

The Union Church of Istanbul is perhaps the oldest congregation of its type anywhere in the world.

It was established by members of the Congregational church, the first of whom – William and Abigail Goodell – arrived in Turkey June 9, 1831. Over the next three years they were joined by several other families, and these formed the nucleus of the Church. The congregational contingent was strengthened by the

arrival in 1842 of Scottish families working in Istanbul and, joining the Church, they provided a strong base of support for its continuing work for many years. In 1857 the incumbent Dutch ambassador to the Sublime Porte, Count Julius van Zuyland van Nyevelt, invited the small congregation to use the chapel on the embassy grounds. The invitation has been renewed by successive Dutch diplomats to this day. This relationship between the Dutch government and the Church may well account for the community's stability throughout the years.

The English-speaking expatriate contingent in Istanbul swelled when Scottish and other British engineers and technicians came to do work for the Ottoman government. Many of these became regular members swelling the congregation. The Cholera epidemic of 1865 hit the Church as hard as it hit all the people, and it spurred the community to organize itself more deliberately. A Covenant and Creed were written and signed by seventeen members in the spring of 1866, and the long debate over a name was settled the following fall; it would be known as 'The Evangelical Union Church of Pera' (Pera then being the name of the district of the city we now know as Beyoglu).

Through this period the Church was unable to support a full-time pastor; it depended for leadership on American and Scottish members. The first formal call of a pastor was issued to a licentiate of the Free Church of Scotland, Rev. Alexander van Millingen, in 1868. He served the church for nine years, and under his leadership it prospered. But the financial collapse of the Ottoman government in 1875-1876, the simultaneous departure of Rev. van Milligen, and the evaporation of its endowment (invested in Turkish stock) plunged the Church into crisis. Generously, the Free Church of Scotland stepped in to underwrite the salary of a resident part-time pastor from 1879 to 1885. The Scots pastor of the period tried to unite the congregation with the Free Church, but the members felt that was inappropriate. It was to remain an autonomous community of Christian believers.

In 1888 the Church's finances had recovered and investment was made in two buildings next to the Swedish embassy that eventually came to be known as the 'Union Han'. The shops and apartments were rented out and occasionally the pastor was housed there. In 1892 a full-time pastor was called, Rev. F.W. Anderson, a Scots Presbyterian, and since that time the Church has endeavored to maintain a full-time pastoral ministry.

The years of the First World War were difficult, but the long-term ministry of Rev. Robert Frew (a Canadian) saw the congregation through, and toward the end of the war the pastor became the honorary chaplain to the Netherlands legation, an act which gave him legal standing and tax exemption. The reordering of Turkey as a Republic in 1923 under the legendary Mustafa Kemal Ataturk did not seriously affect the workings of the congregation. In fact members seem to have shared the optimism of the new nation. As the third decade of the twentieth century dawned the congregation, which had evolved a distinctively British flavor during the tenure of Scots pastors, now had an influx of more Americans and other nationalities. But it was not until after the Second World War that the practice of calling American clergy was begun. 1933 was celebrated as the centenary of the congregation.

The years of the Second World War, during which Turkey was a neutral power, saw the Church struggling to maintain its ministry. It was not until the arrival of Rev. Walter Wiley in January of 1947 that the pastoral situation stabilized. By 1956 the Church declared itself to be fully self-supporting, not needing any subsidy from either the American Board nor even from its own endowment. In 1966 the name was changed: the Evangelical Union Church of Pera became simply 'The Union Church of Istanbul'.

In 1962, with a change in the law governing property ownership by foreigners, the church set up a foundation, the Walter Wiley Foundation to administer its endowment – the Union Han. This relationship continues to evolve as plans are being developed for extensive remodeling and a more rational and deliberate use of the Union Han buildings for church use. Over the years the Union Church has seen and been variously affected by the shifting fortunes of this history-drenched city. Today on any given Sunday morning (when there are two services, because the 'Dutch Chapel' is small) worshipers will be found to represent traditions from the most ancient to the very youngest. For all its diversity, the congregation continues to evidence a remarkable unity and warmth of fellowship.

The 'Dutch Chapel' as the building is commonly known, was built in 1711 with funds raised in Geneva and the Netherlands to serve the local community. At need it has also served as a warehouse and as a prison. Since 1857 the Dutch Chapel has been used exclusively by the Union Church, which takes care of building maintenance. Following the establishment of the Turkish Republic and the shift of the capital to Ankara, the Dutch Embassy was moved to that city, and , like the grand properties of other nations, the embassy of the Netherlands in Istanbul became a consulate.

The short sketch, written by Lew Scudder, draws heavily upon Anna Edmonds' narrative, *The Union Church of Istanbul, a History*, published by the Church in 1986. **Permission to use requested**

Asia

A Brief History of Kowloon Union Church

The Island of Hong Kong was ceded to Britain on the 29th of August 1842. A year later, the Rev, James Legge of the London Missionary Society arrived in the Colony and began to hold meetings in his own house for the English-speaking community. In 1844 a Chapel was built where "the Ordinances of Christianity would be administered without distinction of Denominations". Union Chapel was therefore opened in 1845, the London Missionary Society having contributed more than half the cost. Dr. Legge continued to minister to the congregation during the next twenty years, but by the year 1849, the Anglican members of Union Chapel had seceded, and St. John's Cathedral (Nave and Tower) was opened.

The Congregation of Union Chapel removed to a new building in Staunton Street in 1865, where, under the name of "Union Church" and with a new Trust Deed, it entered upon a more independent existence, although the London Missionary Society was still regarded as its sponsor and guarantor. The years that followed were fraught with many vicissitudes. Dr. Legge left the Colony in 1867, but returned later to finish his edition of the Chinese Classics. Those were prosperous years, but the church would have had to be abandoned in 1885 had not Dr. Eitel, another famous scholar, given his services to it gratuitously.

In 1887, the Church and building were removed to Kennedy Road. And in 1911, during the ministry of the Rev. C.H. Hickling, an Ordinance of incorporation was passed. Under the long and successful ministry of the Rev. J. Kirk Maconachie, and during the years of the financial boom which followed the Great War, Union Church, Hong Kong rose to a very high level of financial and congregational prosperity.

Kowloon, although ceded to Britain as early as 1860, did not attract many residents until the beginning of the century. In 1902, religious services were commenced in the Kowloon British School by the Rev. C.H. Hickling. They were soon discontinued however, owing to the difficulty of finding a suitable hour for worship. A branch Sunday school continued to exist until 1905, when the Church of England, enabled by the generosity of Sir Paul Chater, erected a church in Kowloon. The services there were of a simple evangelical nature and members of all denominations were made welcome. The church was even dedicated to the Patron Saint of Scotland, St. Andrew. Thus the need for a Union Church in Kowloon did not become acute until about 20 years after the Rev. C.H. Hickling's experiment, when a fresh effort was initiated by the Rev, J. Kirk Maconachie. Sir Paul Chater offered to defray the cost of the building if the Government would offer a site.

A petition, signed by some two hundred Kowloon residents, was presented to the government in 1922, appealing for the grant of a site upon which to erect a church building for a congregation similar in principle to the Union Church in Hong Kong. The Rev. J. Horace Johnston accepted the task of forming a congregation in Kowloon and arrived in the colony in 1923. The first congregation met in the Central British School on the first Sunday in January 1924. The first church building, (the existing Church Hall) was opened for public worship nine months later, on the 19th of September of the same year.

Kowloon Union Church was founded in 1927 with the following fundamental aim:

- to provide that fellowship in public worship and in spiritual communion and service which is the privilege and practice of all Christians;
- to spread the knowledge of the love of God in Jesus Christ, and
- to unite in fellowship and the worship of God, Christians of differing traditions and nationalities.

The theological position of the church was Protestant, and its ordained minister or ministers were to be chosen from the ministry of a mainline Protestant church, but otherwise membership of the church was open to those who confess a faith in Jesus Christ as their Saviour and Lord.

The Government promised to reserve a large site beyond the Kowloon Hospital in Ma Tau Wei for a permanent church, but this site was surrendered in exchange for the strip of land upon which our Church, Hall and Manse now stand. The foundation-stone of Kowloon Union Church, was laid on the 27th of May 1930 by the then colonial secretary Sir. W.T. Southorn, and our church building and manse were completed and opened on the 10th of April, 1931.

During the period from December 1941 to October 16th, 1947 the church ceased to function on account of the capture of Hong Kong in World War II.

When Hong Kong was occupied by the Japanese, the church property was left unprotected and suffered severe looting and damage. All church and manse furniture and fixtures, and the roof of the school hall disappeared. The church hall was an empty shell used for the stabling of Japanese horses.

When residents began to return to the colony, efforts were made under the leadership of Mr. A.W. Ingram to reconstitute the Committee of Management and the Trustees. Repairs were undertaken and furniture purchased. This included two of the old pews, found in a second hand shop. The church was again opened for public worship with a rededication service held on October 19th, 1947.

The main problem facing the Church in 1947 was how to obtain a permanent minister. For a few years, missionaries, visiting preachers and chaplains made a wonderful contribution, and the church was indeed blessed by their ministry. In August 1949, The Rev. A.E. Small of the London Missionary Society arrived in the colony hoping that he might be able to get back into China. While waiting, he was invited to serve as acting Pastor, and his first service was held on the last Sunday of August, 1949.

Increasing numbers of servicemen were now coming to the colony, and in order to serve their needs as well as those of church members, evening services were restarted. The service was followed by an hour of fellowship- “the social hour”. For many years this continued but as the services’ population dwindled, this project was finally abandoned. The ladies of the church had faithfully and freely provided food and refreshments each Sunday evening.

In 1950, Mr. Small heard to his dismay that permission to enter Shanghai had been refused. The congregation thus warmly invited him to become their permanent minister. In agreement with the London Missionary Society, Mr. Small accepted the post for a short period initially. Improvements continued to be made and gradually the church was put in a good state of repair.

The years that followed were ones of continued progress and Mr. Small continued to serve as minister. In 1955, new halls for the Sunday school were opened by Mrs. Barbara Whitener. These consisted of a two storey building with a small hall on the ground floor, and a small hall with classrooms above.

Facilities had been granted to other religious organizations who wished to use the church and its amenities. For several years there was a happy relationship with the Hop Yat Cantonese Church and the Mandarin speaking Lutheran Church.

The church was favoured with the continued services of Rev. A.E. Small until May 1961 when he left to take up a new appointment in Bechuanaland. Again there was a long interim period until April 1962, when the Rev. Norman Kemp took up the ministry, and remained until 1966. During the interim, many friends of the church gave freely of their services, including the Rev. E.E. Gates, the Rev. Tom Settle and the Rev. Walton Tonge.

In 1967, it was the good fortune of the church to obtain the ministration of the Rev. James Muir who came to us 'not as a stranger'. 1967 was a difficult year, for both expatriates and local Chinese felt uneasy during riots among the Chinese population. Gradually more and more English speaking Cantonese young people came to our church for spiritual nourishment, and as a result the Cantonese Bible Class was started.

Although language is not mentioned in the Constitution, the Church had always been English-speaking and predominantly "western", the majority of members coming from Europe, America, Britain and Canada with smaller numbers from Australia and New Zealand. The late 60's were to see the numbers of local Chinese and other Asian members grow from a handful to a substantial proportion of the total congregation.

Mr. Muir resigned early in 1973, but continued faithfully as our minister until summer. Rev. E.E. Gates, having retired from his congregation in the United States, returned with Mrs. Gates to Hong Kong and ministered to our congregation for a three year term. When Dr. and Mrs. Gates left in 1976, the Rev. W.M. McLeod from the Presbyterian Church of Australia was invited to become our Pastor. The McLeod family came to us in the winter of 1976.

The differing ethnic, national and church backgrounds of members make for considerable variation and enrichment in attitude toward the forms of worship and the Christian education programme of the church. Sunday school classes, youth groups, adult bible study groups have all continued in various forms according to the membership needs of each period.

Our outreach programme has also been varied. During the sixties the church ran a playgroup for under-privileged children in the neighbourhood, and assisted some with scholarships for later schooling. There was also a social welfare programme to selected families referred to the church by professional agencies. In the mid-sixties, the church hall was made available for use, by high school students as a quiet place for study. In the seventies this study facility continued, and in 1975 both a kindergarten and a playgroup were opened to meet the great need for such facilities in the community, especially among the non-Chinese Asians. Throughout these years the premises have been made available to a variety of Christian groups to hold meetings for evangelism, study, worship or counseling - some on a regular basis for many years. Also, direct financial aid has been given to selected charities.

In 1975, one of our church members, Pastor Le Thanh Nhon was caught here at the time of the fall of his home city of Saigon. Sponsored by the YMCA, Pastor Nhon was able to minister to many Vietnamese refugees arriving in the colony, and eventually in 1977 to welcome his wife and family. Pastor Nhon continued to meet with the Vietnamese in our sanctuary, and received about 35 refugees into baptism and the Christian fellowship of our church. Later he was able to emigrate with his family to the United States.

Through the years some members of the congregation had felt a pressing need for our church to become involved in the education of the mentally disabled. Thus in 1978 negotiations were undertaken, and with the promise of an annual subsidy from the government, the Wai Ji School was opened on March 19th, 1979. This work among the severely mentally handicapped has grown from an initial 6 trainees to a maximum of 50 trainees with 12 full time staff. The training Centre up till now has used our church halls in the afternoon. However negotiations with the Government began in early 1981 for a purpose-built center providing a whole day programme. The new Centre in the Nam Shan estate of Shek Kip Mei is expected to be officially opened in March 1984.

In September 1980, Bill MacLeod and his family returned to Australia at the end of their 4-year contract. For the nine month period of October 80, to May 81, we enjoyed the ministry of Rev. and Mrs. Brad Abernethy, who came on a short term basis. In March 1981 a call was extended to Rev. Clabon Allen who was serving in Hong Kong with the Church of Christ in China. He and his family had been quite active in the church in the preceding years. After helping informally for a few months, Mr. Allen began his ministry in September 1981.

Since its founding as a worshipping congregation on the first Sunday of January 1924, this church has faced many challenges and experienced the guidance and grace of our loving God. The coming years will bring more challenges. In May 1982 the church agreed in principle to investigate the possibility of a redevelopment of our church site. Discussion and negotiations with Government are still going on and we do not know what the outcome will be.

We believe that our members will continue to play their part within the Body of Christ, the church. As we look back over 60 years, **"we are convinced that God has a calling for us"** to glorify God›s name and serve God›s people in the coming years.

[The above article was written for the 60th anniversary of Kowloon Union Church, 1984] **Used by permission**

St. Andrews Anglican Church, Hong Kong

Christians have been meeting at St Andrew's for more than a century.

We belong to the historic Anglican (Sheng Kung Hui) Province of Hong Kong – in the Diocese of Western Kowloon.

Construction on the St Andrew's building began in 1904, financed by Sir Paul Chater. The church was completed and consecrated on 6 October 1906.

Over the years, through God's wonderful provision, the church site at 138 Nathan Road has evolved. The Old Vicarage was finished in 1909. The Lych Gate and steps were added in 1954 to mark the 50th anniversary of the laying of the church foundation stone. In 1978, the St Andrew's Christian Centre (a 6-storey building that includes apartments, offices and a hall) was opened. Finally, the St Andrew's Life Centre was opened in June 2015.

Throughout this time, the community of St Andrew's has been active in the life of Hong Kong. In 1913, a close relationship began with the Diocesan Girls School, which moved to 1 Jordan Road. The church community has experienced the ups and downs with Hong Kong – the church building even being used as a Shinto shrine during the Japanese occupation of WWII. St Andrew's has always been heavily involved in refugee work, particularly after WWII, and during the 1950s and 1970s, and still today. The church community continues to be involved in various ministries around the city, and many groups also come to St Andrew's to use the wonderful facilities.

Today, St Andrew's is made up of people from over 30 nationalities, but is also around 75% ethnically Chinese. We have a vibrant partnership with our daughter churches, Resurrection Church in Sai Kung (planted in 1983) and Shatin Church (planted in 1990), as well as being in active fellowship within the Hong Kong Sheng Kung Hui. Our continuing aim as a church (as stated in our '2020 Vision') is that we will seek to grow in our love of Jesus, becoming more like him, and welcoming many more into his Kingdom. **Permission to use requested**

St. Paul International Lutheran Church, Tokyo

St. Paul Evangelical Lutheran church (SPELC) was founded in June 1960, "*to fill the need to provide administration of the Word and Sacraments to the numerous English-speaking Lutheran Church Missouri Synod (LCMS) missionary families, especially wives and children, in the Tokyo area."*

On September 12, 1965, five years later, the congregation officially re-organized to serve all English-speaking Lutherans in Tokyo. Those present on that day became founding members who voted and reaffirmed with a newly created constitution that the purpose of establishing the congregation was "*to serve English-speaking people in the Tokyo area with a program of worship of God. This is to be accomplished through: preaching the Word; administering the Sacraments; providing pastoral care; teaching Christian education."*

In order to serve the ever-expanding Tokyo area, the new congregation decided to hold Sunday worship services in two locations: downtown and Westside. Therefore, the next Sunday, September 19, 1965, services were held at both the Tokyo Lutheran Center (downtown) and Luther House (Westside). The membership of SPELC at the end of 1965 was 150 (adults and children).

On April 14, 1966, a group of Lutherans from Grant Heights Air Force Housing Activity (northwest side of Tokyo) was invited to join SPELC because the Lutheran chaplain serving the group had returned to his home in the United States. The ministry of SPELC now expanded to a three-point parish. At the annual congregational meeting on October 9, 1966, the total membership was 293 (adults and children).

With an estimated forty percent turnover occurring throughout the year, the congregation continued to grow as evidenced by the total membership listed at the congregational meeting on October 15, 1967, standing at 310.

In the 1970s, SPELC continued to grow as a self-supporting, independent Lutheran congregation recognized by the Lutheran Church in America (LCA), the American Lutheran Church (ALC), and the Lutheran Church – Missouri Synod (LCMS).

They were also recognized by their partner churches in Japan, the Japan Evangelical Lutheran Church (JELC) and the Japan Lutheran Church (NRK). About that time, to better reflect an evolving, growing ministry to the international community in Tokyo, the congregation changed its name to *"St. Paul International Lutheran Church"* (SPILC).

Throughout the early 1980s, growth of SPILC was thought to be certain because of the continued presence of the US military forces, and the ever-increasing numbers of English speaking business people coming to Tokyo representing firms in joint-venture operations. However, as the decade came to a close, the "*economic bubble*" burst in Japan, and as a result, the dynamics of the business community began to change. In addition, sweeping changes were occurring in the world-wide church community as well.

By the mid-1990s, because of changes in the over all "*mission theology*" of the various church denominations, the missionary population in Japan had greatly decreased. The Tokyo international business community was no longer predominantly made up of senior staff brought from abroad to lead joint-ventures. Rather, companies discovered there were any number of young people from around the world who were eager to learn Japanese, and who were more than willing to live and work as locals. Finally, the pastor who had served the congregation almost since its creation was due to retire at this time as well. For SPILC, all of these factors together meant the congregation was about to experience a great sea change.

Upon entering its 4th decade, the congregation of SPILC was no longer predominantly made up of missionary, military or expat business families. Instead, young singles and newly married and bi-cultural/bilingual families with small children were now the faces seen every week at the one worship service held each Sunday morning at the Tokyo Lutheran Center in downtown Tokyo.

Whereas in previous years, the older, more mature members of the congregation had tithed heavily in US Dollars, this newer, younger, more international version of SPILC gave faithfully to the congregation in their time, talent and Yen. These years of transition to a new style of Sunday only ministry were turbulent for the floundering congregation as they gradually came to the painful realization that they would no longer be able to financially support a called pastor.

In late 2012, the now very small but dedicated congregation of some 40 members voted to adopt a member-led worship format so that SPILC could continue to celebrate Christ's cross and resurrection together. From that point forward, Sunday morning worship services were led by a "*Worship Team*" made up of members volunteering to share the duties of Presider, Lesson Reader, Sermon Reader, Children's Message Leader, and Prayer Leader. Periodically, at times of communion, baptisms, and weddings, spiritual leadership was provided by pastor friends of the congregation.

After much prayer and effort by the current members and friends of the congregation, on May 1, 2017, St. Paul International Lutheran Church officially became a new member, and the English language congregation, of the Japan Lutheran Church (NRK) by unanimous vote at their tri-annual meeting. Following 51 years as an independent congregation in Tokyo, the member of SPILC could now rejoice at their new life within this partnership ministry with other congregations of the NRK in the greater Tokyo area.

As of (early 2020) as the mission statement indicates, the congregation of SPILC continues to serve people of diverse backgrounds in deepening and sharing their Christian faith through English language worship, fellowship, education, and service.

Please join us as with God's help, we will all continue to share the common mission of the Church of Jesus Christ in the international community of Tokyo. We give thanks to God, our help in ages past and our hope for years to come. **Used by permission**

Tokyo Union Church

History and Timeline

In 1860 the Japanese and Americans, under the diplomatic leadership of Townsend Harris, proclaimed their Treaty of Amity and Commerce, Article VIII of which gave foreigners the freedom to practice Christianity (when had been punishable by death) and to "erect suitable places of worship." Nine years later the city of Tokyo was opened officially to Westerners, who were confined to the area of reclaimed land called Tsukiji, now famous as the world's largest fish market.

By January of 1870, missionaries of various denominations had begun having Sunday afternoon worship services which they called 'Union Church services'. Two years later in Tsukiji, the first Tokyo Union Church building was completed; funds of its construction were donated by diplomats, missionaries and businessmen. This building served the TUC congregation as well as Japanese and German-speaking congregations until 1902.

At that time, Japan finally allowed foreigners to reside outside Tsukiji, and the church moved out with them. Until 1930 Tokyo Union Church had no fixed home; services were held in various churches, such as Ginza Methodist Church, before deciding to buy land for a new church in Toranomon. The 1923 earthquake which devastated most of Tokyo halted all building plans. After that the TUC congregation worshipped first in St. Andrews Episcopal Church and then at Aoyama Gakuin. TUC eventually sold the Toranomon lot and bought the present site on Omote-Sando. The architect J. Van Wie Bergamini designed the first church on this site, which was dedicate in 1930.

During World War II, Tokyo Union Church entrusted the church to a Japanese pastor, Ugo Nakada, a member of the congregation who struggled throughout the war to keep the church from being taken over for secular purposes. On May 25, 1945, during a fierce bombing raid, Tokyo Union Church was hit by a firebomb that completely gutted the building. By 1947, however, worship services had begun again for the TUC congregation at Aoyama Gakuin, and in November 1951, the rebuilt church, restored to the Bergamini design, was rededicated.

After the war, the composition and character of the TUC congregation changed as the foreign community gradually expanded; the congregation began to include more business and professional people and fewer missionaries. Up to this point, ordained pastors from among the missionary community had always volunteered to lead worship services. In 1952, however, the church decided to call the first full-time pastor for the congregation.

In 1979, after almost thirty years of constant use, the church building on Omote-Sando needed drastic repairs and expansion. The congregation, after much consideration, decided to tear down and rebuild on the same site. The new building, designed and built by Nishimatsu Construction Co., was dedicated on November 16, 1980. Former members of the church who are scattered all over the world provided the furnishing for the building.

Tokyo Union Church is well into its second century of ministry to Christians from many nationalities, races and denominations. We can celebrate the past and look forward to the future of this extraordinary family of God.

For more information on the fascinating history of TUC, please see Robert Hemphill's A Church for All Seasons, a complete history of TUC. Unfortunately, this book is now out of print. However, it is available as a PDF at **https://tinyurl.com/y62dsgk4 Used by permission**

Shanghai Community Fellowship

Beginning in the early 1990's, two groups of international expats started worshiping each Sunday—one group at the Holiday Inn and the other at the Portman Hotel. The two groups combined in 1996 to become the nucleus of SCF and began meeting in the small chapel at Hengshan Community Church. The congregation soon outgrew the chapel and moved to the main sanctuary. Over the next few years, new ministries were added. Children's Sunday School became a consistent part of the church, and Cell Groups began to define the way SCF served its congregation in powerful and personal ways.

Over the years, God has made a place for the international community to come together, worship, and grow as a body of believers. A second afternoon service was added in 2005, and in response to the spiritual needs of the growing congregation, Pastor Dale Cuckow became SCF's first Senior Pastor in 2007. He and a small and dedicated staff serve SCF's continuously growing and dynamic congregation.

In recent years SCF has been instrumental in planting several new international congregations in Shanghai. Future history continues to be written in the hearts and lives of those who share in the unfolding story of Shanghai Community Fellowship.

We are thankful to God for the calling to serve and expand His kingdom here in China! **Used by permission**

A Narrative History Of Taipei International Church (TIC)

During the summer of 1957, just eight years after Generalissimo Chiang Kai-shek, and his Republic of China government and military retreated from Mainland China to take up a position of exile in Taiwan, there was an expatriate English-speaking community in Taipei. Not large, 20-30 families perhaps, it was comprised mostly of American Protestant missionaries, with some diplomatic and foreign military personnel, a few English-speaking overseas Chinese, and a small number of expatriate businessmen. Though there were U.S. military chapel worship services in English, the military and civilian communities were very separate entities in those days, so the need for an English-language worship program became a growing concern.

Led by Rev. Edward Knettler, an American missionary with the Methodist Church Mission in Taiwan, a small group of expats met for an English-language worship service in Oct 1957 in Wesley Methodist Church, in downtown Taipei, and Taipei International Church (TIC), though not yet known as TIC, was officially founded. This group continued to meet in small numbers, perhaps no more than 30 persons, at Wesley Methodist Church under the leadership of Pastor Knettler for three years, from 1957 – 1960, and then for the next three years (1960 – 1963) under Rev. Franklin Smith, who was then also Chaplain of Soo Chow University, in Shih Lin. After Rev. Smith returned to the U.S. in 1963, the congregation continued to meet for worship with the services of various interim missionary pastors until 1966, when it moved to the Taipei Masonic Temple in downtown Taipei. Rev. William Ury served as pastor for two years (1966-1967) until he departed Taiwan for home leave.

In 1967, as the attending membership continued to grow as the foreign population in Taipei also increased, Rev. Dr. Frank Manton became the pastor, and the congregation took its first official name, Taipei International Methodist Church. Dr. Manton continued as pastor until September 1972 when Rev. William Ury, who has returned from leave in the U.S., again became the pastor. Just prior to that, in January 1072, the congregation moved to the downtown YMCA building for its Sunday services and was officially renamed Taipei International Church (TIC). Sunday morning services continued for TIC at the YMCA until again, because of growth in its membership, it moved in 1974 to Taipei American School (TAS), and its previous location on

Wen Lin Road, in Shih Lin, which is now the new campus for Taipei European School.

Rev. Ury was the pastor from 1972 to 1977, when Rev. Mike Vanderpol, of the Reformed Church, was installed as pastor. Rev. Vanderpol played an important part in TIC history for the next eight years, including the combining of the U.S. military community with the expatriate civilian community into one congregation and one united Christian education program (with the closing out of U.S. military installations and withdrawal of U.S. military personnel from 1977-1979) and the formation of Gateway as a ministry of TIC in 1981. After Pastor Mike's return to the U.S., Rev. Gene Wanderwell, also of the Reformed Church, became the new TIC Pastor for the next five years, until 1990, during which time in 1989, TAS made its big move from the Shih Lin location to its present campus on Chung Shan North Shan North Road, Section 6, in Tien Mou.

In Oct 1990, TIC was greatly blessed with the installation of Rev. Dr. Nathan Showalter, of the Mennonite Church, who served as TIC pastor for the next eight years, until 1998, when he and his wife, Christina, returned to the U.S. It was during the ministry of Pastor Nate, in 1991, that the TIC Tagalog Fellowship was established, and in 1993, that Pastor Paul Ko was called as Assistant Pastor of TIC and to minister to the Tagalog Fellowship. After Pastor Showalter's departure in 1998, Rev. Mike Osment, a missionary in Taiwan with the Taiwan Baptist Mission, became the TIC Pastor. Pastor Mike served at TIC until his return to the U.S. with his family in early 2003. TIC was fortunate to have Rev. Doug Beyer to serve as Interim Pastor for most of 2003. Pastor, Rev. Kim Crutchfield, was installed in later 2003.

During these fifty years of faithful witness in Taiwan, TIC has been greatly blessed with lay leaders, musicians, missionaries, teachers, and spiritual gifts in great abundance given to faithful TIC people who enthusiastically shared those gifts abundantly. To mention only a few of the TIC ministries in just these past few years, TIC has been led in its growing commitment to youth ministry, first by Pat Rieck as our first Youth Ministry Director in 1996, and subsequently by our current Youth and Missions pastor, Rev. Doug Street, who brought the Paradyme Youth Worship Program to TIC and soon, hopefully, our first TIC Youth Center.

TIC has sponsored over 25 years of outreach programs to the local community through Gateway; and through Yokefellow, Men's Prayer Breakfast, weekly Bible studies, a rich history of small group ministries and activities; outreach in many areas through the TIC Tagalog Fellowship including Bible Study Correspondence Course (BSCC) and through Kaibigan Magazine aimed at the more than 150,000 overseas contract workers in Taiwan; the AWANA Program for children; Lighthouse Prison Ministry to foreign citizen prison inmates in Taiwan; Tres Dias; Marriage Encounter; YAYA Fellowship; and an active missions support effort for ministries in Cambodia, Philippines, India, China and Indonesia, in addition to the social welfare, music, and educational ministries TIC helps to support which are based here in Taiwan.

Most of all, and most importantly, TIC has for fifty years been a place at which the love of Jesus Christ has been shared on an individual and person to person basis with those around us, every hour, of every day, of every year. **Used by permission**

The English Mission of the Seoul Anglican Cathedral

The English Mission began with the provision of English Anglican services for the foreign community in Seoul in the environs of what is now Seoul Anglican Cathedral on Christmas Eve, 1891. These services have continued ever since at this location except for a few years following Japan's entry into the Second World War and at the times when North Korean forces occupied Seoul during the Korean War. The English Mission provides Anglican religious services and pastoral care to members of Seoul's foreign community who wish to attend Anglican worship services. Some members of the English mission congregation are Koreans who have attended Anglican services or other liturgical Protestant services while living abroad, but the majority of those who attend the services are from outside of Korea. The congregation is truly multinational and includes people of all backgrounds and professions from factory workers to senior diplomats. Many of the members of the congregation are engaged in education, particularly English education, at all levels from kindergarten to university. Many of the members of the congregation were not originally members of the Anglican or Episcopal Church but come and make their spiritual home in the English Mission while living in Korea. **Permission to use requested**

Historical Overview of Seoul Union Church

Seoul Union Church, the oldest Protestant church in Korea, had its humble beginnings in a small Christian service held in June 1885. In July 1886, the Northern Presbyterian Mission appointed committees to confer with the Methodist Mission in regard to the establishment of a church organization and the construction of a church building. There were enough foreigners in Seoul at that time to warrant the construction of a church intended to serve expatriates living in Korea. Committees were formed to draft rules, a constitution, and to look into possible sites and erection of a church building. During the first 50 years, the church grew considerably even though it had many factors working against it. The pastors worked without remuneration and the meeting location changed frequently.

Though the church was not able to settle permanently in one location for many years, Seoul Union Church held regular Sunday meetings for foreigners until 1940. However, war was brewing and American and British consular officials were advising their citizens to leave the Orient. On November 16, 1940, 216 missionary men, women, and children sailed from Inchon on the

S.S. Mariposa. The dwindling congregation continued to meet until December 7, 1941. On December 8, World War II had begun. The dozen or so men of the congregation were escorted to the Methodist Seminary where a classroom became their home until repatriation six months later.

After World War II, by the summer of 1947, some 50 or more missionaries were living in Seoul. The need was recognized once again for a foreigner's afternoon church service so as to not conflict with missionary involvement in Sunday morning Korean church services. Seoul Union Church services were organized once more. The next step was to elect a pastor. Dr. William E. Scott was named, and he consented on the condition that either he or an associate pastor would conduct the service. Prior to that, the pastor had organized and coordinated the speakers, usually preparing a list for 3 months at a time. Except when out-of-town speakers were present, the speaker of the day conducted the entire service. Though this offered great variety, both in speaker and message, electing a pastor brought with it a consistent thread of message, vision, and purpose. The congregational unity continued to grow.

With the "red invasion" on Sunday, June 25, 1950, missionaries once again evacuated Seoul. The communists withdrew after Gen. MacArthur's landing at Inchon, and in September of 1950, some missionaries returned to Seoul. Seoul Union Church services were held in the Adams home, but the Chinese Red army made it necessary to evacuate Seoul once more. By Christmas 1950, Seoul was a ghost town. Late in 1951, Rev. L. P. Anderson returned to Chung Dong, Seoul, but it was another year before there were enough missionaries to hold separate services. According to the diary of William E. Shaw, services were resumed in the Adams home on September 14, 1952 and continued to meet in various homes for about a year. In 1954 the TaiWha Center became available for use. Seoul Union Church continued to meet there until 1979.

In 1957, it became apparent that Seoul Union Church should plan for a farther-reaching ministry. The increasing number of Americans in and around Seoul called for more time and attention than a missionary's schedule would allow. There was also need for extended pastoral availability to un-churched people. A committee was formed to assess the situation and proposed the formal "calling" of a pastor remunerated by the church. Though the church benefited greatly from having a full-time pastor, economic realities periodically caused the congregation to ask missionaries located in Seoul to serve as pastor, or serve collectively as a "College of Pastors." These men directed the services, either preaching themselves or coordinating others to preach as well.

From its inception, Seoul Union Church found it necessary to move meeting locations. However, in 1985, an agreement was made that included the provision of a permanent home specifically granted to Seoul Union Church. The location was the Seoul Foreigner's Cemetery and the construction of the Memorial Chapel in Yangwhajin. For more than 22 years, this was home to Seoul Union Church as it was intended to be. In 2007, a travesty occurred. After more than 22 years of occupying the property, an outside body seized the property. Seizure and control of the Yangwhajin property was based upon the refusal of that body to recognize the official agreement. Seoul Union Church was locked out and forced to abandon her home. Seoul Foreign School allowed the church to gather on its campus for a short time until neighboring Yonsei University opened the doors to its Seminary Chapel as the new Seoul Union Church meeting location. This remains to date.

Seoul Union Church was started to meet the spiritual needs represented amongst the foreign population in and around Seoul. Since 1886, Seoul Union Church has succeeded in developing and providing God-honoring English-speaking ministry and worship based upon sound Scriptural doctrine without the influence of denominational mandate. Both foreigners and nationals have called Seoul Union Church their home church for more than 128 years. One of her strengths, unity in community, is often what many endearingly refer to about the presence and ministry of Seoul Union Church. Though the oldest Protestant Church in Korea, Seoul Union Church remains an independent English-speaking, Bible-believing, and God-honoring church. Over the years, the names, faces, and locations have changed, but Seoul Union Church continues in her mission as a fresh, relevant, and vibrant source of worship, encouragement, fellowship, and love, refusing to grow old.

(Drafted January 2014. For more information on the Yangwhajin property, please visit seoul4ncemetery.org) **Used by permission**

Union Church, Manila, Philippines

The story of this historic church is told in a massive online presentation which is much too long to publish in this book. It is recommended that those wishing to know more about this congregation should see the online history at: http://www.unionchurch.ph/history

St. Andrew's Scots Kirk, Colombo, Sri Lanka

Worship at St. Andrew's Scots Kirk, Colombo, in Princes Street, Fort, began on 21st October, 1842. It was a member congregation of the Presbytery of Ceylon, part of the Church of Scotland, hence the name "Scots Kirk". The congregation enjoyed good relations with its Presbyterian brothers and sisters in the Dutch Reformed Churches of the city. The church experienced good times of growth and had to endure some difficult times especially when one minister had departed and another was still to make the arduous sea journey out from Scotland.

Under the ministry of Alexander Dunn, the church removed to new premises at 73, Galle Road, Colpetty in 1906. The site at

Fort was required for other purposes and the city was beginning to spread south through Colpetty.

After independence was granted to Ceylon in 1948, the Scottish community diminished. Through the second half of the twentieth century, St. Andrew's began to develop a new ministry. Although still a congregation of the Church of Scotland, it has become "International – International – and open to all". It became a member of the Presbytery of Europe in May 2008. **Permission to use requested**

Union Church, Mussoorie, India

Union Church has been serving the Mussoorie community since 1864.

Although the formal beginning of Union Church was not until September 16, 1868, it grew out of evangelistic services that were held from 1864 and perhaps even as early as 1857. On that September day in 1868, the small group of nine men and women resolved that the little body of Christians assembling from time to time for worship be called "the Landour Union Church" and met for worship at least once every Lords day and once during the week and for the breaking of bread on the first Lord's day of each month. In 1869, the church was officially instituted under the name "The Mussoorie and Landour Union Church.

From the outset, the church was intentionally inter-denominational and enjoyed the preaching of ministers from various mission organizations who were appointed for "the season" which at that time was roughly from April through September. However, meetings were also held during the winter months usually in the homes of those few who resided in Mussoorie more permanently.

Early meetings were held in the hall of the building later occupied by the Municipality. Then for several years, the regular

meeting place was at Mullingar. In 1869 the decision to erect a church building was taken and the land owned by Charles Grant was purchased for Rs. 5,000. On December 16, 1872 the foundation stone was laid by Sir William Muir, the Lieutenant Governor of the North West Provinces and the first service in the new building was held on October 1, 1874.

The first Pastor was Rev. Julius Frederick Ullman. He was followed by Rev. J. Gelson Gregson who served the church from 1879 to 1886. During his tenure, the regular church ministries included a Sunday School, mid-week Bible reading meetings in home, meetings at the Soldiers Institute in Landour and periodic meetings at Woodstock. By 1895 150 pupils from the Christian training school at Wynberg had joined those from Woodstock as regular attenders at the services. Special summer conferences for the spiritual growth of vacationing believers were a regular feature of these early years as well. **Used by permission**

International Church of Bishkek, Kyrgyzstan

The International Church of Bishkek began to meet for worship on Easter Sunday, April 15 2001. The church was led by Alastair and Mary Morrice, with an emphasis on worship, preaching and mercy ministry; a retired couple, they came from a Scottish Presbyterian background.

As the Morrices planned to leave in the Spring of 2008, they had difficulty finding someone able to come. Daniel Silviu Danis and his wife, Carmen, were attending ICB at this time; they were from Romania. They agreed to serve for a two-year period; they did so with the gifts God gave them until the Spring of 2010. From October 2010 – March 2013, Tim and Barbara Berends, Canadians, served the church; they came from a Christian

Reformed Church background with active experience and involvement over fifteen years with the International Fellowship of Evangelical Students in Central Asia. As of December 2012, Phil Horton, another Canadian, serves as the lead pastor of ICB. He comes with many years of focused involvement in Central Asia that includes eight years of ministry with his wife, now deceased (2009), in Uzbekistan and other leadership roles with an organization involved in Central Asia. He comes to ICB as a pastor from a Brethren background.

Many people have been involved in the church over these years. Additional summer and interim pastors have assisted. The composition of the church has changed weekly. The situation in the country has changed monthly. Despite these changes, God has shown himself faithful and fruitful. The community has grown even as it has responded to the changes in and around it.

Who Are We?

The Church is registered in Kyrgyzstan as a "local, English-speaking International Church." As such, services are held in English. The church consists of people from over thirty countries of the world. The church views itself as part of the one bride of Christ in Kyrgyzstan. Since ICB is the only English-speaking church in the city, it offers an important service to the Church in Kyrgyzstan.

As one observes the church presently, one sees

- Two Sunday services, morning and evening, which reach a different community of people. In the morning, one sees 150-200 persons gather for worship; in the evening, there are 40-60 persons gather. The morning service offers children's activities through age ten during the service.
- An interactive evening service, called SALUTATION. Many are involved in planning and participating in this service. For the 2012 – 2013 academic year, this service

focused on stories by Jesus and of Jesus in the Gospel of Luke.

- There have been many international students, especially from India and Pakistan. On the second Saturday evening of each month, there is a team of volunteers from the church that host an "International Student Gathering," to which 30-50 international students attend
- Many people from Kyrgyzstan coming; some of these are new to the Christian faith, some come to learn English, a growing number see ICB as their primary church and are giving leadership in various ways. Those who go to a local congregation come to the evening service at the ICB.
- Various foreigners attending the church. Some see ICB as their primary church; some also attend a local church. Some come every Sunday; some come when they are in Bishkek while living in other places in Kyrgyzstan and Central Asia. Many of these foreigners are serving in Kyrgyzstan as volunteers and therefore have active ministries outside the church. This affects their involvement in ICB
- Increasingly, more and more people are attending the church from Asian backgrounds (e.g. Singapore, China, Korea). This also corresponds with a trend in the expat community in Kyrgyzstan.
- Life Groups meeting and new ones forming. The twofold goal of these Life Groups, or small groups, is to help people grow individually in Christ AND to strengthen ICB as a community in Christ. In light of uncertainty about how certain restrictive laws might be applied, these groups grow and multiply through word of mouth.
- A growing hunger to be formed in God's story and discipled into Christ; many of those who come are from Hindu, Muslim and other worldviews; the church takes seriously the desire to communicate the biblical story, centered in Christ, in ways that they can understand and respond.

- An increasing number of people taking on leadership in the church. While all leadership in the church must be "unofficial" except for the pastors who have "religious certificates," it is encouraging to see people get involved in focused roles. While the foreigners attending the church, including the international students, have many demands on their life, there is a growing willingness in some to give time each week to specific tasks. As people come and go, ongoing effort is required to replace volunteers departing with new volunteers.
- A growing commitment to discipling one another and praying with one another for fuller experiences of Christ's forgiveness, healing love and joy.
- A developing website at http://www.icbishkek.com/ that provides audio of sermons, some study helps and questions for Life Groups (i.e. small groups), useful information for newcomers, weekly blog updates that inform, and opportunities for comments, questions and interaction.

Reflections by the founding pastor, Alistair Morrice:

The initial request

In the late `1990s there were a number of folk with various missionary agencies who thought that it would be a good idea to have an international English speaking church in Bishkek. The need was felt in a number of areas.

1. Nobody was reaching the expats who were in Bishkek on business, embassy and aid projects. The local churches operated in Russian or Kyrgyz and were inaccessible to those who only had a European language.
2. There was a perceived need among those Christian workers with families to have a church where their children could be nurtured in the faith in their own language.
3. There was a perceived need also for those who were

Christians to have a place where they could be spiritually fed without constantly struggling with the language in a local church. These did not wish to leave local churches. They were very committed to them, but an English speaking church with a service at a different time, might help to meet this need.

The story of the start.

The needs were discussed at a conference in 1999 where I was the guest speaker and we sensed that the Lord was possibly calling us to respond to this. We came at the beginning of 2001. The church had its first service on Easter Sunday in the Silk Road Lodge Hotel and met thereafter in our home over the summer at 5 p.m. Sometimes we would have over 40 in our apartment.

In the autumn we began morning services in the Dostuk Hotel and used the Bible Seminary building in the evening. The events of 9/11 led to the immediate departure of nearly all American citizens and the morning service was drastically diminished, but carried on without a break, with the evening services continuing.

The Bible Seminary became available in the morning as well and that became our venue from 2002 until we left in 2008.

The emphases of ministry

We had the vision of a church that would be accessible to the widest range of people of a Christian background, and so the services were simple in form. At various times we came under a little pressure to conform to the ideas of church of different individuals. Some wanted extensive periods of singing.... expression of spiritual gifts....emphasis on particular doctrines, but we resisted this. A typical service might open with a hymn, continue with prayer an address to the children, a hymn, reading of Scripture, hymn, sermon, hymn, prayers for others hymn and closing blessing. This style of service, though not fitting perfectly with any of the many different Christian backgrounds was not threatening to any and so we had people coming and fitting in who were with the embassies, involved in banking or business, as well as those serving with NGOs. The emphasis in the Bible teaching was straightforward Bible exposition consecutively following through portions of Scripture week by week which was a pattern I had followed at home. It seemed to fulfil the need for spiritual nourishment among a good number.

Developments.

From the beginning we had local people with good English who were key members of the congregation, and as time went by more came, particularly to the evening service. On the whole these were young people who were attending their local fellowship in the morning and would come to IC in the evening. Their ability in English varied considerably, and we had a group meeting with those who wished to have a better understanding where they went over the evening message beforehand so that difficult words and ideas could be explained. A number of those were definitely spiritually helped during these years and continued to serve in their local congregations, looking to the IC to provide fuller teaching than they were receiving locally. There was also the sense of fellowship that developed with all the different backgrounds meeting in the church.

So as time went by the two services developed a different character, the morning service meeting the needs of a Western type of clientele....the evening service more youth orientated towards those whose first language was not English, but at the heart of both services the exposition of Scripture with the central focus on Christ and His work. Christian workers who supported their local church in the morning would come for preaching in English in the evening as well as providing pastoral support for the local friends who came. We had baptisms of infants and children and adults, confirmations too, always seeking to meet the needs as they arose.

Africans came, and Indians came, and Pakistanis came and found a spiritual home. By the time we left we would have a regular morning congregation of almost 100 with a Sunday School for the children, and an evening service of a similar number. We also sponsored a youth group for children of Christian workers which met during the week. We had some special events, the most notable being the Christmas Celebration at the beginning of December. In the later years we hired the Setek theatre and would have 400 people of all nationalities celebrating Christmas. A choir was gathered for the occasion and some could sing solos. The last year we had 32 nationalities in the hall.

The organisation of the church

From the beginning to the end of our time, it was essentially very simple with a Core group helping us to organise, discuss plans and give advice. Financially we were able to help work with the homeless and support the work of the Bible College as well as other projects. We were fully supported ourselves so needed no financial support from the church. The church had to be registered as a religious organisation and we were religious workers recognised by the state.

Pastoral care

In the normal work of a pastor at home there is ministry to the elderly, dying and stewardship of staff and buildings. We had the blessing of little of that. Pastoral work was following up people from the services who would usually come to our home. This set us free to be involved in other ministry in the Bible College, with homeless, prisons and the old people home in Bishkek. While all of this was administratively separate from the church as such, we were enormously supported in prayer and fellowship in doing what we did. **Used by permission**

Middle East

History of the International Community Church (Beirut) Founded in 1823

The International Community Church history dates back to 1823. It is nearly as old as the Protestant mission movement in the Middle East, which began in 1819. With three locations under consideration for stationing the work of church planting in the region, Jerusalem, Damascus, and Beirut, the last was chosen and the community church began in 1823 under the joint pastoral leadership of well-known missionary William Goodell (he translated the Bible into the Armeno-Turkish language) and Isaac Bird.

Ever since its nascence the Community Church has aimed to serve the international community in Lebanon. Its pastoral leadership has also been diverse, composing of approximately 10 denominations, while benefitting from the administrative leadership of and support by the Congregational church in England and America, Presbyterian Church of America, and the Scotland Mission Society. In the mid-20th century the church became independent after the Scotland Missionary Society recalled its last pastor.

Recent history of the church very much mirrors its past, showing that regardless of war, instability, resistance and persecution, and the transciency of its expat membership, the church of Jesus Christ in this city remains, sometimes as few as 3 to as high as 200 plus members. Indeed, the Community Church has gone through all the major wars in the region: the Greek War of Independence, with members and pastors evacuating to Malta; WWI where low membership almost prompted its dissolution;

WWII, where it ran a hostel and added church services to cater to Allied troops stationed in Beirut; the Lebanese Civil War, that again necessitated evacuations to neighboring Cyprus; and the more recent July War of 2006 that left many homeless, particularly the refugee population that was the church's focus group for outreach during that period.

Recent timeline of leadership, including significant events and facts, (1973-2018)

1973-2018

1973-5: Rev. Richard Wilcox (United Church of Christ

1975-1982: (No full-time pastor) Rev. Dennis Hilgendorf (Lutheran missionary, Wisconsin) took the main responsibility for the congregation. He left Beirut in 1989 after having escaped three kidnapping attempts and being held captive by terrorists for two days in 1985. During this period, the members organized and led the Sunday services upon the consensus of the church council.

1982-1987: Rev. Dr. Harvey Staal (Reformed Church missionary, Michigan) served as full-time pastor. During this time he worked on an ancient Biblical manuscript found in Mt. Sinai in the 1800s, transcribed and published the Mt. Sinai Arabic Codex 151 that was developed in 867 A.D., possibly the oldest existing Arabic translation of the Bible. Toward the end of the war, Rev. Staal stayed in his house for around one year because of the danger of being kidnapped.

1971-1986: The Community Church worshipped in the Gulbenkian Amphitheater with average attendance of 200 plus on Sundays. (Although by 1986, only a handful of members were still left in the country.) During wartime most of the social activities and Bible studies were interrupted. Four members of the congregation were kidnapped, and the last service was held on June 1986 before the church stopped all activities.

The restart of the Community Church

In 1998 Rev. Dr. Habib Badr finalized the reconstruction of the National Evangelical Church building. As the need for an English service became more pronounced the Arabic congregation service became more pronounced the Arabic helped restart the Community Church. June 2002 marked the first worship service for the community church since the civil war.

2002-2008: Rev. Wilbert van Saane (Protestant Church, Netherlands, served as full-time pastor. In the first few months the church grew in numbers. As the congregation desired to embrace different ethnic groups and nationalities the name was changed to "International Community Church." A steering committee was formed to assist in church leadership.

During the period after the July War, ICC and NEC held joined worship because combined attendance dropped to an average of 20 to 25. Rev. van Saane himself left the country for a few weeks and returned soon after the war. As many refugees from Africa left Beirut, the congregation had to start from scratch once more. The three focus groups remained while work with and among refugees decreased.

The Philemon Project: In addition to pastoral care, the Church was providing practical relief in the form of provision of food, clothing, blankets, assisting in homelessness relief and healthcare. The Philemon Saturday School offered computer, craft, and business and trade classes. Philemon Preschool "Rainbow Kids Daycare" was open in 2013, followed by the Project transitioning from being a parish ministry to an independent nonprofit charity.

2008-2014: Rev. Robert Hamd (Lebanese-American Presbyterian pastor), took on full pastoral leadership. After 2010, attendance increased and a board of elders was formed in 2011.

2014-2019: Dr. Karen Shaw (American missionary, Connecticut) came on as full time pastor in 2016 (after having assisted Rev. Hamd and assuming the role of interim pastor from2012-2016).

2018: The ICC Board of Elders voted to relocate from Riad del Sohl near the government palace to Achrafieh. The church maintained its Congregational status and worship style, and shares space with an interdenominational Lebanese church. **Used by permission**

Latin America

Union Church of Monterrey, Mexico

It is not known when the English-speaking Christians in Monterrey began to assemble for worship, Bible study and prayer in their native tongue. It is known that as early as the 1930s, in the basement of La Trinidad Methodist Church on the corner of Washington and Escobedo Streets, a group of 75-80 persons met regularly for a Sunday School class in English. On occasion, visiting ministers came and held English services for the group.

In the spring of 1945 one such visitor, Methodist Bishop Ivan Lee Holt, a church leader with a keen interest in Union Churches all over the world, shared a series of messages which the Holy Spirit used to encourage the English-speaking community in Monterrey. They had been praying and dreaming for some time about the formation of an official church body. As a consequence, on March 29 of the same year, some men from this group met at the Ancira Hotel to discuss the possibility of organizing a church. Those present were Dr. H.D. White, E.H. Weil, T.G. Gehring, Ramon Noble, Octavio Casavantes, Walter Thieme, M.E. Smith and Bishop Holt. Plans soon became a reality. On July 1, 1945, Dr. Warren Johnson, Pastor of the First Methodist Church of Fort Worth, Texas, following his sermon, presided at the organizational meeting of The Union Church of Monterrey. In this meeting, the first members were received.

Visiting ministers and local leaders shepherded the young congregation during its early days. On July 28, 1945, R. Drew Wolcott became the first pastor. Rev. Wolcott served the church in a two-part ministry for a total of 27 years. He is lovingly remembered for his pastoral care. Under his leadership, the church moved from La Trinidad Church to the Seventh Day Adventist Church on the corner of Vallarta and Matamoros Streets, using those facilities until construction and occupation of the present building in 1953 located in Colonia Chepevera.

These words of Rev. Drew Wolcott on the 30th Anniversary of the dedication of the present sanctuary are still descriptive of our church:

"The intervening years have been a succession of people from many lands and many communities who, in loving tolerance of differences but in firm commitment to Christ, have sat and stood and knelt in prayer and listened to the proclamation of the Word. Here in the fellowship hall and adjoining garden they have met in Christian comradeship and laughed together and loved one another and lingered awhile and left to serve the community in countless ways in the name and spirit of the risen Christ.

The Union Church of Monterrey has provided Christian evangelical worship and ministry in Monterrey now for 75 years (as of the summer of 2020). We continue to offer worship in English and now with simultaneous translation into Spanish. Over the years, the Union Church has also assisted in the starting of other evangelical churches in the Monterrey area in Spanish. We are thankful for God's continued guidance and blessing as we move ahead to follow Him faithfully and to serve Him and others in the spirit of Christian love. **Used by permission**

A History of International Baptist Church, Costa Rica

Say the words International Baptist Church of Costa Rica, or simply "IBC" as most locals call it, and many will immediately think of the distinctive and beautiful church building in Guachipelín de Escazú in the central valley just west of the capital city of San Jose, Costa Rica. It is a beautiful building, but talk to its members and visitors today and you will see that it is much more than a building. IBC Costa Rica is a rich body of believers in the Lord Jesus Christ whose roots go back over 40 years and span the globe from more than 80 different countries. On March 18, 2012, IBC Costa Rica celebrated part of this wonderful history with a 10-Year Anniversary celebration of the Opening & Dedication of its remarkable facility as well as its rich history that started in the early 1960's.

Where did we come from?

In the early 1960's many missionaries from the United States' Southern Baptist Convention (SBC) who were serving in Costa Rica began to gather regularly to worship God with English-speaking services. Though their mission was with the local Spanish-speaking community, there was a common desire to worship God in their native tongue and to grow fellowship and closeness among the missionaries who were far away from home.

In 1963, construction was completed on the International Baptist Chapel which was later named the Baptist Center in San Pedro and many of the missionaries and others from the English-speaking community gathered together for regular Sunday evening worship. Just as this early church started to grow, the SBC urged its missionaries to focus on, and become more involved in, the local Spanish-speaking churches. Graciously, though, they assigned a rotation of various ministers to preach at the newly planted

English-speaking church. During the 1970's and early 1980's the congregation, which numbered near 50, continued to be ministered to and led by SBC missionaries who had full-time responsibilities elsewhere.

In 1985, the SBC asked missionaries Frank Lay and his wife Margaret to dedicate 60% of their time to leading the church. Frank served as pastor from 1985 to 1990 and then had to take a yearlong furlough for health reasons. In the interim, Reverend Steve Henning, a teacher at the International Christian School, served as pastor. In 1991, Frank Lay returned and continued leading the church as pastor until 1996.

In 1997, attendance was averaging 80 people each Sunday morning. With this growth, the church saw the need for a dedicated pastor and called Dr. Tom Hill of New Mexico to come and serve the growing church. Dr. Hill and his wife Connie arrived on January 3, 1997 and quickly moved the congregation from the seminary chapel which only seated a maximum of 70 people to facilities at the radio station, Faro Del Caribe (a Christian radio station), which seated up to 120. Committees were soon formed and the hunt began for a new permanent facility.

The search led to the west side of San Jose to a hilltop in Guachipelín de Escazú. The search criteria were: to be close to a large English-speaking population; to be clearly visible; easily accessible; and most of all, affordable. Locations in Pavas and Escazú were considered before God directed the leadership to the current location.

The property was purchased at a considerable discount—approximately one eighth of the market value at the time. It was an exciting time for the church, but sadly, during this time, there was division on the direction and future vision of the church and some of the members left in 1999 and began another English-speaking church on the east side of San Jose—a church which remains active to this day.

In October 1999, Dr. Hill retired and suggested Dr. Richard Steel of Baytown, Texas as his replacement. Dr. Steel and his wife Betty graciously agreed to come and stay on board to see the church through its building phase.

On January 28, 2000, ground was broken on the building project. By that Easter, on April 23, 2000, part of the sanctuary was built and a sunrise service was held in the midst of the partially constructed building. A record attendance of 260 was set on that day.

With the new attendance numbers becoming consistent, the church moved from Faro Del Caribe to the top floor ballroom of the Gran Hotel de Costa Rica. The church met there every Sunday for fifteen weeks in 2001.

As Easter of 2001 approached, there was a sense among the church that it was time to start meeting at the new home in Guachipelín even though the construction was still not yet complete. On April 15, 2001, the church again met in the still unfinished building to celebrate the resurrection of Jesus on Easter Sunday. One member recalled that without doors, two small dogs joined the service and seemed right at home.

On March 17, 2002, after five years in the planning and building stages, the new church building was dedicated. Even more remarkable than its beauty or the one million dollar price tag was the fact that not a single penny was borrowed for the project. All proceeds were donated by both its members and by many others outside the church who cheered the project on and wanted to be a part of its history.

With the building complete, and his mission complete, Dr. Steel helped the church search for its new pastor. The search led the church to Paul Dreessen of Houston, Texas. Paul, his wife Dina, and daughter Denae moved to Costa Rica and began their ministry with IBC in August of 2002 and continue to serve to this day.

Currently, with Pastor Paul and our church staff serving our congregation, IBC continues to experience strong growth hitting a record attendance of over 700 in the spring of 2016. With an emphasis on family and community, and with an energetic blend of contemporary and traditional worship, we pray that our congregation will continue to be influential to English speakers in the San Jose area.

Today, the church continues to experience amazing growth because of its unwavering dedication to the mission of Knowing Christ, Showing Christ, and Sharing Christ. We hope and pray that you will consider making IBC your church home and join us in this commitment to share the good news that Jesus Christ is Lord! **Used by permission**

English Fellowship Church, Quito, Ecuador

After almost 80 years in Quito, English Fellowship Church is increasingly international and intercultural (which we believe includes interdenominational and intergenerational). "EFC" was born in the hearts and minds of D.S. and Erma Clark. They were a British couple from Jamaica who had come to Ecuador with the Christian and Missionary Alliance and played a major role in the founding of the international Christian missionary radio station HCJB.

In 1934, the Clarks began opening their home to the English-speaking community on Sunday afternoons. They wanted to minister to people who were far from home and had a desire and/or a need for Jesus-focused fellowship in their native language. Mrs. Clark also began hosting a weekly tea for women, which grew into weekly Bible studies. Before long, the "Sunday English Fellowship" was meeting in a number of missionary homes.

In 1939 the core fellowship moved into the third floor of the HCJB office building in what was then "downtown" Quito.

By the 1950's, they had moved to the Southern Baptist Church in the same area. In April of 1957, the English Sunday Fellowship began to meet in the Iñaquito Church next door to Hospital Vozandes, just a short walk from EFC's current location.

In August of 1962, the EFC Board approved construction of a church on the present site – a piece of property owned by HCJB. The move to the new building was made in October of 1963. It was officially named the Peggy Lord Memorial Chapel. Peggy was the daughter of D.S. and Erma Clark. She had grown up in Ecuador and wanted to return after graduating from Wheaton College. Rheumatic fever had weakened her heart and changed her plans and left her bedridden the last years of her life. Upon her death, $5,000 was contributed to the church as a memorial – almost half the total cost of construction.

The past few years have seen a significant transformation of the church – both its structure and its Sunday morning atmosphere. We completed a lengthy process of becoming a completely independent church, moving out from under the legal and administrative umbrella of HCJB. We have worked through the structural change of becoming an Elder-led church while also defining church "bylaws" for the first time.

EFC started as a "missionary fellowship" and that was its predominant identity for decades. That led to much concern with the relocation plans of many mission agencies in the mid-90's. Instead of a drop in attendance, we have watched in wonder as things have gone the other way. By God's grace, we have seen that happen through an exciting and growing international community in Quito and a common interest in English; a steady flow of college-age folks from North America and Europe; and some new bridges into the diplomatic corps and business sector. The doubly exciting thing is the way a number of long-time missionaries are seeing the church's renewed vision and are turning here as well! **Used by permission**

Santiago Community Church, Chile

A Brief History

The first church in Santiago for the English-speaking community was the Union Church of Santiago, founded in 1885 and incorporated in 1906 as an inclusive interdenominational Protestant fellowship. Membership included people from many countries.

In 1904 members of the British community founded the British Protestant Church under the chairmanship of the Anglican Bishop of South America and the Falkland Islands. Services were initially held in homes of the members until a church was built in Calle Santo Domingo in 1922 in downtown Santiago – called St. Andrew's.

By the end of the Second World War most of the English-speaking community had moved out to the eastern suburbs, so the present site was bought on Avenida Holanda 151. The new and larger St. Andrew's Church was completed in time for Easter 1947.

In 1963, the Anglican diocese of South America was divided into smaller units and Chile finally became a diocese in its own right. This meant that St. Andrew's became the Cathedral Church of the new diocese, which now ministered not only to the English-speaking congregation but also to the fast-growing Chilean Anglican church.

The Union Church was prospering as well, with over 200 families worshiping together at the church at the corner of Pedro de Valdivia and 11 de Septiembre in Providencia.

However, this ecclesiastical glory was not to last. The political upheavals of the early 1970's resulted in a major exodus of many English-speakers (and others) who were able to leave Chile. It became clear that the English-speaking community was not large enough to support two churches.

In November of 1971, the Union Church building was sold and its congregation joined with that of St. Andrew's to create the Santiago Community Church, an interdenominational church which continued in the Anglican tradition. In 1979 the statutes were formally changed to recognize the new name and in 2005 a new internal regulation re-affirmed the international, interdenominational focus of it ministry.

The Anglican Church of Providencia ("Iglesia Anglicana Providencia") also uses the church building for services and meetings under an amicable rental agreement. **Used by permission**

Christ Church, Montevideo, Uruguay

In 1968, the two English speaking Protestant churches in Montevideo, Emmanuel (Methodists and other free church worshippers) and Holy Trinity (Anglicans & Episcopalians) considered the idea of uniting. Both the Methodist and Anglican congregations had existed in Montevideo since the mid 1800's. They set up an Exploratory Committee to study the forming of a joint church in a new building and in new surroundings. During succeeding years a great deal of time and work was devoted towards furthering the unification project and in 1971, joint services were started at Holy Trinity. The name of CHRIST CHURCH was adopted for the uniting church.

Early in 1977, the legal entity "Asociación Civil Christ Church" was constituted. There were 81 founding members of which approximately 1/3 were Anglican, 1/3 were Methodist and 1/3 were of other denominations. Land with an area of 2297 sq. metres was bought with Emmanuel funds, (Emmanuel Church having been sold to the Uruguayan Methodist Church).

From the beginning, it was made quite clear that the founding members were aiming towards an inter-denominational united English-speaking church, and not in terms of two separate congregations using one church building. It was also clearly expressed that the united church would maintain connectional links with both the Methodist Church and the Anglican Diocese in Buenos Aires, but in October of 1977 the Anglican Synod in Buenos Aires decided to change the existing arrangement with the Methodist Church which, unfortunately, brought about an end to the union..

In May 1978, Christ Church Trustees agreed to build a new church. The foundation stone was laid in October of 1978. The “Light of the World” window was removed from Emmanuel Church and incorporated in the construction. In November 1979 the new building was completed and the Consecration Service held on November 18th.

Until 1983, the Methodist Church supported Christ Church by providing it with regular pastors. In 1984, this support was suspended as the Board of Global Missions reduced their financial assistance to overseas churches. In the intervening years since 1984, Christ Church had to rely on the invaluable assistance of visiting pastors to keep our Sunday services going and to them we owe an eternal debt of gratitude. Our present pastor John Hamilton has been with us since 2005.

In 1994, arrangements were made with the Carrasco Baptist Church to use our buildings for their Spanish speaking work. This arrangement continues today. Over the years Christ Church has been used for brief periods by several Spanish-speaking groups such as The Church of Grace under Pastor Arnie Selfors, The Methodist Church under Pastora Violeta Cavallero and The Church of God under Rev. Nehiel Rojas

Despite difficulties, the local residents in our congregation have kept Christ Church going, not only for themselves but because they are convinced that this is also a church for expatriates.

International expatriates have always been a power of strength, supporting and assisting Christ Church not only by their presence but also by their service.

Christ Church has a purpose and a mission in Montevideo and with the Lord's help it will gain in strength and continue to be a witness for Christ and a place of worship for people of all denominations. **Used by permission**

Streams in the Desert: The History of Heliopolis Community Church

In your wanderings through the streets of Heliopolis, it is not likely you would by chance discover the building where Heliopolis Community Church meets. However, in a little street called Seti Street, just off Baghdad Street, you can find one of the more picturesque sights in Korba. Although the Church of St. Michael and All Angels is surrounded by a wall lined with trees, behind the iron gates is nestled a charming stone structure that is reminiscent of times past in Heliopolis. This is where Heliopolis Community Church (H.C.C.) has been privileged to meet for the past 35 years.

The history of English language worship in Heliopolis is a long one, and H.C.C. has played its own significant role in continuing to provide a venue where expatriates living in Egypt can find a community of fellow believers in Christ. The foundation stone for the Church of St. Michael and All Angels was laid on April 12th, 1925 by H.E. the High Commissioner Lord Allenby (you can still see the stone above the entrance to the church). However, English language services were discontinued in 1956 due to the departure of the British. Then, from 1962 until 1973, Bishop Ishaq Mosaad held English services once a month.

In 1979, the intern pastor at St. Andrew's Church, Dean Bard, and the Provost of All Saints' Cathedral, Derek Eaton, reached out once again to expatriates in Heliopolis and recommenced English-language worship services. Heliopolis Community Church was officially established, and today is still blessed to gather on the premises of St. Michael's Church. One former member of H.C.C. referred to Heliopolis Community Church as an oasis, or "streams in the desert," during their sojourn in Egypt, and H.C.C. continues to carry on the call to provide a community where expatriates can find friendship, fellowship, and above all a place to worship God in English.

Here is the story of the beginning of HCC in the words of Rev. Bard:

I am delighted to have an opportunity to extend hearty greetings and congratulations in the Name of our Lord Jesus Christ on this 25th Anniversary* of the Heliopolis Community Church. During the academic year 1978—1979, I served as an intern pastor at the English speaking congregations in Cairo, and together with the Rev. Derek Eaton, Dean of All Saints Cathedral, led the first worship services at St. Michael and All Angels that resulted in the formation of the congregation. At that time, English speaking expatriates living in the Heliopolis area had very little community resource to support and enrich their lives in Egypt. To help build community life, Ed and Sheila Knopp from Colorado State University, Fort Collins, together with other interested persons, organized monthly community events called the "Heliopolis Happenings." This process led to the formation of a number of interest groups and organizations and also formed the basis for beginning worship services in Heliopolis. After I left Cairo in the summer of 1979, the Rev. Michael Shelley was sent as a missioner to Cairo with responsibility to continue building this worshiping community. At the time, I was told by long-term Presbyterian missioners in Cairo that HCC was probably the first Christian congregation to be established in the country during the past fifty years.

Pastor Mike Shelley, the first permanent pastor of HCC, and his wife Joanne share about the beginnings of the church*:

We remember our years at the Heliopolis Community Church with much fondness and happy memories. The HCC was the first church Mike pastored. In the early days, Derek Eaton (now a Bishop in New Zealand) was instrumental in getting the HCC going, and then worked with Mike for two years, coming out from All Saints' Cathedral to share in preaching and leading the services on Sunday evenings. When we arrived in October 1979, the HCC was but six months old, and there was a church constitution to write, a council to be formed, a Sunday School to begin, along with other foundational work. Those were challenging days!

The HCC saw us through the birth, baptism and early years of our sons, Matthew and Timothy. We made many dear friends during those early years. Many brave souls took turns babysitting our little ones while Joanne attempted to take some Arabic classes. In many ways, the church was an extended family for us. Our sons had lots of honorary grandparents. Those years created such an amazing opportunity to get to know people from all walks of life and all corners of the globe.

Joanne remembers being involved with the choir, and still has wonderful memories of some duets and ensembles with Rebecca Atallah and several others. Being involved in the music was a great blessing for her. As a young mother, it helped her stay involved in her beloved field of music.

So much has happened since those early days of the HCC, in our lives and in the lives of all who have worshipped there. We are pleased to know that the HCC continues to play a very significant role in the Heliopolis community and as a church home for so many. We pray for God's continued blessings upon its ministries, and for bountiful blessings upon all those who have and who continue to enter its sanctuary. "IL HUMDU LILLAH!" **Used by permission**

Africa

International Evangelical Church, Addas Abbaba, Ethiopia

History of the IEC

The IEC began as most international churches do – expatriates living in Ethiopia seeking to have a worship experience in their own language and culture. The following is a summary of its 75 year history.

Most of the missions in Ethiopia including the SIM, Society of International Missionaries (at the time, the Sudan Interior Mission), left Ethiopia during the Italian occupation. Following the expulsion of the Italians, the Emperor in his desire to modernize the country gave permission to the missionaries to come back to Ethiopia. The permission for the missionaries' activities, however were conditioned by a decree, issued in 1944. The decree stated open areas (the southern and eastern Ethiopia), and closed areas (areas where the Ethiopian Orthodox was dominant) for mission activities.

Using that opportunity, the SIM mission including several other missions came to Ethiopia. It was during those days that the missionaries in Addis Ababa desired a place of worship where God's word is preached in English. Motivated by this the SIM started a small chapel in a rented house in the Piazza area of Addis Ababa. It was not a registered church at the time, but it was just a fellowship of believers worshiping on Sunday afternoons. Some Ethiopians who knew English joined, though not many.

The pastors of the Chapel were recruited by the SIM and it increased to the point that the chapel could not hold all the attenders. At the end of the '50s the Chapel moved to the compound of the SIM Headquarters, near the Black Lion Hospital. After some time, an extension was built to the chapel due to its steady growth.

It was at that time, when Dr. Peter Cottrell was the pastor (1970-76), that the church offered two morning services and an evening service. Dr. Cottrell was a part-time pastor because of his responsibility in the SIM as the Secretary of the Bible Schools. The morning service was more traditional while the evening service had short sermons, music, poetry and drama so as to appeal to the needs of the young people.

Despite the fact that so many people attended both the morning and the evening services, there was no membership. That was mainly because, there was no doctrinal statement that would be acceptable to everyone in the congregation. At the time the congregation was comprised of Baptist, Anglican, Methodist, Presbyterians, etc.

Dr. Cottrell left Ethiopia in 1976, two years after the communist revolution, then Pastor Bark Fahnestock took over in 1978. Pastor Bark came to Ethiopia in 1967 as SIM missionary to serve in the north and southern parts of Ethiopia. The threat posed by the Communist regime to the evangelical churches, forced the Elders of the Chapel to restructure the Church so that it might have the proper Board of Elders and Constitution.

During the time of the Communist Revolution in Ethiopia most of the SIM mission stations were taken away by the Dergue (Communist government) and missionaries were not allowed to move freely. The Dergue closed Protestant churches and wanted to take the SIM Headquarters including the Gospel Chapel. But, seeing that most of the people who attended the Chapel were from the international community including a good number of foreign diplomats, the Communist regime refrained from taking the SIM compound fearing the repercussions it could cause to the regime. Ethiopians attending the Chapel at that time were allowed to attend but were restricted from holding official positions in the church.

Since the Communist regime took away almost every mission station, and restricted the movements of the missionaries, most of them left Ethiopia. The church ministry then focused on the many foreigners who came to Ethiopia for diplomatic purposes. Based on this, in 1978 the board of the SIM Gospel Chapel changed its name to the International Evangelical Church (IEC).

After the name change the SIM gave sole responsibility of managing the affairs of the church to the IEC board of elders. In 1983, the IEC issued a statement defining the relationship between the IEC and the SIM, which was approved by the SIM Council. The statement included the following:

> *IEC and SIM are severable organizations while they are partially dependent, they are not wholly so. Each is self-governed with separate and distinct work to perform and obligations to discharge. However, despite the organizational independence of each, there does exist a cooperative and complimentary working relationship between the two entities with the IEC being under the umbrella of the SIM. The IEC is not dependent on the SIM for the administration of its internal affairs. IEC is governed exclusively by its own Board of Elders who are, in turn, responsible to the congregation.*

Although the SIM provided the physical facilities to the IEC for use, the SIM on the other hand received remuneration from the IEC for those services. Having its own governing body, a statement of faith and a constitution, paved the way for the IEC to become a strong independent entity.

The Communist regime that came to power in 1974 closed many of the Protestant churches in Ethiopia. Except some of the international churches including the IEC, all Pentecostal, Baptist, Mennonite and most of the Kale Heywot (Word of Life) churches had been closed. It was during these terrible years that the IEC became a place of worship for hundreds of Ethiopian believers who understood English. Furthermore, as many Ethiopians heard about the service at the IEC, attendants of the Sunday service increased greatly, making the ratio of Ethiopians to expatriates to about three to one.

The IEC also allowed other church and par-church groups to use the church's premises for Bible study, prayer meetings and related Christian services. As a result, different groups from different organizations began to shelter under the umbrella of the IEC. For instance, some of the groups that used the church premises in 1983 were:

- Medical students' prayer meeting
- University Graduates Christian Fellowship
- Hospitality Workers Christian Fellowship
- UN Prayer and Bible Study.

Due to the growth of people who attended the Sunday worship of both the morning and the evening services in the beginning of 1980's, the Board of Elders of the IEC began to consider ways and means of handling the matter appropriately.

In 1982, about 60 – 70% of the congregation were Ethiopians. The Board felt that it was a phenomenon that changed the character of the IEC and also noted that some of the international community stayed away from Sunday service because of the problem of overcrowding. The Board, nevertheless, decided to take a prudent step of adding another morning service, avoiding any intention of segregating the internationals from Ethiopians.

In the first half of 1983, the Kale Heywot Church (KHC) approached the IEC regarding the establishment of a Bible training school. Its target group were people interested in biblical education from the IEC and non-IEC churches. The name chosen for the school at the time was the IEC Biblical Training Institute. After careful preparation, the evening program was begun in January 1984.

In May, the IEC Board of Elders, as suggested by the SIM Council, changed the name of the school to IEC Evening Class (IECEC). Four years after its establishment, IECEC was allowed to have its own Administrative Council.

The IEC Evening Class tried its best to meet the demand for biblical theological and ministerial training from the many evangelical churches and fellowships in Addis Ababa. In 1991, by the decision of the Board of Elders of the IEC, the name Evangelical Theological College (ETC) was adopted.

The ETC recognized by the Ministry of Education and accredited by the Accrediting Council for Theological Education in Africa (ACTEA), continued to provide Ethiopian church leaders with evangelical training at the SIM Headquarters until the new IEC-ETC complex was completed in 1995.

To complete this new facility the IEC board of elders in 1992 procured from the government the land on a 50-year lease, raised over US$400,000 within the communities in Ethiopia and $1.4 million from Germany, UK, USA, Australia and New Zealand. Joe Harding and Girma Demissie shared IEC's vision with different congregations in these countries. People became very excited about being a part of God's work in Ethiopia after the fall of ungodly Communist regime and responded generously.

Ethnicity of the Congregation

Shaped by our history of starting as a fellowship of expatriates and becoming a place of worship for Ethiopian church leaders during the time of the Communist regime, the ethnicity of IEC has been strongly Ethiopian. Today the IEC appeals to the 'international-Ethiopians' (for lack of a better term) who are desiring a more international environment because of their education (all university education is done in English), profession (working for an international organization or trained outside of Ethiopia), global business connections, diplomatic role (with an embassy or Africa Union), or because of international travels and thus are more global in their thinking. The IEC uses this as a means to reach the influencers in society.

In a survey of the congregation the ethnic composition would be described as following:

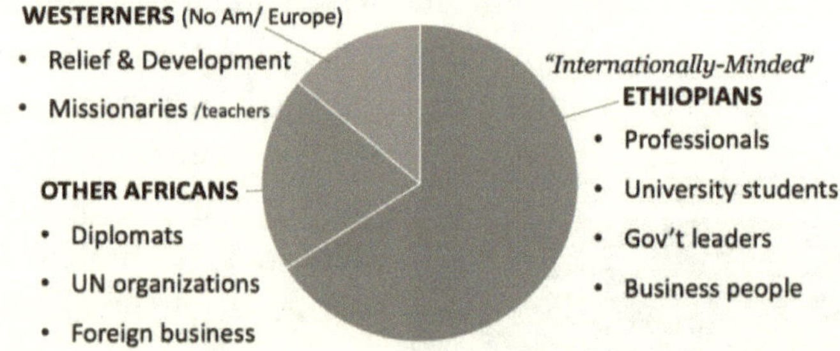

(about 66% Ethiopian, 20% other African, and 14% Western nations)

Church Planting

The IEC has started congregations with specific foreign ethnic groups who have come to Ethiopia for various assignments. These include a Korean congregation, a French ministry (half of the embassies in Africa are French speaking), and a new Chinese ministry (about 100,000 Chinese are reported to live in Addis Ababa, mainly for construction projects).

The IEC has also started a new church plant on the East side of the city and has taken in a church plant to the south of Addis Ababa (Debra Ziet) which has a strong Dutch community doing various NGO projects.

IEC Vision Statement

Who we are The International Evangelical Church (IEC) is an interdenominational and multi-ethnic church in Ethiopia seeking to reach the 'international-Ethiopian' and expatriate communities.

Our mission *(why we exist)* "To become a community of disciples, making disciples of the nations for the glory of God."

Our vision *(how we accomplish our mission):*

Meet: - Meet Jesus together in worship, study and service

Mature: - Mature the believer through intentional discipleship to become more like Jesus

Mobilize: Mobilize the believer to use their spiritual gifts in service to others for Jesus

Multiply: Multiply through evangelism, missions and church planting the church of Jesus

- What do we mean by the term "international"? *At IEC, when we say that we are 'international' we mean that we seek to be a community of people who intentionally transcend national and cultural boundaries through the use of languages which are commonly used in a wide variety of national and cultural contexts.*
- What do we mean when we say we are an "international church"? *At IEC, we understand that we are an international church in that we seek to be a community which intentionally draws upon our cultural diversity to honor God in our worship and fellowship and which cultivates in others an ability to transcend cultural boundaries for the sake of the gospel.*

What makes IEC unique?

While most international churches have a mission of providing English worship services for expatriates, the IEC has a mission of using English as a means of connecting with influencers in society who are more global in their thinking.

As a church we have sent missionaries to other countries, trained Christian education workers for other Addis churches, and are looking at expanding our vision to other cities in Ethiopia where there are significant university populations or international workers.

Our passion is to "make disciples of the nations" – either those nations who have come to Ethiopia or Ethiopians who have vocations connecting to other nations. **Used by permission**

International Baptist Church of Dakar

Introductory Narration of the History of IBC

The International Baptist Church of Dakar was founded in the summer of 1979 by Pastor Edward Segars, a Southern Baptist Convention pastor. He had come to Dakar as a missionary of the SBC, but did not have enough French to witness to the French-speaking community. In May 1979, he met Brother Michael Mah'Moud who had a small prayer group of English speakers meeting in his house. Pastor Segars got interested and visited the group the following week. He announced to the prayer group his plans to start an English-speaking fellowship, the first of its kind in Dakar. The inaugural service had about 30 worshippers, including people from the small prayer group that was meeting at Dr. Mah'Moud's house. The congregation came from different church backgrounds, including Baptist, Methodist, Assemblies of God, and Presbyterians. The inaugural service was also advertised on radio in Dakar.

The name chosen for the church at the time was The International Church of Dakar. Pastor Segars wanted the name to reflect mainly the international nature of the fellowship rather than his own affiliation to the SBC.

The Church grew gradually and by October 1979, the congregation had expanded to include the Ambassadors from Nigeria, Ghana, and Japan as well as several exchange students from Ghana. Under Pastor Segars, the church's place of worship shifted from Temple Evangelique, to the American Embassy cafeteria, and the later, one of the American Embassy's vacant houses when the Iranian conflict deepened. Pastor Segars had a medical emergency and had to depart suddenly to the US in the summer of 1980. Indeed, we received tremendous support from the missionaries at the time, and several of them helped with the preaching.

In 1983, the SBC sent Rev. Warren Rush to pastor the church at a time when the church was worshipping at the Dakar Academy. Membership had grown considerably and so Pastor Rush encouraged the church to make its affiliation to the SBC clearer. Therefore, after considerable discussion within the Church Council and meetings with the congregation, the reorganization was announced.

The International Baptist Church of Dakar was formally established as a church on Sunday, 6 November, 1983 based on Baptist principles and doctrines. Thirty four members covenanted to begin the church on that day. Others who could not transfer their membership from their home countries joined as associate members.

Pastor Rush also believed that the church should reach out to the lost in Senegal, rather than ministering only to the English-speaking community. The church began an outreach program with Brother Seck, in Ndiaganio a few miles from Mbou. A multi-purpose building to house the church and serve a social center was built and used successfully to train women in sewing. At one baptism occasion, 105 villagers were baptized. Unfortunately, the work went down when the Missionaries left.

By the time Pastor Rush left, the IBC of Dakar had been firmly established. Brother Ogunniyi was elected to lead the church in the absence of a regular pastor. Dakar Academy served the church with a year's notice to look for another place of worship. The matter was discussed at length within the council and at church business meetings and it was decided that we would look for a building to purchase. A four member Building Search Committee was appointed to look for the permanent place of worship. The church bought the current place of worship in August 1987 through special fundraising and a loan from the bank. By 1992, the loan had been paid off.

After the retirement of Brother Ogunniyi, Brother Mah'Moud was appointed as the Church Leader and served with other volunteer pastors like Pastor Jackson of the Mission Baptiste de Dakar. In 1989 Pastor Gerald Taylor was called by the SBC as the second pastor of the International Baptist Church. He rebuilt the evangelization ministry of the church, including the founding of a Wolof Church. He saw the church through the conversion of the residential building the church had acquired into the new church building and permanent worship center.

Pastor Taylor left in 1993 and since the church did not have the burden of paying mortgage or rent, the congregation decided to appoint its own Pastor. Furthermore, the church did not want to continue to depend on the SBC for a pastor. .Consequently, on 24 August 1993, after a period of searching by a committee headed by Brother Joseph Darko, Pastor Kwashie Amenudzie, who was then a Pastor in Togo and President of the Baptist Convention there, was invited to become the first African pastor of the church. Under Pastor Amenudzie, the church expanded to a double service in 1999. The church engaged in an outreach to Seamen at the Dakar Port. The WMU began a ministry to the Leper Colony in Keur Massa through prayer and gifts on a regular basis. Several mission efforts were successfully launched including the founding of the Grace Baptist Church in Parcelles Assanies where Brother Damien Bassene was posted to as the Pastor in charge;

In 2002, Pastor Amenudzie felt the Lord leading him into full time ministry as a missionary church planter. He therefore resigned as the resident Pastor in the same year. A five-member Leadership Team, headed by, Elder Wilfred Amoako, was called to lead the church, while a Pastor Search committee was set up under the leadership of Brother Dan Ole Shani.

On 15th May 2003, the church, after much prayer and consideration of the entire pastors interviewed, called Rev. Kwame Owusu-Baafi to be the second African Pastor of IBC. Under his leadership, IBC has experienced study ministry and personal growth in spite of the initial two years of turbulent sailing.

May the Lord who has brought us thus far, continue to guide and strengthen His church into a higher realm of spiritual experience growth for His own glory. And so, we continue to say, "God is good, all the time; and all the time, God is good. The best is yet to come; for we have not seen anything yet!" **Permission to use requested**

Arusha, Tanzania

A Short History of Arusha Community Church

The congregation began many decades ago as the English language congregation of Christ Church (Anglican), Arusha. Over the years, the denominational base of this part of the congregation widened, and eventually a new interdenominational community of faith emerged. Other facilities were sought, and on February 23, 1986, at 10 am, the congregation met for the first time as "Arusha Community Church" at the Greek Club (Meru Club) in the Kijenge area of Arusha. That first week, there were 36 in attendance, and by the next week the number had grown to 62. Bibles, hymn books and more chairs were purchased to accommodate the increase in attendance.

By 1992, the administration was shared among various committees, and the congregation had grown too large for the Greek Club. This was particularly true of the Sunday School. Once again it was felt that alternative premises should be found to accommodate the growing community of faith.

Two years later, no suitable premises had been found, and so a survey was held among the members to determine the way forward. The most favored choice was for the congregation to build a multipurpose facility for worship. A proposal to erect such a building was presented to the Annual General Meeting in January 1994, was accepted by a clear majority, and fund raising began.

The Diocese in the Arusha Region of the ELCT offered a plot of land, and at the Annual General Meeting of 1995 it was agreed to start formal discussions with the Diocese regarding the building of a worship facility on the offered plot. Ground was broken on January 28, 1996, and on January 18, 1998, the building in which the congregation now meets was dedicated -- with no debt on the building. TO GOD BE THE GLORY! **Used by permission**

In the news

International churches have often caught the attention of a wide audience through newspaper, magazine and wire service articles. What follows is a compendium of such news stories and features from the past several decades.

Religion in America; Churches overseas welcome out to U.S. travelers

By DAVID E. ANDERSON
UPI Religion Writer | May 24, 1985

Vacationing Christians, whether in Alexandria, Egypt or Caracas, Venezuela, or Paris, France don't have to miss church on Sunday.

These and some 93 other cities around the world all offer churches with English-language worship services.

The congregations, ranging from the well-known American Church in Paris to a small worship and Bible study group that meets in an apartment in a Middle Eastern nation, have become an important and enduring means of helping Americans traveling or living abroad continue to practice their faith.

'We try to help these churches meet the spiritual and fellowship needs of thousands of Americans living and traveling overseas,' said the Rev. Russell Spry Williams, who directs the International Congregations and Lay Ministries program of the National Council of Churches.

'So many times these people feel uprooted, particularly spouses who come to settle with someone on assignment abroad,' Williams said. 'While the people working have a social network, their wives or husbands may not. These congregations help them ease the transition and the loneliness.'

The 96 English-speaking congregations overseas are all associated with the council program.

Council officials said each of the congregations has risen out of the particular needs and circumstances of the people it serves.

Often the churches are interdenominational. Many of them began as a small gathering of American Christians drawn together by a missionary or other religious person serving abroad, who, 'after teaching and preaching in the language of the people, hold an English language service for their own sake.'

In other instances, such as the Philippines or Frankfurt, West Germany, a large U.S. military installation has been the catalyst.

Other places, such as Tokyo, regularly play host to a large number of Americans visiting on business and yet other places, such as London or Paris, attract many English-speaking students.

Williams said students, though deeply immersed in learning of the culture they are experiencing, may seek reassurance and comfort from worshipping in their own language.

On the other side of the coin, Williams said that many of those who participate in the services may be natives who have returned to their homeland after years spent in the United States or another English-speaking country and who participate in order to maintain their English language capability.

Many of the churches, Williams said, are full-service parishes where pastors are frequently called on to perform marriages or to minister to those in local hospitals and prisons. American pastors play a crucial role, he said, because they often are the only source of English-language counseling available overseas.

Each congregation is independently run and financed although the National Council of Churches offers support in a variety of ways. It provides personnel services to 65 of the interdenominational congregations, placing pastors in these churches for four-year assignments. Training sessions and consultations for the pastors once they are abroad also are offered.

In the past, before some of the financial constraints that have limited the council's activities, the office also provided some grants for construction of churches in places where an active congregation could not pull together the funds itself. **https://tinyurl.com/y2dtbg8a Permission to use requested**

One of the most disturbing newspaper references to international churches was the reporting in the *New York Times* and other publications of an armed attack on one such church in Islamabad, Pakistan in 2001. Here are excerpts from the article by Raymond Bonner in a March 18, 2002 article:

A Nation Challenged: Islamabad; 2 Americans Killed in Attack on Pakistan Church

"Two men walked into a Protestant church close to the American Embassy this morning, in one of the most guarded areas in one of the most secure cities in Pakistan, and threw several grenades. Five people were killed, including an embassy employee and her daughter, a high school senior.

At least 40 people were wounded, many critically, most of them foreigners…."

The attack targeted the Protestant International Church, a nondenominational church in the diplomatic enclave here, 400 yards from the sprawling embassy compound, where glistening razor-wire coils along the top of brick walls. Life had been returning to normal at the embassy, with relatives of the diplomats only recently having come back after being sent home after Sept. 11.

The attack appeared to be directly aimed at the Americans and at the government of President Pervez Musharraf of Pakistan….

The Americans killed were Barbara Green and her daughter, Kristen Wormsley, a senior at the American school here.

Mrs. Green was an employee in the human resources center at the embassy. Her husband is a diplomat, Milton Green, director of the computer section at the embassy, the State Department said. He and their young son were also injured, but not seriously, American Embassy officials said here this evening....

The church was only about half full, with 60 to 70 worshipers. Many diplomats and foreign aid workers have still not returned to the country....

The glass was blown out of every window and huge holes were punched in the ceiling. Blood soaked the floor throughout the room, about 80 feet by 80 feet. **https://tinyurl.com/y6656sas**

Churches may now be in terrorists' cross-hairs

By Lisa Hoffman
Scripps-Howard News Service
March 18, 2002

For pastors of English-language Christian churches overseas, dodging danger is simply part of the job of ministering to expatriate Americans and other worshippers.

But until now, there was a sense that these churches were somehow removed from the anti-American sentiment driving terrorists to acts of violence against U.S. targets overseas.

That is likely to change in the aftermath of the deadly grenade attack Sunday on the Protestant International Church in Pakistan that killed two Americans and injured 14 others, the Rev. Scott Campbell, interim head of a 160-congregation global network that includes the Islamabad church, said Monday.

Campbell, who leads the Network for International Congregations and was a pastor at international churches in Paris and Brussels, Belgium, said terrorists may be seeking "soft targets" like churches and schools attended by Americans now that heightened security has made U.S. government buildings abroad less vulnerable.

"Up until now, churches have felt relatively safe and exempt from these attacks," Campbell said. "My guess is there will be a ripple effect, and the churches will tighten their security."

That is the same message contained in a "worldwide caution" issued Sunday by the State Department, which advised U.S. citizens abroad to avoid areas where Americans congregate, or at least be extra vigilant at restaurants, places of worship, schools, outdoor recreation events and other similar situations.

"As security is increased at official U.S. facilities, terrorists and their sympathizers will seek softer targets," the alert said.

No official count exists of English-speaking churches worldwide, although estimates range from 600 to 1,000 in countries where the language is not dominant.

Hundreds are missionary outposts tied to a particular denomination, but equally large numbers are interdenominational "international churches" that cater to a variety of Christian faiths everywhere from Warsaw, Poland, and Tokyo to Indonesia and the war-battered Balkans.

An estimated 15 million Americans live overseas and many turn to such churches for everything from a place for familiar worship to fellowship with other U.S. expatriates to help in negotiating a new culture.

"Ranging from charismatic to liberal, contemporary to traditional, these churches provide a home away from home for diplomats, missionaries, soldiers, students, businessmen, travelers and others living abroad," is how Kenneth MacHarg, former pastor of three such churches in Panama and Ecuador, described them in an article for the magazine *Christianity Today*.

While many of these churches are attended mostly by Americans, a growing number of congregants are English speakers from other countries. For instance, those wounded in the Pakistan grenade attack, believed to have been staged by Islamic terrorists, were people from 10 nations, including England, Canada, Switzerland and Germany.

Security concerns are nothing new for overseas Christian churches.

A Minnesota family started an English-language church in Sarajevo, Bosnia, as the war there wound down and snipers still threatened the city. When MacHarg was a pastor in Ecuador, a rash of kidnappings led some U.S. congregants to bring bodyguards with them when they worshipped, said MacHarg, who now is communications coordinator for the evangelical Latin America Mission. Less than two weeks ago, the U.S. Embassy in Bogotá, Colombia, warned Protestant evangelical churches in rural areas of the civil-war-wracked country that they could be targets of guerrilla attacks.

Campbell said that when he was pastor of an international church in Paris during the 1990-91 Persian Gulf War, a time of anti-U.S. tensions, a security system was installed at the church.

Regular church goers were given the security code to unlock the entrance during the week. But, reflecting the desire of the church to welcome all worshippers, the security system was unplugged on Sundays, he said.

Campbell and MacHarg said many U.S.-linked churches struggle with that same dilemma – that visibility is important to attract congregants but also can bring serious risk. MacHarg said that if he were pastor of an English-speaking church overseas now, he would consider holding services in a private home, an office building or some other less public venue.

Campbell said the international church in Paris hired security guards after the Sept. 11 attacks, and that he expects others are taking similar measures. But he said that vulnerability is just a fact of life for such overseas churches.

"You proceed with caution, but also with an element of faith," the United Methodist minister said.

"Unfortunately, we are unable to confirm we own the rights to these archives. While it is possible that we surrendered our rights to the archives to a local library or university, we have no

records or historical knowledge of such a transaction.... Scripps will not object to your use of the materials as you describe..... Please be aware, however, that because our records are inconclusive as to our ownership of the material (we) are unable to grant you permission with respect thereto and you are not to indicate that your use is done with our permission". --Scripps

Tulsa couple pastored openly Christian church in Saudi Arabia

***Tulsa World*, Tuesday, 01 November 2016 13:44**

Brandon and Misty Macal have been key leaders for eight years in what they believe is the only openly worshipping Christian church in Saudi Arabia, a technically illegal congregation of some 1,200 people who meet weekly in a rented hall.

Last week the Macals (pronounced Motzals) talked about their experiences, she sitting in her Broken Arrow apartment and he on her laptop via Facebook Messenger from the church in Riyadh, with services going on the background.

Misty was born and raised in the Tulsa area and met Brandon while they both were students at Mounds.

They married in 1995, two years out of high school, and for most of the past 21 years have lived overseas while Brandon served in the U.S. Air Force. Their son, Brandon Jr., was born in Germany and their daughter, Brooklyn, in Japan.

Brandon left the military in about 2004, and they returned to the Tulsa area.

In 2008, Brandon announced that he had accepted a job in Riyadh, Saudi Arabia, as a military adviser to the Royal Saudi Air Force.

"I was so mad," Misty said. "I never expected to find myself going to a place where the Bible is banned and open Christian worship is banned.

"I thought I was going to a place where I would be miserable."

Brandon moved to Riyadh, and she followed several months later with their two children.

Culture shock

The culture shock was severe.

"As a woman, I had to wear an abaya, a full-length black gown with a head covering, whenever I was out of the house, and my daughter did too, once she was older than about 11. It was very hot. ... And I couldn't drive."

"I got to wear shorts and flip-flops," Brandon chimed in from 8,000 miles away.

"My third week there, I had a breakdown," she said. "I was sitting on a curb to eat a powdered doughnut because women weren't allowed in the doughnut shop. White sugar was dropping on my abaya. I was crying like a baby. I didn't realize that this would be my life."

"After that, I got through it, believing Jesus that I was there for a mission and a reason."

Misty said she was raised in an Assembly of God church in Sapulpa and felt called to the ministry in a powerful dream when she was a teenager. Brandon, however, had wanted nothing to do with church until he had a conversion experience while he was stationed in Tokyo.

After they moved to Saudi Arabia, the couple got involved with a small group of expatriate Christians who met first monthly and then weekly, and later formed a church that met in their spacious Riyadh home. After about a year, when the group grew to 100 and became more visible, they were asked to stop meeting in the house for fear of authorities.

They decided to rent a building in Riyadh for their Friday morning meetings.

"It's on our visa that we are non-Muslims," Brandon said, "so we decided we were going to be who we are. If we get kicked out of the country, we'll hold our head high."

Christian services in Saudi Arabia are allowed only in foreign embassies and compounds.

Brandon served as administrator of the church, called Grace Outreach Riyadh, and later as pastor. Misty was the worship pastor.

'A great achievement'

The church grew to 1,200 people, all of them expatriates, most from Asia and Africa, with a few Westerners from the United States, Europe and Australia. At one point they had members from 46 nations. Saudis were not allowed to attend, for their own safety. IDs were checked at the door.

To their surprise, they have had only minimal difficulty with authorities, in part, Brandon believes, because they are open about what they are doing and cordially invite questioning authorities to visit the services.

"We don't hide what we do. We're very transparent. Very honest," he said.

The church has a Facebook page with GPS coordinates for the services, which are live-streamed. They have told their story publicly.

"The police come by and tell us, 'If you have any problems with anyone, call us,'" Misty said.

She said it was a "great achievement" that they have been able to have weekly Christian music in a nation that forbids music.

Brandon distributed a booklet to help Christians in Riyadh understand exactly what their rights are under Shariah law.

In 2011, they had an event they think is unprecedented in Saudi Arabia: public revival services attended by about 8,000 to 10,000 people, including many people from the some 200 underground churches they say are in Riyadh. Tulsa evangelist Chresten Tomlin sang, and Greg Webb of Muskogee spoke.

God's love

Misty said her attitude has changed greatly since the day she sat on a curb with a doughnut and cried.

"Here you see God's love; you are directed by God. You have fellowship with all these people. It is just an extension of God's love that brings us together. This is what heaven is going to be like."

This summer, Misty returned to Tulsa to give her daughter the experience of living and going to school in America for her senior year. Brooklyn attends Union High School. Their son is a student at College of the Ozarks in Missouri. Brandon continues to work in Riyadh and remains active in the church, though he has stepped down as lead pastor.

What will they do next?

They don't know. Both said they were eager to get back together, either in Tulsa or in Riyadh.

Misty said she plans to continue to minister through preaching and singing, wherever she is.

https://tinyurl.com/yyzem72p

Permission to use requested

In Arab Nation, Christians, Buddhists and Jews Emerge to Worship; U.A.E. celebrates religious tolerance and prepares to welcome Pope Francis

By Asa Fitch Jan. 27, 2019

The Wall Street Journal

A band performs at Fellowship, a Dubai church based at a hotel conference center. PHOTO: ASA FITCH THE WALL STREET JOURNAL

DUBAI—Every Friday, on the fourth floor of a hotel conference center in this Arab business hub, several thousand Christians arrive to worship in two-hour shifts at what may be the world's best-hidden megachurch.

There is no sign outside the center to guide people to Fellowship.

The Protestant congregation sprang up roughly a decade ago in a place where Islam is the official religion, non-Muslim practice has long been closely monitored and sanctioned church buildings are limited and regulated.

But restrictions on places of worship have gradually loosened in the United Arab Emirates. The government has designated 2019 the "year of tolerance" to reinforce the idea that, in a region torn by conflict, people of diverse cultures and religions can find common ground.

The U.A.E. will display its more accommodating stance in February when it hosts Pope Francis for the first visit by a sitting pope to the Arabian Peninsula. The pope's itinerary includes engaging in an interfaith dialogue and celebrating Mass at a sports complex with a capacity of around 120,000.

Fellowship started with a handful of people, but now attracts roughly 4,000 a week from all religious backgrounds to services at two hotels. The services reflect the opening to non-Muslims in the U.A.E., which has accelerated in recent years as the government cultivated ties with Western powers that value the freedom of worship and explored ways to undermine the pull of Islamic extremism.

Churchgoers attend Mass on Christmas eve at Santa Maria Church in Dubai. PHOTO: AHMED JADALLAH REUTERS

As a result, a Buddhist temple catering to Sri Lankans, Cambodians and Thais is now operating out of a villa in Dubai. Leaders of a Jewish synagogue, which had been operating in secret, revealed its existence recently. A large Hindu temple is under construction. The religious institutions serve a population composed almost entirely of expatriate workers from Asia, Europe and beyond.

Rulers in the U.A.E. have allowed the establishment of churches since the 1960s, and have traditionally been more religiously permissive than neighboring countries like Saudi Arabia, which bans any form of non-Muslim worship.

Diverse Beliefs Religious groups in the U.A.E., where most of the over 9 million people are expatriates: Source: Association of Religion Data Archives Muslim 74.6% Other 5.2%Hindu 7.3% Christian 13.1%

But religious freedoms here have limits. The U.A.E.'s constitution guarantees freedom of worship as long as it doesn't clash with public policy or morals, according to the U.S. State Department in its religious freedom report for 2017. The country's laws also prohibit blasphemy and non-Muslim proselytizing.

The U.A.E. shows little tolerance for political Islam, too, and authorities provide guidance for the content of sermons in mosques, the State Department said.

The U.S. government has been supportive of the U.A.E.'s push for tolerance, and State Department officials have met with local religious leaders, according to people who attended the meetings, amid efforts to foster better religious understanding across the Middle East, partly to combat terrorism.

Pastor Tim Maxson leads Communion on a recent Friday at Fellowship, a Dubai congregation that sprang up roughly a decade ago. PHOTO: ASA FITCH, THE WALL STREET JOURNAL

The path toward open worship in the U.A.E. hasn't been without its bumps.

There are about 45 officially sanctioned church buildings in the country, but more than 700 Christian congregations, leaving them to share limited space for services. In the lobby of the

Evangelical Church center in Abu Dhabi, the capital, a board lists more than 50 congregations that worship there. Church services in the U.A.E. generally take place on Friday, the Muslim day of worship and a day off for most residents.

Local religious leaders said they would like to see more land allocated for church-building. But many also recognize that it isn't their decision to make.

"There's certainly a need for it," says Rev. Andrew Thompson, the British chaplain at St. Andrew's, an Anglican church in Abu Dhabi. "But I also caution Christians to say at the end of the day it's not our country, and I'm concerned about the sense of entitlement."

In Dubai, the phenomenon of hotel churches began a few years ago, after the Christian population became too large for designated church facilities. Congregations started meeting all over the city, but authorities eventually banned the practice last year, citing existing regulations for religious institutions.

Only three churches—including Fellowship—were allowed to continue meeting in hotels following an appeal to Sheikh Nahyan bin Mubarak al-Nahyan, a member of Abu Dhabi's ruling family who has been the country's minister of tolerance since 2017.

Concerns about Christian congregations that couldn't meet because of that move came up in discussions between a delegation of American evangelical leaders and Abu Dhabi's Crown Prince Mohammed Bin Zayed in November, according to several people who were there.

The Ministry of Tolerance didn't respond to requests for comment about Emirati policy.

Local religious leaders said they are encouraged by gradual progress and are hopeful for the future. Many of the evangelicals came away from their meetings reassured that the problem stemmed not from deliberate persecution of Christians but from the lack of clear bureaucratic procedures to approve new churches, according to members of the delegation.

At a recent Fellowship service, there was no sign of security forces or government monitoring as people shuffled in and out. In a conference-center ballroom, a nine-piece band led by a Filipino woman in stonewashed jeans sung a rendition of Matt Redman's Christian pop hit "10,000 Reasons (Bless the Lord)."

Tim Maxson, one of the church's pastors, led Communion for a congregation that looked like a cross-section of Dubai's expatriate workforce, a mishmash of nationalities including Filipinos, Kenyans, Australians, Americans, South Africans and Indians.

"We have Presbyterians, Baptists, Pentecostals, Roman Catholics, Mar Thomas, Anglicans, Episcopalians, Assemblies of God," said Jim Burgess, the Oklahoman who became Fellowship's first full-time pastor about 10 years ago. "People," he said, "are not as concerned about the label as they are with what's inside."

Write to Asa Fitch at asa.fitch@wsj.com

Appeared in the January 28, 2019, print edition as 'U.A.E. Slowly Loosens Constraints on Religious Freedom.' **Permission to use requested**

If It's Sunday, This Must Be Belgium or Germany, Or...

By Bruce Buursma, *Chicago Tribune*

In an excellent article in the August 4, 1986 *Chicago Tribune*, journalist Bruce Buursma explored the international churches. Here are excerpts:

"There are, of course, homilies to preach, ceremonies to officiate and confirmations to perform. But there are also several unfamiliar languages with which to contend, cultures to learn and customs officials and currency exchanges to confront with almost every parish visit," said Bishop A. Donald Davies, the then-bishop-in-charge of the Convocation of American Churches in Europe (a fellowship of eleven Episcopalian/Anglican churches).

The churches mentioned in the article, several of which had been established for more than a century, served as sanctuaries principally for American expatriates and diplomats living in those cities, but they also attract tourists and a growing number of European-bred students who were eager for exposure to the English language. The Convocation, was administered and financed by the U.S. Episcopal Church as an overseas diocese.

Although the Convocation was founded by the Episcopal Church, the U.S. branch of the Anglican Communion, the parishes were considered self-consciously ecumenical, with representation from numerous Protestant groups.

The churches were hampered, Bishop Davis said, by the free-flowing transience of the expatriate community in Europe. "*Every Sunday", the prelate said, "I meet someone who is heading out to return to the U.S. or to a posting in another country. It`s difficult to maintain the continuity of a program."*

The key demands on the clergy in the Convocation, the Bishop told the *Tribune*, centered on providing a ready ear for parishioners who were having difficulty adjusting to life away from home.

"There are many Americans over here who are lonely and whose biggest fear is that people back home might forget them," he said. **https://tinyurl.com/y4cn6g8k**

A church surrounded by nightclubs

Is the red light district the best place to have church activities? "When I try to imagine where Jesus would want a church, I definitely think it would be here", says the pastor of International Church Prague.

FROM PRAGUE
Author: Nelleke Wolters 16 July 2016

A church family game night has been organised by the International Church of Prague (ICP). I am walking with my family to the place. It's as busy as usual in the city centre.

Then, one of my children asks: "Mummy, the lady in the video on that building is dancing very strangely in her underwear, why is that?"

I am reminded again of the place where we actually are: the red light district of Prague.

We're just passing another night club. In general, we're a very open family and talk about everything that comes up. But confronted with reality, so unexpectedly through the eyes of my child, I have to think what to say.

But I realise something else. It is a bit uncommon for a church to organise a family game night in the middle of the red light district. A church building there is unusual too. There must be a story behind it, so I decided to ask pastor Drew Stephens a few questions. We meet in my favourite coffee place, La Boheme.

Question. The International Church of Prague meets every Sunday in a church building of the Seventh Day Adventists. And, recently, you opened 'The Bridge Center' in the middle of the red light district. Why?

A. Our church didn't have an office space for quite a while already. We really needed a church office again. And we needed a place to get together with the youth ministry on Fridays as well. They had been meeting in a variety of different places over the past view years. A place of their own would be good.

Also, we wanted to be a visible presence, to engage with the city and to serve it. We had been looking for a place for about a year, and finding a suitable building wasn't so easy. Many landlords were not eager to rent their places to a church and they simply refused to give it to us.

At some point I decided to stop looking. It felt as if I was in the way of getting the right building by looking for it myself. So I started to pray that God would bring us the building we needed instead. Within a week after we started praying God answered. I got in touch with the owners of the building where we're meeting now and they believed we could have a positive contribution to this neighbourhood.

It is a street with many night clubs, true enough, but there are also other things going on. Like a cafe that trains disabled people to serve. And a copy shop that prints for the blind. There is also a swimming club for mothers with toddlers. In the future we hope to be able to connect with these neighbours as well.

Q. What is the main purpose of 'The Bridge Center'?

A. We want to be a bridge between churches, ministries and cultures. A bridge for the gospel also.

Q. And has the famous Charles Bridge here in Prague anything to do with this?

A. Only a little bit. The logo of our church is a cross with the Charles Bridge on it, so there is a small link between the bridge and our church. But the name is mainly connected with the purpose that we see for this building and our church.

Q. Is there already cooperation between your center and other churches, organisations and ministries?

A. Yes, there is. A Czech church, Kresanske spolecenstvi, needed a place to worship on Sundays and right after the building was ready and open they started having their church services there every Sunday morning.

Also during weekdays there are many ministries using this building. The International Baptist Church has a homeless ministry and every Saturday they come here to cook and bring food to the homeless on the street, and they share the Gospel with them.

Youth With A Mission (YWAM) have an office in our building and they also minister to the homeless, but also to ladies who work in the sex industry. Before they go out on the streets they first pray together at 'The Bridge Center'.

Also there is the group called Journey. They have a heart for young people who call themselves agnostic or atheist. Journey cooks for them and invites them over to 'The Bridge Center' to talk with them about the important questions in life.

In the future we hope to start with other activities as well. This building has so many possibilities.

Q. So, the building can be a blessing for a lot of things. But how about the location? It's impossible to avoid sex and erotica in this city with so many sex shops all around, but you don't have to go into the area of the night clubs and sex clubs if you don't want to. Yet there are Youth Praha meetings in the new 'The Bridge Center' every Friday evening. What to think of the fact that you deliberately have impressionable and maybe vulnerable teenagers every week coming into this street full of night clubs?

A. Yes, this is a good question. Of course we've thought about that, but when I try to imagine where Jesus would want a church, I definitely think it would be in the red light district!

So if Jesus wants a church there, then there is no better place to have one. But, indeed, we have to deal with the challenges that come along with it. We've talked with the police about safety issues.

They said that there could be illegal things happening, but only inside the night clubs and definitely not on the streets, where the police are present. One of our measures is that we have the teenagers go in groups escorted by an adult always, to get them to places where it's safe enough for them to continue on their own.

Q. Yes, that's the safety part. But how about the seductive side of a night club? The moving images outside the buildings are not particularly subtle.

A. Yes it is a tough neighbourhood for the youth. There are ways to minimize the risks. When you come from Wenseclas square you have to pass a lot of night clubs, but when you walk in from the other end of the street you don't. But then still you have to pass a few clubs and also the adult book store.

It's impossible to avoid it completely. More important than shielding this from them is teaching our youth about it. So one of the things Youth Praha do on Friday evening is, they split up in small discipleship groups. And in these groups one of the things we discuss is how they can guard their eyes and hearts in an environment that is at odds with what the Bible and the church say about sexuality."

Q. Now there is this great place that is an answer to many prayers. When you think about the future, what are your hopes and expectations? What will 'The Bridge Center' look like in, say, five years?

A. Five years from now? I hope it will be a safe place to have spiritual conversation. A place of transformation that builds the Kingdom. A place to be at home and do live and faith together.

I hope many other churches and organisations will use this building for Kingdom purposes. As an international community we want to serve many different cultures. I hope the staff that we have will have developed new projects and outreaches and that we as a church will have established firm connections and relationships with the people in our neighbourhood. **https://tinyurl.com/y5btedsl Used courtesy of Evangelical Focus.com**

Missionary tends to international congregations in Germany
A UMNS Report By Kathleen LaCamera*

A growing number of international United Methodist congregations now exist within Germany, where their members range from Americans to Africans, diplomats to asylum seekers, students to business people.

All, according to Bishop Rosemarie Wenner of the Germany area, are welcome within the United Methodist Church in Germany.

Wenner believes that differences in language and culture need not create barriers within the church but, rather, can offer rich opportunities for connection and exchange. To help support these non-German-speaking congregations, German United

Methodists and the United Methodist Board of Global Ministries have worked together to appoint the Rev. Carol Ann Seckel, a board missionary, as coordinator for English language and migrant ministries.

Seckel, an American, has extensive experience working in cross-cultural settings. She has served as conference superintendent in the denomination's Alaska Missionary Conference, where she also worked with Alaska Children's Services. From 2000-2004, both she and her husband, Kevin, served as missionaries in Latvia. He is now doing similar work with English language congregations in the south of Germany, starting new churches.

Seckel said she already is impressed by the commitment of German United Methodists to support those coming from outside the country. She recounted one recent experience where she came across two older German women taking part in an English language service aimed at foreign students. "They said even though they didn't understand English, they wanted to be there to support this ministry," she added.

While officially installed in the Frankfurt-based position in January, Seckel has been on the job for the past eight months.

Diverse congregations

Currently, about 40 international United Methodist congregations are in Europe-20 of them in Germany. They serve a wide range of people with diverse abilities, challenges and socio-economic situations. Most of the congregations are small and a number serve economically disadvantaged migrant communities.

Seckel said these congregations face the challenge of "how to live faithfully with limited resources, struggling to be the church we are called to be."

English is the primary language for most of these congregations. However, both preaching and pastoral ministry also are conducted in French, Russian, Vietnamese and African dialects.

The largest group of these international church members come from Ghana, West Africa.

One particular challenge within the Ghanaian Methodist community is getting parents-who are anxious about European influence and its effects-to encourage their young people to meet and get to know young European Christians.

Seckel's responsibilities include outreach to American military chaplains. She says many chaplains don't realize that United Methodist congregations are close by. She thinks she is in a unique position to offer support as a chaplain to "the chaplains."

According to Wenner, it is important to offer pastoral care for clergy colleagues doing a difficult job during wartime. She welcomes the exchange of insights and perspectives that these links can bring. "We are sisters and brothers in one church," she explained. "We must get to know each other, start conversations about ethics, exchange insight and perspectives."

Cross-cultural training

In addition, Seckel will train German pastors and lay people who desire to work more effectively within cross-cultural settings. And she will help strengthen relationships among international English-speaking and migrant congregations in Germany and those in other parts of Europe including Sweden, Demark, Russia and Belgium. Under Wenner's leadership, leaders from these European international congregations have started to meet annually.

"I have joked that I feel like I'm on this significant learning curve that continues to go straight up," Seckel told United Methodist News Service. Seckel began learning German only last spring. A map of Germany is an essential tool for her work, and one is pinned to the wall of her office.

In Wenner's opinion, the work with international congregations in Germany can be a model for others, showing how to build one inclusive church rather allowing separate parallel Methodist churches to develop.

"We have sisters and brothers who come to live here in Europe who have made all those transitions in their lives and in their families' lives. They are part of the church here in Europe," Wenner told UMNS. "In future, we need to build up the (pastoral) leadership of people within these people coming from abroad."

**LaCamera is a UMNS correspondent based in England.*
Used courtesy of United Methodist News Service

Kingdom Faces
May 28, 2010

Alliance international workers Mark and Pattie Brinkman have served in Hong Kong and in the Balkans. Today, they are the pastoral couple at Trinity International Church of Strasbourg, France. The following is Pattie's reflection of Trinity's "way-station" ministry to a continually changing congregation of multinationals.

The coffee and tea are ready on the back tables, chairs have been lined up in our rented Catholic youth center, and cords run over the cement floors. Amps are plugged in, and greeters are stationed at the door. Another Sunday worship service begins.

Our worship leader adjusts his microphone, pushes back his dark bangs, and strums a chord on his guitar. He looks around and smiles at the faces gathered before him, and we swing into, "Light of the world, you stepped down into darkness . . ."

As the worship leader closes his eyes to sing, it is my turn to look around the room and smile as well. Six months ago as I looked out at the congregation, I wondered if I would ever know everyone's name. Today, I can name probably 60 percent of the worshippers, who have come together in France from Benin, Brazil, Germany, Peru, China, France, the United States, Ireland, Gabon, Hong Kong, Ecuador, Bulgaria, Korea, and more.

If I were in an American church, I would feel guilty for not recognizing the other 40 percent, but in this church, it is not an unusual day. Each service is a first-time experience for 20 percent of the attendees; they are visitors from out of town, have lived here for only a month or so and finally found us, or they have always lived here but have come today mostly out of curiosity about the church.

Another 20 percent have been here once or twice. I might have met them at some point in the past six months. The 60 percent I do know arrived between one month and four years ago, and only a few can say with relative certainty that they will still be here in another month, year, or two years.

In one of the most secular regions of the world, our international church plays a key role in pushing back the darkness. Trinity International Church is a community of believers from many backgrounds, worshipping Jesus as they draw into Kingdom life their neighbors and friends who are searching for meaning.

Metro Stop

International churches have been compared to a metro, an urban train that stops often to let people on and off; the doors slide open people come and people go. A river, with streams flowing in and out, also has been used to describe what this church constantly experiences.

You get the idea-international students, business people, and diplomats from other countries; transient military families; couples in bicultural marriages; locals with out-of-country experience; those restlessly seeking new adventures or hobbit-like creatures of comfort who are unhappily relocating-we all are a bit surprised to be here and unsure exactly how long we'll stay.

What is it we are looking for? Why did we step in from our platform this morning? And by the time we step back off this particular metro, how will God have matured us, pruned us, and used us in this place?

Faces in the Crowd

A family in the front row catches my eye. As happens each week, the father juggles an energetic, blond three-year-old toddler. While the mother carries the baby in a front sling, another blond, giggly son sits beside her with several little friends. Elle and Francois, a local French couple, just became Christ followers early last summer.

God moved them into a new house next door to one of Trinity's typical families-an American who grew up in South America who is married to a French woman with international experience. The two families struck up a friendship, and the Christian couple ministered to their new neighbors, who had recently lost a child. Their conversations were deep and God-centered, and Elle and Francois found the God of comfort and hope.

Although Elle and Francois could not speak much English, they came to church to grow. God took the seeds planted in the soil of "good and honest hearts" and helped them through biblical preaching and a loving community. After nine months as church members, Elle and Francois find themselves moving precipitously to Africa for an employment opportunity. We all are praying for a church that will nurture these young believers. They leave here with a firm foundation in truth and a real picture of love as the Body has reached out to nurture them in spirituality and practicality. They have begun their journey toward being conformed to Christ, living like Him in faith and fruit.

A Step Closer

Just behind them sits Sabine, a young northern European woman who is dressed and coiffed with precision. She was invited to the church by friends with whom she works locally. Sabine is still grieving the loss of family members several years ago, trying to control her life so that tragedy will not mar it again.

Sabine knows that there is a Father who cares for her, but she is not yet at the point of accepting that there is also a Lord who is asking her to give up control. We all pray for her to find that joy and release someday soon. She is here, searching; if she leaves, she will do so a step closer to the God of the Bible, having seen what life in His Body looks like. Sabine is on her way to becoming more like Jesus in faith and service to others.

The Jesus Student

Across the aisle toward the back windows sits Luc, a local master's student. He spent some of his undergraduate years in the Midwest of the United States and found Jesus there, with the help of Asian students and their church. He came back to France, looking for that kind of community again.

Today, Luc is involved in ministry to Asian students here as well as being discipled in a home group. When Luc graduates next spring, he will leave with more biblical truth in his head, more selflessness in his heart for having served, and more love given and gained through the church-more like Christ.

The Faces of Maturity

On the right side toward the back sits a couple my own age with their son, a local family who met Jesus in Paris after several years of searching for meaning in Buddhism, the biker lifestyle, and whatever else they could explore. They are mature Christians now, living lives of faith before coworkers and neighbors. In their year or so at Trinity, they have had opportunity to encourage all of us with their lives of trust in God, and they have seen more of God's Kingdom in the church and in the world. They are growing more like Jesus in faith and humility.

Everyone Has a Story

Scattered behind me are more individuals with their own stories. I see a young man from Peru with gifts in theology. He will leave here soon for Bible school in another country, having been gently challenged and encouraged in his enthusiastic ponderings. Nearby is another man from Benin, who, having just recently begun his journey within this community, is struggling with God about why He has not provided employment and conflicted about his family background, which includes witchcraft.

I wish I had time to tell you how the French military man is stronger for having been here, how the South American MK received rest and a place to use his gifts, how the Irish lawyer understands her faith in the real world more fully, and how the American space engineer has had a place to bring her Indian and Asian classmates.

Another Stop along the Journey

We come, needing truth, wisdom, and salvation from God; we need guidance from our brothers and sisters, a place to worship, tasks through which we can express God's love, and a community in which we can explore who God is and what He offers and requires.

When we leave, we move out those "sliding metro doors" a bit more like Christ-trusting our Father, serving Him in His Body, loving, knowing, and telling truth. We leave with more gentleness, joyfulness, and with His peace, ready for His next stop.

The church together sows the seed of God's Word and the love of His community. Sometimes we see harvest; many times we see only a small step on our friends' journeys, either before or after they find Jesus. Either way, we rejoice to live our lives of faith and love together.

"So here I am to bow down . . ." I have sung "Here I Am to Worship" in other languages and other countries, and roads from France east to the Balkans and China are in my head as we sing. It is easy to imagine the many, many roads in others' minds, connecting us to all continents. May God use His church in this town-beautiful and lost-to make Himself known here and around the world as we come and go.

Reprinted with permission, The Christian and Missionary Alliance.

(Note: Items marked **Permission to use requested** indicate that multiple requests for use were submitted but no response was received)

Published articles concerning international churches from church and academic sources

The International Church for a Global World

By Dr. Warren Reeve

The International Church is a *kairos* call to a profound need and compelling opportunity. God is sovereignly and supernaturally planting and building International Churches in unparalleled numbers around the globe. The unprecedented diaspora scattering has created cutting-edge potential for the International Church to reach every tribe, tongue and nation.[8] The International Church is the collection of God's people diverse in nationality, culture, colour, class and church background, gathered together in many cities and locations around the globe to worship God, hear from God and tell others about God.[9]

---

[8] Missional International Church Network (2017). *Strengthening the International Church Movement for Missional Impact* (Brochure) Calgary, Canada: Ken Driedger, Ken Paton, Warren Reeve

[9] Ed Teo, Warren Reeve (2016, April 12). *Why The International Church is Such a Big Deal.* Quick Talk presented at Global Church for a Global World conference hosted by the International Christian Assembly, Hong Kong. Host Pastor Ed Teo and Warren Reeve met together to define and describe the International Church as succinctly as possible for our joint presentation. The above is a modified version of that discussion. We wanted to communicate God's sovereign genius explaining the kaleidoscope of people collecting in a Church called International.

There are versions of the International Church dotted across Church history landscape. Geographically identified as the church at Antioch, perhaps this body of disciples is more appropriately called the first International Church (Acts 13:1-3). It started with Jewish expatriate believers meeting in current day Syria. They heard and acted on Jesus' Great Commission to be witnesses at home, in the region, in the country and abroad (Acts 1:8). They invited Greek and Roman Gentiles into the church despite the obstacles of contrasting nationalities, differing cultures, a mosaic of colour and mixed classes.[10]

Then the Jewish-Gentile International Church sent the gospel to the least reached people groups. The first International Church was a launching pad for kingdom movement. Within twenty-five years, kingdom expansion had spread exponentially. It started in Antioch, and then moved to Asia Minor and across to Europe, as far as Rome. The capital super city, Rome, was where the Acts of the Apostles ended the biblical church history account in chapter Acts 28. However, the movement continued, and continues today.

The Jewish-Gentile first International Church not only went west but east! In fact, Church history records that the Church, for the first one thousand years after Christ's ascension, was more Asian than European. Philip Jenkins unveiled the little known history of the Asian church. Nestorian and Jacobite missionaries were commissioned from Syria to the Far East long before the Silk Road was travelled by any other Christians.[11] These missionaries landed in Mongolia, China, India and perhaps as far as Vietnam, Philippines and Korea.

---

[10] Reeve, Warren. *"Unleashing Great Commission Potential through the International Church"* in Tira, Joy and Yamamori, Ted ed. *Scattered and Gathered: A Global Compendium of Diaspora Missiology* (Ragnum Books International, 2016) 195.

[11] Jenkins, Philip. *The Lost History of Christianity: The Thousand-Year Golden Age of the Church in the Middle East, Africa and Asia—and How it Died.* 1st ed. (New York: Harper On, 2008) 70.

By the year 1000 AD, Asia was populated with 17-20 million Christians who could trace their faith back twenty five to thirty generations.[12] This history only serves to strengthen the understanding and impact of the Acts 13 narrative. The International Church then, and now, is an invitation to the diaspora to join God's accelerated spiritual growth plan and to unprecedented numerical growth, a key to unlocking the nations to engage with the gospel. The International Church of Acts 13 impacted the East on an unprecedented scale and, from the first century, became the kingdom of God without borders.

Leveraging Expatriates in a Global World

The International Church is the Bride of Christ at the crossroads of the scattered peoples of the world, offering a warm welcome in the name of Jesus. The composition of this gathering is multi-national. Within the cities and mega-cities of the world there is untapped potential inside the Christian expatriate community already living overseas, self-funded, planted and prepared to obey the Great Commission. They are globetrotters that are generally highly educated, entrepreneurial, people of comparable means and full of adventure. However, in certain regions of the world expatriates are composed of migrants that are historically required for the host country's economic benefit. Ratios in some countries can be as high as four expatriates to every one national. Expatriates comprise everyone from street cleaners, maids, and taxi drivers to bankers, surgeons and lawyers including everyone in-between. Among most expatriates there are biblically literate Christians desiring to make an impact for Christ in their corner of the world.

When expatriates are collected in International Churches to encounter Christ, are discipled into Christ, and are commissioned by Christ, there is tremendous leverage for the Kingdom of God.

---

[12] Ibid

This leverage initiates the communication and demonstration of the gospel through otherwise impossible relationship networks. Least reached people from diverse nationalities are encountering and engaging Jesus in places often presumed to be impossible to reach for Christ. This is happening cross-culturally. Without the International Church these expatriates are left to collide at the intersections of other traveling nomads. Since one in eight people live away from home today, it is clear to International Church leaders that God is sovereignly and supernaturally extending his kingdom through a diversity of travelling, globe-trotting expatriates/internationals meeting host country citizens. Never before in the history of humanity have so many people been on the move. This is a *kairos* moment in history when the nations are meeting in the urban centers of the world in the diaspora. The church to reach these people is naturally international, expediting the flow of the gospel to a globalized world.

Varied Cultures Provide Context to Reach People

The International Church is the face of the diaspora. Where there is a gathering of the nations it follows that there is a cultural mix. First-hand experience could describe the culture mix as a "taste of heaven."[13] The apostle John describes this experience through a vision in Revelation 7:9 *"I looked, and there before me was a great multitude that no one could count, from every nation, tribe, people and language, standing before the throne and before the Lamb."* The International Church is a tangible picture of this biblical vision on earth. Like a kaleidoscope of colour, it is the splendour of the kingdom's great multitude gathered into one assembly.

In "Look Who God Let into the Church," David Packer writes of "tight" and "loose" cultures. He describes the degree

---

[13] C. L. (2000). Bandung International Church monthly elders meeting. When asked what does the International Church mean to you? Cindy Lewis responded, "a taste of heaven."

to which social constraints are placed upon individuals in certain cultures to behave a certain way. "Tight" means that social norms in behavior are well-fixed and everyone within the group is expected to follow them. "Loose" means more flexibility, that social norms are not as rigid, that either there is no norm or there is tolerance with deviations from the norm.[14] The International Church is a melting pot of tight and loose cultures requiring astute leadership. There are no cookie cutter solutions when leading the various cultures that are sometimes in conflict. Ultimately, International Church pastors must shepherd and love over and through these different cultural expectations. Authentic love can provide a different opportunity to experience God's love than simply through one culture or one way. Jesus sacrifice of love penetrates all cultural expectations. So must the shepherd's love of the International Church.

God created the diaspora. When the diaspora is brought together from various diverse nationalities there is an obvious compelling opportunity for the Church to reach the nations. When the International Church engages the diaspora through contextualized, incarnational servant-hood, then missional becomes the norm. Missions is not delegated to a person in a place, rather, missional is a shift in thinking for the whole Church as an active and transformational presence in each culture, equipping one another to serve people within the diaspora. Missional is the mental shift from formulaic and institutional programs to relationships of word, deed, sign and power. The International Church aims to facilitate creative thinking to catalyze active participation in God's mission within the diaspora context.[15]

---

[14] Packer, David. Look *Who God Let into the Church: Understanding the Nature and Sharpening the Impact of a Multi-cultural Church* (Amazon Digital Services, LLC. 2013) 1295 – 1298.

[15] Missional International Church Network (2015). Bangkok Conference Book: Graham Chipps ed.

The Diaspora as a Rainbow of Colour

The International Church is a canvas of colour, drawing scattered people into a rainbow of grandeur. If it were possible to assemble the world's international migrants to live in one place it would be the world's fifth largest country with more colour than any country on the planet. However, this international mosaic of migrants does not live in one country, the people are scattered around the world. During 2016, the rainbow of colour in descending order, painted across the world's canvas, includes India (15.6 million), Mexico (12.3 million), Russia (10.6 million), China (9.5 million) and Bangladesh (7.2 million).[16] The mandate of the International Church is to create a masterpiece by gathering the colours of the nations.

Traditional mission strategy is geographically bound. Seizing the diaspora opportunity through the International Church is one way to engage people on the move. Who would consider Australia a mission field? Yet 28% of the Australian population is born outside their country. Melbourne boasts the largest Greek speaking population, next to Greece, in the world. The International Church is no longer constrained to "overseas" but today must be understood as a viable and essential deal breaker for completing the Great Commission. Collecting the colours of the diaspora is to experience the rainbow of the International Church.

Mixed Classes are a Viable Ministry Partnership

The International Church includes expatriates that have left home for bigger and better. This quest for opportunity exists in people of every occupation in every class. The supposed greener grass on the other side of the fence is a strong incentive towards

[16] Conner, Phillip (2016, May17) *Pew Research Center: Global Attitudes and Trends, International Migration: Key Findings from the U.S., Europe and the World.* Retrieved from www.pewresearch.org

migrating. Sometimes the result is increase, and sometimes it backfires. Class separation in the International Church is often deep and wide, while at the same time the ambition to succeed can be found in every class.

One challenge for the International Church is to teach and motivate all classes toward the reality that God has a bigger and better plan than material success. From Adam came every person from every ethnos to be placed in a time and a setting. He determined and appointed each expatriate in His *kairos* time, to His designated place, so that the different classes would "*reach out to Him and find Him*" (Acts 17:26-27). When expatriates of any class find God's higher migration calling within the diaspora, more people meet Jesus.

The same class levels reach one another with greater understanding even though the interaction may be cross-cultural. For example, a Nigerian diplomat connects with a British environmentalist because both are highly educated. Similar classes naturally understand and relate to one another despite different nationalities, colours or cultures. A taxi driver reaches out to a street cleaner and he *"finds God."* A banker communicates with a doctor and a divine encounter inspires a "*reach*" to the living God. Class connections and networks are created and discovered, leveraging kingdom growth.

Conversely, mixed class connections can also expand the kingdom. Expatriates with greater resources make provision and create pathways for less privileged expatriates to find their newly discovered, diaspora calling. Often the profound "pure belief in Jesus" faith of the less privileged expatriates is profoundly impacting to the complex and sometimes chaotic world of expatriates with greater means. This dynamic is authentic, viable and presently happening through the International Church globally. There is hardly a mission strategy that could make this kind of mixed class partnership so productive for the cause of Christ except through the International Church.

Center Set Inclusion versus Bound Set Exclusion

The International Church is planted by denominations, military or independently organized believers. When denominational International Churches emphasize their own distinctives, contrasted against participating members, those bodies forfeit the best International Church potential. When military International Churches remain nationalistic, they evolve into an extended chaplaincy service. When independent organized International Churches refuse connection with an outside body they set themselves up to be isolated and invite possible conflict without objective input. Conversely, having stated these cautions, each specific church background of the specific International Church calls for celebration and connection.

When the International Church is more centered set versus bound set, more inclusive than exclusive, then health, scope and impact are increased. Twenty-five years ago, the International Church was understood to be primarily American and English speaking. Today, the International Church is emerging into the global church for a global world. Missiologists Michael Crane and Scott Carter write:

"International Churches around the world are making an invaluable contribution to the church's mission to make disciples of every nation. Around the world God has used International Church's as instrumental in sowing seeds of the gospel of Jesus Christ on the frontiers of lostness.[17]

From the Past to the Future

Movements of God are identified when God circulates the same vision to different people in different places at the same time. Staggered within the last twenty years, God has imparted

[17] Crane, Michael and Carter Scott, Gateway to the Nations: *The Strategic Value of International Churches in a Globalized Urban World,* (unpublished paper, August 28, 2014) p.1.

the similar International Church vision to reach the nations for Christ to several servants from several different locations. Below are the known unfolding networks of International Churches that have emerged.

1) *Fellowship of European International Churches* in thirty-eight European countries
2) *China International Fellowship* in the most populated nation on earth
3) *International Baptist Convention* in Europe, Middle East, Africa and the Americas
4) *Global International Church Network* a global relational network for international churches
5) *Missional International Church Network* starting and strengthening International Churches

The above network leaders and members agreed to combine their annual conferences in 2016 and come together for the first united Global Church for a Global World conference. The name "Global Church" was chosen to include both International and National churches. Delegates attended and participated, speaking and listening to what God was saying to each other and from each other.

Keynote speakers Ravi Zacharias, Os Guinness and Rodney Woo challenged participants attending the Global Church for a Global World conference in Hong Kong, hosted by the International Christian Assembly. With some excitement, at commitment time, 232 International Church leaders signed the Global Church declaration included below. The Global Church for a Global World is emerging as an alliance that collaboratively bridges God's vision between International Church networks and International Churches around the globe. The Global Church for a Global World:

DECLARES to all nations that the Global Church is rising to meet the demands of a global world

AFFIRMS that God is scattering people to accomplish His global mission

CONNECTS: leaders everywhere to advance the global church movement

Fellowship of the Emirates International Church in Dubai hosted the second triennial Global Church for a Global World conference from April 29 to May 2 in 2019. The International Church is on the move. God is collecting people from the diaspora into the International Church all over the globe to play a unique role in the Great Commission mandate.

Biodata

Warren Reeve served with his wife Debbie as Lead Pastor of the Bandung International Church in Indonesia from 1998 to 2009. The three Reeve children loved the environment of the International Church while growing up in Southeast Asia. From 2010 to 2015 Warren was the Senior Pastor of the Lighthouse International Church Kuwait. Warren founded the Missional International Church Network in 2000. In 2014, Terry Hoggard of the Fellowship of European International Churches, Jon Davis of the China International Fellowship and Warren co-founded the Global Church for a Global World network through Ken Driedger acting as facilitator and Ed Teo acting as host through the International Christian Assembly in Hong Kong. Today, Warren is chairperson of the Global Church for a Global World steering committee.

Other significant articles by Dr. Reeve concerning international churches can be accessed online at www.micn.com, including: The Profile of an effective international church pastor by Dr. Reeve and Dr. Graham Chipps: **https://tinyurl.com/u8rarmz Reprinted by permission**

Ministering to American Families Overseas

Dr. Robbins W. Barstow

Recently I received an urgent letter from a concerned mother in Iowa, whose son had accepted a business position in another country. He and his bride were about to sail for a two-year term, and the mother wondered what they might find in the way of church life over there. Would there be services in the English language and Chris tian fellowship for these young people who had been active in church life all through their school and college days? Or would they be more or less orphaned, spiritually, while away from their normal home surroundings?

This letter pinpointed an important aspect of our total church responsibility by its reference to one category of overseas Americans who have received too little attention on the part of most of us here at home. We all know at least something about our missionaries, and through our benevolent giving we are privileged to help support them in their varied types of work, evangelical, medical, educational and social, among many different peoples in all parts of the world; and we all know about our armed forces abroad, and are glad to think of the devoted chaplains, who are sharing in their dangers and ministering to their spiritual welfare.

Too few of us, however, have given thought to the thousands of civilian citizens living in other countries, in the midst of other cultures. They are engaged in a wide variety of activities, diplomatic, technical, commercial, and professional. Many of them have their families with them, particularly if their assignments or operations are of several years' duration. Most of them are concentrated in the principal cities of Latin America, Europe, the Middle East, and the Far East, with lesser numbers in lower Africa.

These individuals and groups represent the United States in cross section, coming as they do from all parts of this nation and setting up American homes and community interests wherever they find themselves located. In fact, these persons interpret to other nations the culture and standards of American life more directly and more effectively than do the radio broadcasts, the propaganda booklets, and the other official attempts to "make friends and influence people." They are flesh and blood realities as they are seen on the streets and in the shops, and what they say and do and are is carefully noted

For these reasons, it is most enheartening to realize that in half a hundred such situations there has been a sort of coagulation of earnest Christian men and women who have been keenly conscious of the importance of religion in their own lives and in the lives of their children. They have felt the need for the cultivation of their own spiritual experience and have been glad of an opportunity for quiet public witness by their observance of Sunday and their conduct throughout the week. They have been led to organize interdenominational Protestant Sunday Schools and preaching services in the English language and, often from small beginnings, there have developed substantial congregations, many of which now have their own union church buildings and full-time pastors. The earliest of these were in Beirut (1829), Istanbul (1817), Mexico City (1867), and Bogotá (1868), and the story is far from finished, for new congregations are even now in process of organization in a number of places

Sometimes it is asked why there should be separate churches for these overseas Americans. "Why," some say, "should they not worship with the local congregations? The first answer has to do with language, for most of these families are on limited appointments and do not master the local tongue so that they are sufficiently at ease with it to profit by sermons or services of worship. A second answer has to do with educational levels and cultural compatibility. For the most part, the preaching to national Protestant congregations has a different focus and, even if language were no barrier, the services would hardly be mentally stimulating or spiritually satisfying to the American families who in the nature of the case represent a higher than average level of education and a very different general cultural background. This difference is even more significant in the area of religious education for the children.

It should be added quickly, however, that the existence of separate English language churches does not mean a complete separation, nor does it imply any superiority complex. The missionaries who are working with the nationals in so-called "mission areas" are usually active in the life of the American Union Churches and form one link with the body of local Protestant believers. English-speaking nationals are welcomed at services of worship and social events and form another link. There are many such in almost every foreign city, including individuals who have studied in the United States and had connections with church and youth groups or have at least studied in missionary colleges and have a good command of English. Furthermore, the Union Churches often give very generously through their benevolent budgets to local Protestant programs or institutions, and sometimes even take over a particular project for full or partial support as an expression of their fellowship in Christ. Thus, there is a very definite integration into the various aspects of church life.

By and large, however, there seems to be sound justification, amply sustained by the experience of the years, for churches especially designed to minister to the Americans and other English-speaking individuals in these distant and scattered locations. In many instances, it is an Anglican or Scottish or other chapel, established in the era of Britain's far-flung colonial empire and commercial expansion, which serves the entire English-speaking community. In fact, when I was in Baghdad, the following paragraph appeared in the weekly calendar of St. George's Mesapotamian Memorial Chapel, which is ably served by Archdeacon Roberts and welcomes all Americans. "IT is uplifting to see the various nationalities and Christian denominations attending this church. Here we emphasize our agreements. We are all far from home: long may it be that our church is one where we can come together as a group of Christians and realize our common heritage. I am deeply conscious of this growth of unity and family spirit among us. It is a source of strength to the Church of God." One is tempted to interpolate that if this gracious spirit were more prevalent at home as well as abroad we would surely feel a more rapid movement toward fuller ecumenical understandings."

An analysis of these Union Churches would be interesting. I myself have visited nearly two score of these strategic spots in the last fifteen months. In set-up and program they vary widely, all the way from the American Church in Paris with its extensive institutional activities for many different groups such as students, service men and women, Scouts and others, across the full range of church life to small companies in out-of-the-way places, meeting only occasionally in a home or a mission chapel for an English-language service when a missionary or visiting minister is available. Many of them have organizational patterns and schedules of events quite like the average church here in the States - women's groups, men's clubs, fellowship suppers, adult Bible study courses and even annual bazaars!

Some of the churches serving the entire English-speaking constituency are sponsored by a denomination, usually one having active missionary work in that area. In this case, whether or not it is called a Union Church, it follows the denominational pattern as to membership, by-laws, and general polity, and the minister is appointed by, or at least is a member of that denomination. But most of the Union Churches, whatever the name, such as American Church, Community Church, Protestant Fellowship, or some other, are organized as independent congregations, with their own constitutions and by-laws, usually reflecting common denominators in the thought and experience of the churches from which the original members came. In many instances statements of faith and polity have been written, drawing freely and richly from many sources, but emphasizing in all cases the most widely accepted essentials of Protestant belief and practice, and avoiding emphasis upon matters which still cause so much division.

In point of fact, these Union Churches are more inclusive in their fellowship than any existing ecumenical organization, bringing together in harmonious, spiritual unity representatives of almost every line of tradition or strain of faith, fundamentalist, conservative, moderate or liberal. In such alien surroundings, and often in circumstances that are tense and difficult, the differences in creed or manner of worship which split our home communities into overlapping and competing parishes fall properly into the background. Episcopalians and Baptists, Lutherans and Congregationalists, Methodists and Quakers, Orthodox and Pentecostals, Presbyterians and many others, discover that in Tehran or in Athens, in Tokyo or Manila, the common faith in Christ Jesus as Lord and Saviour that unites Protestant Christians is vastly more significant than the inherited variations of phrasing or interpretation or liturgical custom that kept them apart back home.

It would be dangerous and unfair to attempt any comparison or evaluation of these many overseas churches, for each one has grown out of and is specially adapted to local conditions. From my own recent observation, however, I venture to comment on the American Church at Caracas, Venezuela, as one outstanding example, In addition to its own normal program which keeps its pastor and its minister of education very busy, this church has appointed a third staff minister to serve three of the oil settlements to the east. Over and above this extension work, the Caracas church is giving very generously to help in the resettlement of refugees and other immigrants from Europe through the program jointly sponsored by the World Council of Churches and the Lutheran World Federation.

I would mention also the Lago Community Church at Aruba, Netherlands West Indies, which has a Church School of which any church might well be proud, enrolling over 500 children, some 95 per cent of the nominally Protestant girls and boys in the settlement, and with unique equipment by way of separate open-air patios for the various departments. One is tempted to extend the catalog by mentioning that the Union Church in Tokyo has received more than a hundred new members in the past year, many of them on first profession of faith. Many other churches deserve citation, did space permit.

Indicative of the vigor of these overseas congregations is the fact that within the past few years, mostly through local resources sacrificially contributed, the war-destroyed sanctuaries in Manila, Tokyo, and Kobe have been replaced or restored. New church edifices have also been erected, with a minimum of outside assistance, in Monterrey, Mexico; in Gamboa and in Margarita in the Canal Zone; Guatemala City; La Lima, Honduras; and Sao Paulo, Brazil. To reach back a bit further we must include Caracas and Aruba. Splendid building programs are now in process or contemplated for the near future by the Union Churches in Mexico City; Lima, Peru; Rio de Janeiro, Brazil; and Bogotá, Colombia. The church at Bad Godesberg in Germany occupies a beautiful new interfaith chapel, the Stimson Memorial, erected by the State Department for the use of Protestant, Catholic, and Jewish groups within the HICCG community, for, of course, in any assemblage of North Americans there are Roman Catholics and Jews, as well as Protestants, and some, alas, of no faith at all.

One hears much in these days of the unpopularity of Americans abroad and the lowering esteem in which the United States is held. Anybody who travels much becomes painfully aware of this. There are many and varied reasons or explanations for these regrettable attitudes. Probably the major factor is the wealth and strength of this nation, which is bound to stir up envy and a measure of fear. A great world power is never loved by lesser nations. Another factor is rooted in post-war policies of the United States or, perhaps more accurately, procedures. Without being unduly critical, it is pretty generally recognized that some of the things we have done and the unilateral ways in which we have done them have not been calculated to build friendship and international admiration.

Then we must remember that too large a proportion of the movies which this country sends abroad gives a disgustingly distorted picture of American life, gun-play and seduction being the two principle themes Furthermore, personal attitudes and actions of Americans are frequently such as to repel, rather than to attract. Government officials, businessmen, and tourists have too often displayed a spirit of superiority, of arrogance, of callousness to other cultures, and of just plain coarseness in their lavish spending, their drinking, gambling, and other personal habits. These matters of conduct all reflect adversely upon the nation and the Christian tradition which we like to feel is our foundation.

It is against this negative background that the importance and the wholesome influence of these Protestant Union Churches stands out the more clearly. Their very existence means that there are many United States citizens for whom religion really has a priority value. Thank God that there are so many, diplomats and business men as well as teachers and missionaries, who endeavor to be truly Christian in their thinking and their living! They themselves recognize the need for the cultivation of their own spiritual experience. Over the years, the initial planning of services of worship and programs of religious education has always been by way of local "spiritual spontaneous combustion," not something demanded of them, or even suggested, by outsiders or "statesiders."

In the light of all this, it can be seen that these Union Churches, whether large or small, mean several things. First, they help their own members to be at their best. Their services of worship serve to "maintain the spiritual glow." A United States ambassador, with a long and distinguished career, said to me, "I have always noticed a difference in the morale and the whole quality of the life of the American community in places where there is a strong Union Church." One of these churches, which has just completed its first year with a full-time pastor, reports that "the church is full almost every Sunday now, and the feeling of unity and real Christian fellowship is greatly strengthened in the American community." Of course that is a universal experience, the Church providing guidance and strength for the followers of Christ and, also, offering wholesale social opportunities for mutual encouragement as well as enjoyment within the frame of reference of Christian standards.

Then, in addition to the benefits to the individual members of such congregations, one cannot measure the positive influences that reach out into the city and the nation. The very fact that people of natural prestige because of position and personality place their religion in the forefront of their thinking and living is a powerful witness. Men and women whose Christian faith is vital always radiate a wholesomeness that is the best possible counteragent to the adverse factors previously mentioned. In all candor, many observing persons have remarked that the daily walk and conversation of a lay Christian abroad may be far more effective in spreading the Gospel than the direct preaching of an evangelist. Perhaps it is not too much to say that some of the most telling Christian witness in non-Christian lands is being given indirectly and sometimes even unconsciously by the men and women who are sincerely expressing their faith in their own lives, whether in business or in governmental offices, or as wives and mothers, or whatever their occupation may be.

In conclusion, let it be said that these Union Churches merit greater recognition than they hitherto have had. The Department of American Communities Overseas of the National Council of

Churches is the channel through which cooperatively, in addition to many direct personal contacts, the home denominations are expressing their interest and concern. As has been indicated, most of the churches are independent and congregationally governed. They call their own pastors and too high praise cannot be given to the men who, whatever their own denominational background and standing, are serving unselfishly and so successfully these interdenominational parishes.

Through this Department this network of isolated Protestant congregations, many of them in a predominantly Roman Catholic or non-Christian environment, is being welded into a free association for mutual helpfulness. Specialized service is being rendered them, such as assistance in finding pastors, or the securing of educational and program materials. Ministers of families which are going abroad on any governmental or business assignments are urged to acquaint such people with these Union Churches and, simultaneously, to let the Union Church pastors know of the coming of new families. In addition, this Department is also seeking financial assistance for special situations where local personnel and resources are not adequate. It might be in the matter of a major building project for which some outside help is needed, or, in some cases, a local group might require some subsidization for a year or two to enable it to have a full-time pastor to organize the congregation more effectively and bring it to the point of self-sufficiency. The fact that most of these churches have become financially independent is one of the strongest arguments for assisting the others toward that goal. There are few ways in which comparatively minor investments of consecrated money will show such effective major results so quickly.

Important as has been the influence of these Union Churches in the past, conditions today and in the foreseeable future give them a role of even greater significance, with the increasing numbers of Americans going abroad under technical assistance programs or for private reasons. As we in the Protestant churches here at home are striving to bring the patterns of our community and national life more into line with the Christian ideal, we are meanwhile being interpreted abroad by these thousands of unofficial ambassadors. The Union Churches are one of the finest means possible for trying to make sure that the men and women who represent us in the eyes and the minds of the world are encouraged and assisted to represent us at our best, as true disciples of our Lord and Saviour, Jesus Christ.

Dr Barstow was a Congregational minister and executive director of the Department of Overseas Union Churches. Missionary Research Library, Occasional Bulletin, 1954 **https://tinyurl.com/y5qncvbd**

Meeting the Spiritual Needs of the U. S. Minority Overseas
Posted on April 1, 1978 in *MissioNexus*
By Ronald C. Smeenge

They are among the 1.7 million Americans, plus other English-speaking people, who live in foreign countries.

John Doaks is a white, Anglo-Saxon Protestant, and yet a member of a very distinct minority group. Stranger yet, Rodrigo Gutierez, Leopold Korseniowski and George Jones and Afro-American, all belong to the same minority. They are among the 1.7 million Americans, plus other English-speaking people, who live in foreign countries.[1] They comprise but a fraction of a percent of the population of their adopted countries.

These Americans are in business, economics, technical aid, the diplomatic corps, the professions, advisory roles and the military. An estimated 290,000 retirees are living outside the U.S. on Social Security benefits, mainly in Canada, Mexico and Italy.

This American community living abroad is on the average made up of more highly educated and younger persons than Americans living at home.[2] They are an invigorating, resourceful combination of people. They are sent overseas because a corporation, agency or government felt they had a contribution to make.

Other foreigners are also a part of this emerging community. European and Asian expatriates sometimes equal in number the U. S. citizens abroad.[3] As English is a second language for them, they relate well to Western culture and social life.

Members of this minority community seek each other. Language is not the only common denominator. Together they face the "ordeal of change."[4] For the first time some endure discrimination and harassment.

They have all been up-rooted from a home town, friends and family where belonging has been part of their emotional security. They go through culture shock, disillusionment, frequent depression and loneliness.

The secure props of a previous life-style have been removed. The strength of the familiar is gone. The initial excitement of being assigned to an exotic foreign post soon dissipates. Miles of tropical beaches are not the paradise of the travel poster. The squalor of the deprived, the miserable living conditions of the majority of the world's people, the pathetic look of a poor child in tags begging from the "rich foreigner" all have an unsettling influence. Value systems are challenged. In living in the pressure-cooker of alien culture, and in learning about the other side of the world, these Americans have come to learn also more about themselves.

This community of people is open to the gospel – even more so than back home. There is an increase in their responsiveness because there is an increase in their awareness of need. In that they have had to endure some change, they are open to even more change. They are learners again. And this is where the credibility o£ the gospel has an opportunity to come to their attention.

The apostle Paul saw the need of reaching diverse people in unique circumstances. He said he would go anywhere and be anything to accommodate the needs of people so that they would be won to Christ. He was ready to "get alongside of any man."[5] This is where a minister must begin, if he is to reach the diverse community of English-speaking people who live in non-English countries.

Who is reaching the English-speaking minority? There are sixty-five congregations affiliated to some degree with the Overseas Division of National Council o£ Churches.[6] The Christian and Missionary Alliance maintains four overseas congregations. There are no statistics from other groups. The rising consciousness of the evangelical is, however, beginning to be felt abroad. New fellowship of Christians are emerging around the world as a result of aggressive evangelistic efforts. There are some interdenominational congregations that are developing effective, far-reaching ministries. Some denominations have assigned personnel from their mission staffs in a particular country to cover an English service. Too often these have only been an adjunct of their primary mission goal.

The field is ripe for a more concerted effort by evangelicals. This ministry may not demand learning a new language, but it suggests the need o£ a generous amount of the Apostle Paul's adaptability.

How can a very proper Presbyterian from the East, a Bible church fundamentalist from Wheaton, Ill., and Lutheran from Missouri worship together with a Southern Baptist and a smattering of Methodists, Episcopalians and a Pentecostal from Brazil? In spite of the walls denominations have too often built, a unity of the Spirit can emerge. If the stress is on doctrinal distinctives, often there are not enough persons of identical persuasion to have a congregation.

This proves to be an asset rather than a liability. The inter-relationships of Ephesians 4 can be experienced. The gifts and ministries of Romans 12 and 1 Corinthians 12 can be more clearly brought into focus. Add to this already delightful blend of people and gifts another segment comprised of nationals, who, through westernization have come to appreciate English and a broader base for fellowship than local congregations offer, and you have an international, interdenominational and interracial congregation.

I am now pastoring in Haiti, having served previously two churches in Puerto Rico. We have thirty-three church backgrounds under one roof.

Services are not the extension of anyone's seminary. No one is bothering to check out spiritual pedigrees before fellowship can happen. We don't demand new members all agree on some matters o£ eschatology. We accept the deity of Christ and the authority of the Word, which implies the necessity of salvation and the second coming of Christ.

We practice the unity of all believers and seek to be the salt, light and yeast in our communities. We're so busy working with doctrines where we do agree we don't have time to polarize on our "positions."

Look at our harvest field! They are people of influence – gifted leaders and motivators. Paul went to people like that at the centers of his world. It was part of his strategy because these people would in turn influence countless others. Members of our congregation do this as they crisscross the globe from one city to another.

An attorney from Miami said he felt his home church had planted some seeds, but he never had time to see those seeds grow until he landed overseas where this congregation began to nurture his spiritual life. A business man said he had never had a pastor call on him. I had dropped in one night unexpectedly and found him facing the deepest personal crisis of his life. He opened his home and life to me in a unique way.

A young medical student on vacation came to church with friends because there was no other place to go on Sunday. He found the Christian message believable, intelligible and worthy of more serious study. He spent his month's vacation devouring books on Christian evidences and attending several home Bible study groups. He had become a pagan; he left a committed Christian. These are not uncommon experiences.

Many families term that their experiences in an overseas church brought them together for the first time. Many have found their skills useful in third world countries, and, in cooperation with the English church and national churches, have gone to work on social and economic problems. The pooling of efforts and expertise of Christians meeting in key cities overseas can have world-wide effectiveness in evangelism and development.

Some suggestions to mission personnel considering the launching of English-speaking ministries among Americans:

1. Though missionaries may initiate the fellowship, lay leadership from the community should be sought. Even outside pastoral help may become more effective than an established missionary. He may be better equipped to relate to the American or western community. The missionary may not be free to function in leadership roles, but can certainly have a part as advisor and/or teacher. Just creating a prayerful spiritual climate is a tremendous ministry.
2. Advertise the church services in hotels, restaurants, corporation bulletin boards, embassies and supermarkets. Foreign elements may seem scattered or lost in masses, but they do surface at some of these key areas.
3. Meetings themselves can be held in hotels. We've used also used a restaurant, a concert hall and schools. It is perhaps best to stay off of mission compounds. There is often an initial wariness of the professional religious personality on the part of non-Christian business leaders.
4. Never let a church service for expatriates be the extension of your mission-staff prayer circle. You may frighten that economic advisor right out of his Guayabera by your theological semantics. Keep it low key.

5. Cooperate with organizations like Christian Women's Club, Christian Businessmen's Club or International Christian Leadership. They usually have resource persons visiting. Our services or study groups have been stimulated by some of these key leadership people. Work also with servicemen's centers and chaplains in the military. Campus Crusade for Christ, Navigators and Inter-Varsity are constantly enlarging overseas ministries. Your ministries can complement each other.
6. Give strong consideration to keeping the format interdenominational. There is so much to a contributed from a variety of traditions. Of course we also recommend the use of non-denominational Sunday school materials.
7. Try Christian concerts. Many artists are delighted to travel abroad. They'll never have a more appreciative audience. Special interest seminars so attract divergent communities. Family life conferences, hobby and craft workshops, personal witnessing seminars and a variety of Christian life and d Bible study opportunities will always draw interested participants. The English church can be a veritable meeting place for these unique minority groups who speak English. Don't overlook resource people like professors on sabbaticals or retired church leaders.
8. Surprisingly, you'll find expatriates increasingly interest in your missionary endeavors. Most have never been exposed to Christian missions, their philosophy and activity. Some will volunteer to assist in practical areas.

Diplomats may be more cautious of meeting you than you are in meeting them. The ice is worth breaking. One ambassador literally came to open the doors of his office for mission work and frequently lends his chauffer and vehicle for mission guests. He became the official greeter at the English church. (We have members of three embassies attending services and a fourth promising to come. They are spiritually hungry people and often are caught up in social cycles that are unfulfilling of their basic needs.

9. Telephone ministries are extremely helpful. Foreigners face personal crises without finding adequate resources for help. Advertise a phone number and indicate that people in trouble can call night or day. You will find rich witness opportunities. It can be an entire ministry in itself.
10. National church leaders are not always sympathetic to a congregation of foreigners meeting by themselves. They would have wanted them in their own churches. They can, however, be made to understand that all people – including their own – seek a homogeneous unit in which to worship. They can perhaps also see that a strong congregation of foreigners can well be of great assistance to a local national church in other practical ways.

The author invites response from readers about this area of ministry. International Fellowships of Christians is now being formed to pool resources and aid in the establishment of new international congregations. When IRS approved, IFC can be of significant assistance in channeling funds through a U. S. office. A newsletter linking overseas evangelicals is planned as a forum for communicating ideas and relaying information on the movement of people and corporations in the international circuit. A directory, essential to all of this, is now being compiled. We will appreciate your assistance. Ron Smeenge, c/o Missionary Flights Int., Box 1 EGGS, alert Palm Beach, Florida 33405 U.S.A.

N.B, Endnotes 3 and 4 are missing from the website where this article was obtained.

Endnotes

1. U.S. Citizens Residing in Foreign Countries (Washington, D.C.: U. S. Department of State, 1976), p. 4.
2. United States Department of Commerce News (Washington, D.C.: Bureau of the Census, 1973).
5. 1 Cor. 9:19-23 (William Barclay commentary).
6. International Congregations and Lay Ministries (New York: National Council of Churches).

https://tinyurl.com/yyu52zo9
Reprinted by permission. Source: EMQ April 1, 1979 (www.missionnexus.org/emq).

Globalization and the Missionary Potential of International Churches

Posted on July 1, 2005
By Dan P. Bowers
MissioNexus

During the latter half of the twentieth century, globalization has caused the dispersion of millions of English-speakers to the ends of the earth. Throughout major cities of the world today hundreds of international churches have been planted to make disciples of English-speaking expatriates. Many work with nationals from the host country's middle and upper classes. Through this contact, thousands of English-speaking nationals have become involved in these churches. What is the missionary potential for international churches reaching out to indigenous people?

Globalization Creates Opportunity To Reach Indigenous Peoples

"Globalization" is a buzzword to describe the emergence of worldwide interconnectedness in areas such as economics, communication and pop culture (Menconi 2001, 6). Daniel Sanchez referred to this phenomenon as "the CNN culture" (Pederson 1999, 4). Global communication empires use English to transmit news and entertainment worldwide.

Does globalization create an opportunity for international churches to reach out to indigenous peoples? Richard H. Bliese described two opposing components of globalization: the forces of "homogeneity" and "particularism." While particularism creates borders, homogeneity makes borders porous by "universalizing markets, ideas and technology from without" (1997, 204). Particularism appears to raise barriers for reaching indigenous people, while homogeneity facilitates such outreach.

Historian Andrew Walls suggests two forces that can facilitate Christian mission. One is an "indigenizing" principle that creates a sense of identity in diverse communities. He identifies the other as a "pilgrim" principle that tends to "universalize" the vision of the church (1996, 43). The indigenizing principle suggests that an international church could retain its identity as an expatriate ministry while welcoming any indigenous people attracted to the church.

International churches (ICs) appear to be moving away from being a "confined cultural island" as more English-language churches form overseas. During the 1980s a few mission boards planted ICs with the aim of reaching into the expatriate community. One example is Crossroads Christian Church in Geneva, Switzerland, which initially targeted the international community. In time, English-speaking Swiss were attracted to its "seeker-sensitive" ministry.

Tension Between Isolation and Integration In The IC

Most ICs are finding that their worship attracts English-speaking nationals. Since ICs exist in a foreign country, many struggle with the tension between isolating and integrating nationals. Integration is the active assimilation of indigenous people into the worship and leadership of the IC. Isolation means that the IC resists becoming involved with those who are from the indigenous community. Isolation also involves a conscious choice to keep the indigenous participation in the expatriate church to a minimum (Pederson 1999, 58). It seems necessary for ICs to preserve enough non-indigenous elements to maintain a witness to the expatriate community.

Many ICs are naturally inclined to isolate themselves from the local people. Lonely foreigners may think of the IC as a safe haven, a "slice of life" back home. Security concerns may also dictate isolation over integration. In restricted access nations, such as China and most Middle Eastern countries, the government may mandate the isolation. For example, to attend the Beijing International Christian Fellowship, one must possess a foreign passport.

An IC may opt to isolate itself to preserve its expatriate identity. For many years the Seoul Union Church prohibited nationals who had never lived overseas from becoming members. Eventually this policy was overturned in an attempt to integrate English-speaking Korean Christians. The International Baptist Church (IBC) of Manila has evolved into an English-language Filipino church. The concern is that if ICs stop focusing ministry on expatriates, the national pastors and churches would have little interest in evangelizing them.

Must international churches choose between isolation and integration? Should expat congregations integrate with the indigenous population as part of the overall mission strategy of the church? David Pederson believes that choosing between the two is not necessary. As an expatriate church receives proper teaching and leadership, it can be both an oasis for expatriates and a launching pad to the indigenous people (1999, 65-66).

When the International Christian Fellowship of Caracas (ICF) was planted, its leaders decided not to isolate themselves from the nationals but rather welcome them with a view to planting a Spanish-language church. This decision seems to have enabled ICF to keep its identity as an expatriate fellowship.

Christian Associates International (CAI) is deliberately planting expatriate churches in Europe as launching pads to reach the continent for Christ. The "high impact" English-language churches they are planting aim to reach Europeans and train them to be "high impact" leaders who can kindle national church renewal.

Using English To Reach Indigenous People

How can the English language be used to reach out to the indigenous people? During the 1970s, a Baptist missionary to Austria found that because Baptists were considered a sect there, few nationals would have anything to do with his ministry. He changed his strategy and started an English-language church he said was for Americans. Parents let their children attend because it improved their English and introduced them to the international community.

Christians are not the only ones taking advantage of globalization and the English language to reach indigenous peoples. In the article "Using English to Promote Islam" published in the Muslim World League magazine, the author argued that since English has become the universal language, Muslims should seek to work in that medium to help make converts to Islam. He suggests teaching English as a foreign language and holding Quran study sessions in English for students and business people. Mormons and Jehovah's Witnesses also make use of the English language to make converts outside of Anglophone countries.

The European Baptist Convention gives this rationale for English-language ministry: "Since English is the most widely used language in the Western world, English-language churches have a great opportunity to reach people from many nations with the Good News of Jesus Christ." Wagner suggests giving fresh thought to missionary activity in English. He suggests five ways that North American missions can use English-language ministry in Western Europe:

1. Working with various cultural minorities living and working in Europe;
2. Working with Americans, Australians, Canadians and other native English-speakers;
3. Working with Europeans for whom English is their mother language;
4. Working with other Europeans for whom English is their second language;
5. Use English-language international institutions to train young people for Christian service (1993, 171).

Most international churches were begun using English to reach out to native English speakers (2 and 3 above). Many found that the use of English and the presence of expatriates attracts nationals (4). Some are reaching out to other cultural minorities through English-language ministry (1). Does the trend toward the global use of English and the presence of expatriate churches abroad signal a greater opportunity for reaching indigenous peoples?

The Missionary Potential of International Churches

Today's dispersion of Christian expatriates abroad bears some similarity to the scattering of God's Old Testament people among the nations (Ezekiel 11:16). J. Christy Wilson suggested that this dispersion presents a great opportunity for English-language churches to not only minister to expatriates, but to reach out to indigenous people. He proposed three main purposes for international churches: (1) to provide fellowship, renewal and growth for Christian workers serving abroad; (2) to bring a gospel witness to the growing numbers of non-Christian expatriates; (3) to serve as a base for witness to the indigenous people.

"In conjunction with the ministries of missionaries, these congregations can be stepping stones to cross-cultural witness which must take place if the world is [to be] evangelized" (Wilson 1980, 120). This suggests a two-fold mission for international churches: to the expatriate community and to the indigenous community.

International Churches Ministering To Expatriates

Historically, some of the earliest Protestant missionary endeavors were directed at expatriates. During the colonial era, English-language churches were planted in North America and throughout the British Empire to minister to the spiritual needs of British settlers abroad. Henry Martyn went to India to minister to English-speaking civil servants of the British government. C.T. Studd served in south India from 1900 to 1906 in an English-language church as a minister to planters, soldiers and government officials (Wilson 1980, 121).

After World War II, the Southern Baptist Convention (SBC) began planting ICs in Europe to minister to US military personnel. The SBC's Foreign Mission Board (now called the International Mission Board) established more than one hundred English-language congregations around the world. Today most of these churches are not only self-supporting but are also able to help support missionary work to the indigenous people.

While some may question the validity of investing precious mission resources in international church ministry today, others believe that mission agencies should target English-speaking expatriates. In a 1987 Fuller Seminary study titled "Unreached Peoples: Clarifying the Task," Americans living in Geneva were classified as an unreached people group (Wagner 1993, 157).

Addressing the needs of expatriates in sensitive and stimulating ways will not only help them grow spiritually but also can impart to them a vision for taking the gospel to the others on their next overseas assignment. For example, the International

Christian Fellowship of Caracas rekindled the faith of a Trinidadian family. As the family grew in the Lord, the expat wife became burdened for other wives in her husband's oil exploration company. She began a Bible study that ten women attended. Several professed faith in Christ. Her husband got involved in a street children ministry in Caracas. In 2001 the family was transferred to Stavanger, Norway, and went with a vision for outreach to both expatriates and nationals in their new home.

The Mission Of International Churches To Nationals

David Pederson believes ICs must move away from being "a haven for people out of their culture" and become vital congregations not limited to reaching expatriates. "The IC is not the only means for mission…but a vital key in world evangelization" (Pederson 1999, 30). He cites the example of Greater Europe Mission's three-phase strategy: plant an international church, then a daughter church for nationals and finally a leadership development center for nationals.

Linus Morris, founder and director of Christian Associates International (CAI), believes that the multiplication of English-language expatriate churches "can serve as a first step leading to the revitalization and growth of national churches in adjacent areas." CAI has planted fifteen international churches, mostly in western European cities. All are designed to reach and equip nationals to reach their countrymen with the gospel. These English-language churches intentionally seek to attract nationals through their worship and outreach (Pederson 1999, 64).

Union Church of San José, Costa Rica, is an example of an international church launching out to the indigenous people. The church has worked to overcome its "rich gringo" image by targeting Costa Ricans for outreach. It has evolved from a congregation of mainly foreign English-speakers into a bilingual church which ministers primarily to permanent residents.

It serves as a bridge to the local community by partnering with nationals who rescue prostitutes, feed children and evangelize the lost (Bowers 2003, 139).

A number of ICs share facilities with national churches and help support ministry to the indigenous people. An IC in Stockholm shares a building and finances with two other congregations, one Swedish, the other Korean. They work cooperatively in community outreach and plan to plant another non-indigenous church that will be multicultural, using English and Swedish.

Some ICs in countries closed to missionaries have amazing opportunities to touch the indigenous people. J. Christy Wilson's church in Afghanistan is an example. Tentmaking teachers planted Community Christian Church of Kabul in 1952. When Wilson was called as its first pastor, services were held in a home in Kabul. With the growth of the expatriate community, homes were not large enough for worship services. The church sought and received government permission to construct a church building in Kabul in 1970. God used the church to reach out to thousands of world travelers who flocked to Afghanistan in the 1960s and '70s to do drugs and study Eastern religions.

A funeral for a Canadian worker at a British military cemetery presented a unique opportunity to preach the gospel before a largely Afghan congregation. Afterward, the church decided to start a work among the many blind people of Afghanistan. The church recruited Christian teachers who taught Braille in the local language. A project was also started to bring eye doctors and nurses to Afghanistan. But persecution began because of Afghan conversions. In 1973 the church building was destroyed, the work with the blind was shut down and Christian teachers were given one week to leave the country (Wilson 1980, 121-124). Since the overthrow of the Taliban in 2001, however, efforts have been made to re-establish an international church ministry in Kabul.

Issues In International Church Outreach to Nationals

One concern of ICs in reaching out to the indigenous people is the possibility that they may lose their identities. This happened recently with a former Southern Baptist church in Caracas. During the 1970s, missionaries of the Southern Baptist International Mission Board planted an expatriate church. Fluctuations in the expatriate population meant the church struggled to become self-supporting. After the missionary pastor left, an expatriate member became the lay pastor. As the number of Venezuelans attending increased, worship services were translated into Spanish. In time, Spanish-speaking members outnumbered English-speaking members. When the lay pastor resigned, the congregation called a national as pastor. Today the ministry is entirely in Spanish and is largely indigenous. While there is nothing inherently wrong with this, the church lost its identity as an expatriate ministry. Perhaps if this church had had a vision for planting a national church it might have been able to keep its international identity.

Although ICs exist on foreign mission fields, many serve the original target group with little consideration for impacting nationals. To reach nationals, ICs must develop plans for ministering to the needs of indigenous people. A new breed of international churches planted since 1980 is breaking new ground. They envision reaching English-speaking nationals and internationals who will impact the host country by planting national churches.

It appears that most North American boards have not considered the mission potential of ICs. Few have been involved in planting them. In some cases boards have advised their missionaries against contact with English-speaking expatriates (Bowers 2003, 192). It is understandable that mission boards would require their personnel to be involved in national churches and cross-cultural ministry while on foreign assignment. But isolating them from expatriates and expat ministry may lead to missed opportunities to partner with ICs in launching out to the indigenous people.

Conclusion

Those involved in international church ministry must realize that as English-language congregations, they exist in a mission field with great potential for reaching nationals for Christ. Many ICs can plant churches among middle- and upper-class nationals. Most are in world-class cities. Some are in countries closed to traditional missions. All ICs must consider their strategic position to become launching pads for mission to the indigenous people.

North American mission boards should re-examine their view of and relationship to international churches. Globalization opens doors for using English-language ministry as a launching pad to indigenous peoples. ICs and mission boards could enter strategic partnerships to target nationals in major cities of the world.

References

Bliese, Richard H. 1997. "Globalization: A Challenge for Lutheran Missiology in the 21st Century." Currents in Theology and Mission, 24 June, p, 204.

Bowers, Dan P. 2003. "International Churches as Launching Pads for Mission to Indigenous Peoples." Doctoral dissertation. Denver: Denver Seminary.

Menconi, Peter. 2001. "The 'Global' Church." Focal Point. Spring, p. 6.

Pederson, David. 1999. Expatriate Ministry: Inside the Church of the Outsiders. Seoul, Korea: By the author.

Wagner, William Lyle. 1993. North American Protestant Missionaries in Western Europe: A Critical Appraisal. Bonn, Germany: Culture and Science Publishers.

Walls, Andrew F. 1996. The Missionary Movement in Christian History: Studies in the Transmission of Faith. Maryknoll, N.Y: Orbis Books.

Wilson, J. Christy. 1980. Today's Tentmakers. Wheaton, Ill.: Tyndale House Publishers, Inc.

***Dan Bowers** served two years as pastor of the International Christian Fellowship of Caracas, Venezuela. Prior to that he served nineteen years as senior pastor of Hope Baptist Church, Manchester, Maine. He holds a D.Min. from Denver Seminary. His doctoral research project was on the International Church as a launching pad for mission to indigenous peoples. For access to his research go to:* **https://tinyurl.com/y3bvxrmr** *or contact him at: revdanbow@juno.com*

Reprinted by permission. Source: EMQ July 1, 2005 (www.missionnexus.org/emq).

English-speaking international churches seen as 'lighthouses' for all nations *SEPTEMBER 11, 2008*

By Ken Camp, Managing Editor, *Baptist Standard*

English-language churches planted in non-English-speaking countries may seem like a small niche market. But a former missionary and pastor of international Baptist churches insists they have the potential to become "spiritual lighthouses for all the nations."

American expatriates who may have had little interest in religion in the United States—and homesick English-speakers from other countries eager to socialize with other people who share their native tongue—often are drawn to English-language churches overseas, said Thomas Hill, former pastor of international Baptist churches in Germany and Costa Rica.

Hill, now a pastoral care assistant at Park Cities Baptist Church in Dallas, served 33 years with the Southern Baptist Foreign Mission Board.

After his retirement from the board, he began working with international Baptist churches in Europe and Latin America. He served five years as pastor of Bethel International Baptist

Church in Frankfurt, Germany, and three years at International Baptist Church in San Jose, Costa Rica.

The Frankfurt congregation was one of the founding members of the small European association of English-speaking Baptist churches formed 50 years ago that grew to become the International Baptist Convention.

International Baptist churches in Europe began after World War II primarily due to the initiative of twin brothers Herman and Herbert Stout. The Stouts had helped establish Sunday school classes for children when they were stationed at the Army Air Force headquarters in Weisbaden, Germany, in 1946.

After they completed their military service, they returned to the United States, finished their undergraduate education at Hardin-Simmons University and enrolled in Southwestern Baptist Theological Seminary.

While in seminary, the Stouts contacted the Southern Baptist Foreign Mission Board, asking to be sent to Germany. However, at that time, the board had no plans to send missionaries to Germany.

Herman Stout secured his own financial support, and he founded the first English-speaking international Baptist church—Immanuel Baptist in Weisbaden, Germany—in 1957.

Another new English-speaking congregation, Bethel Baptist Church of Frankfurt, called Herbert Stout as pastor and was constituted in July 1958.

One month later, the two churches led by the Stout brothers formed the Association of Baptists in Continental Europe. Those two churches sponsored 19 churches and missions in a short time, and the association became the European Baptist Convention in 1964.

"In the early years, the churches were about 90 percent military personnel," Hill said. But the drawdown of American troops in Europe during the 1990s forced the English-speaking churches to reconsider their mission, he added.

"They had to reach out to other people," Hill said. And in the process, the churches became what they had claimed to be all along—genuinely international.

In 2003, the European Baptist Convention was renamed the International Baptist Convention. Its membership now includes close to 70 English-language churches and missions in two-dozen European, Middle Eastern, African and Latin American countries. Only about one-third of the affiliated churches are comprised primarily of military personnel.

Hill, who serves as a liaison between the International Baptist Convention and the regional group of English-speaking churches in Latin America, hopes to see international Baptist churches mobilize their members for missions outreach.

"We need to harness the potential of people who are overseas already—not only provide them a spiritual home, but also make them missionaries," he said.

Hill also wants to engage churches in the United States to commission as missionaries their members who move overseas, to develop partnership relationships with international Baptist churches and to provide initial funding for church starts overseas.

"We need a strategic effort to find areas where international Baptist churches can be planted to meet legitimate needs and to seize opportunities for the spread of the gospel," he said. **Used by permission**

International Church Impact: A Unique Pastoral Opportunity
John Spadafora in Blog: International Church Pastor

English-speaking international churches represent a unique opportunity to impact the non-believing world, particularly in places with little religious freedom. Bruce Dingman, president of The Dingman Company, writes from his experience of working with international churches about the pastoral opportunity it presents.

A Unique Pastoral Opportunity

I have lived as a businessman in several countries and been a member of international churches in São Paulo and Panama City. As a search consultant serving Christian organizations, I have occasionally assisted international churches with their senior pastor searches. What started as a hobby has now become a purposeful effort. I can tell you from experience, this is a unique and rewarding opportunity for pastoral ministry.

What makes international churches unique?

First, they're nondenominational and acknowledge that some members may believe or practice their faith differently than others (i.e. baptism by immersion versus sprinkling). International churches concentrate on the gospel, the major points of salvation, and the integration of Christ into their lives, rather than focusing on theological differences that might divide. Compared to the fragmented North American religious scene, international churches provide a unique opportunity to focus on the unity of essential gospel truths.

Second, it's likely the congregation will be primarily international expatriates (people from all over the world who have moved to work there) and English-speaking nationals. This presents a few unique challenges. Many expats have a short-term assignment at their job, so there's ongoing transition within the congregation. During school vacations and holidays, many families travel to their home country, so at times there can be a big drop in church attendance.

What does an international church provide?

Christian expats may not know any other believers in their new host country, and they yearn for a place to fellowship and worship. International churches can provide those as well as a wonderful feeling of community that may not be available anywhere else in the city. Relationships become deep and heartfelt.

Besides creating needed community, international church pastors can equip their people for gospel impact. Many countries prohibit proselytizing nationals, but believers everywhere can learn to live their faith in deed and word outside the church without proselytizing. And the international church pastor can help them do that. What kind of person would make a good international church pastor?

This opportunity could be ideal for someone with a seminary degree who loves working with other cultures. Though preaching is important, even more important is pastoral care. Depending on the church, you may have little or no staff working with you, so you need to be wise in making strategic, tactical decisions. Regardless of location or church specifics, you'll have a unique opportunity to equip people to be disciple-makers where they live and work.

Jacob and I recently visited an international church in East Asia, where we met *Craig*. Craig's story is unique but not uncommon today — many believers find themselves in high-level positions at multinational companies overseas. They know Jesus, but they don't know how to bring Him into their workplace. As you'll see, the potential in coming alongside marketplace workers like Craig could be a game-changer for the Kingdom.

Mentoring for Global Impact

By Jacob, *a faith-work mentor*

Craig came to faith five years ago at the age of 35 and is on fire for Christ. He was recently hired to lead an edgy, high-profile firm in East Asia in need of a turn-around.

Craig told his employers of his faith before they hired him. "I'm a Christian, and I will bring my Christian values with me if you appoint me to this role," he said during his interview. "Fine," they said. "We need things shaken up."

With permission granted to "shake things up," Craig wondered where to start.

Addressing LGBT benefits or sexually driven marketing? Tightening the highly creative but largely unproductive work environment? Many employees feared Craig's outdated Christian values, and threatened to quit just weeks after his appointment.

When Craig and I met at a faith-work integration event, he wanted to talk further about how to bring his faith into his business role. So we met for lunch the next day. "Is the company in imminent danger of collapsing?" I asked him. "Or do you have time to better assess the situation before making critical decisions? Will leadership grant you time to do some critical discovery to understand the landscape and make informed decisions?"

"The company's not in imminent danger," Craig said. "But the trend is strongly negative and I've been hired to fix it. I have a great relationship with the owners. They trust me and will give me time and space to move as I see fit."

"Do you know who your most critical players are? I asked. "Who would it be very damaging to lose? Who are your problem people, and who are you far better off without?" "I don't know yet, though I'm gaining a sense of this."

One more question: "Do you have a plan for effectively integrating your faith in how you lead through all this change? A plan to introduce people to the transforming person of Jesus Christ even as you seek to transform the company?" "No, I don't," Craig said. "Can you help?"

Like many others I've met in my travels, Craig needs a mentor. The Lord has scattered thousands of Craigs all over the world in places closed to mission workers but open to Christ-following marketplace workers in business, engineering, design, management, medicine, education, construction, hospitality, agriculture, government, and more.

Many of them already see their careers as belonging to the Lord and themselves as stewards to integrate their faith with their work. Many others don't have that global marketplace vision yet. But they all need mentors who can help them catch the vision and carry it out where they live and work. They need mentors who will help them be "living letters of Christ" (*2 Corinthians 3*), bringing the transforming power of the gospel to the darkest places on earth.

Scott MacLean is the pastor of the Milan Bible Church (MBC) in Milan, Italy, an international church that has been around since the 1980s. When my wife and I were living in Italy, MBC was primarily a haven for expatriates to find fellowship. In recent years, it has shifted focus to be a gathering for safe community *and* a strategic place to equip God's people to be on mission where they live and work.

A Pastor's Perspective

By Scott MacLean, pastor of Milan Bible Church

Living in another country and culture is not without challenges. Often there is a tendency to grab on to anything familiar — like expats from your own country who share your language and cultural values. Yet as Christ-followers in Italy, we have the opportunity to make disciples in a spiritually dark world. And that opportunity should push us out of our comfort zone and into cross-cultural relationships where people can see the difference Jesus makes in our lives.

My wife and I embraced this challenge when we moved to Italy in 2000. We sought, and struggled at times, to find ways into the lives of those around us.

When I became the pastor of Milan Bible Church in 2015, we saw my role as a way to multiply the work that we had been doing in Italy. We now encourage and prepare a whole church of believers to take up the challenge. God has placed each of them in a circle of neighbors, coworkers, and friends that need to know the love of Jesus. It's an amazing opportunity, and we long to help them see how they can be a strategic part of God's plan to make disciples here in Milan.

Being expats ourselves, we can identify with many of the struggles our members face. As we go out and evangelize together, they learn how to better explain the gospel in Italian. As we spend time together, we encourage them — and they encourage us — in prayer and with stories of how God has opened doors.

As an international church pastor, I get to equip these believers for God's purposes, and I have a front row seat to see how He uses them to draw others to Himself.

Christian Zebley is the pastor of the West Tokyo Union Church and the church planter of the Redeemer Church of Roppongi. He gives us a brief history of English-speaking churches in Japan and, in doing so, provides a compelling illustration of the potential of collaboration between English-speaking international churches and national believers.

Collaboration Between Churches

by Christian Zebley, Pastor of West Tokyo Union Church

Japan's population of nearly 127 million is considered the second largest unreached people group in the world, just behind Bangladesh. The Japanese church is growing as young people embrace faith in the backdrop of increasing globalization, the breakdown of traditional values, new immigration, and the daily influx of thousands of tourists.

English-speaking churches have been forerunners in Japan since the Protestant mission period begin in 1859. Japan had just reopened to the outside world from an isolated period of more than 220 years.

A few years later, in 1872, the first three Protestant missionaries to enter Japan worked with Japanese believers to organize two of the first Protestant churches in the country:

the English-speaking Yokohama Union Church and the Japanese-speaking Kaigan Church.

As Christianity began to emerge, local believers and missionaries worked together to evangelize, disciple new believers, plant churches, create Bible translations, and establish Christian schools, hospitals, and orphanages.

In those days, missionaries often worshiped in Japanese with local believers in the morning and in English with missionary colleagues in the afternoon. This pattern was obviously colonial in many respects. However, from these missionary roots grew the informal Union church network in Japan.

These Union churches are now multicultural and not just for expats — Japanese *and* foreign believers come together to worship and fellowship in the English language. Often, the Japanese believers in a Union church have relationships with national churches, too. In this way, the Union churches in Japan function as a link between the foreign and local Christian communities.

My church, West Tokyo Union Church, is also planting a bilingual church in the urban center of Tokyo: the Redeemer Church of Roppongi. Today, Japanese and foreign pastors often work together on church planting teams. I work alongside local pastors who are leading their own congregations

International churches are growing in Japan because foreigners in cities like Tokyo, Nagoya, and Osaka launch new congregations to which Japanese are drawn to attend. Some are led by foreign pastors; others are led by Japanese pastors. All have some element of bilingual worship and teaching.

The division between national churches and foreign churches from the 1800s is giving way to a new wave of bilingual, multicultural churches that represent the diversity of this country.

In Japan, "The harvest is plentiful, but the workers are few" (*Matthew 9:37*). God has continuously called both Japanese and foreign workers into this harvest over the centuries. Please pray for God's church in Japan. **Used by permission**

Expatriate Churches: Mission and Challenges
By Thorsten Prill

An exploration of the motivation, challenges, and validity of expatriate churches around the world.

The increase in global migration has led to an expansion of expatriate churches around the world. In spring 2008, for example, a German-speaking Protestant congregation was founded in the United Arab Emirates.[18]

The new church meets for its worship services at a local Anglican church which also hosts Tamil, Korean, and Afrikaan congregations. There are also African, Chinese, Hispanic, and Iranian churches mushrooming all over the world. But what is the motivation of those who attend or actively participate in the life of such churches?

What are the challenges these expatriate churches face? Is the expatriate church a valid model of church at all?

Reasons for Attending Expatriate Churches

The reasons why people attend expatriate churches can be divided into five categories: linguistic, cultural, sociological, theological, and missiological.

1. Linguistic. Expatriate churches are often the only forum in which expatriate Christians can worship and have Christian fellowship in their mother tongue. This

[18] Not all international churches are covered in this book. The author and his wife once attended an English-language church in Madrid, Spain which had African roots—the participants were mainly from Ghana and Nigeria. In addition, as indicated, international churches in languages other than English are common. While serving as the pastor of an English-language international church in Costa Rica, the author lived near a German school and neighboring German-language Protestant church. And, nearly 15 years before this book was written, Deutsche Welle, the German international television service, aired a 30 minute program in English featuring the German pastor of a German-language church in Beijing.

function is especially important to those expatriates who have little or no command of the dominant language of their host country. Due to the nature of their work and the limited time they are in the host culture, there is often very little need or opportunity for expatriates to learn or improve their knowledge of the local language.

2. Cultural. Besides being a place where Christians can worship in their mother tongue, expatriate churches often function as a cultural oasis where foreigners can meet people of the same or a similar ethno-cultural background. They are places that remind people of their home country and their native culture. In addition, expatriate churches are places where the home culture is passed on to the next generation. Thus, expatriate churches often celebrate traditional festivals and run classes where the home language is taught and which are attended by children from church families and non-Christian families who otherwise have no links with the church.
3. Sociological. For some people, expatriate churches also function as a refuge from racial discrimination or what is perceived as such. The church becomes a safe environment. Negative experiences in indigenous churches prompt others to join an expatriate church. In these cases, it is the inability of indigenous churches to integrate foreigners into their communities that causes them to found or join an expatriate church.
4. Theological. Less common, but still important, are theological reasons why foreigners become members of an expatriate church. It is certain distinct theological traditions and teachings that attract them. This is especially true for expatriate churches which are part of a particular denomination. Retaining their liturgical tradition or staying faithful to some fundamental theological beliefs become the determining factors.

5. Missiological. Finally, there are those who believe that expatriate churches are better equipped to reach out to their fellow countrymen and women. They hold that they are better placed to evangelize and disciple members of their own ethno-cultural group and provide pastoral care for them than indigenous churches.

Challenges Expatriate Churches Face

While there are good reasons for the existence of expatriate churches, it is also true that these churches often face a variety of problems and challenges. The most common challenges are missiological, theological, sociological, geographical, and in leadership.

1. Missiological. By their nature, most expatriate churches limit their mission to people who belong to the same ethno-cultural group. They are exclusive insofar as they do not feel responsible to reach out and minister to members of different ethno-cultural backgrounds. The danger for ethnocentric and insular churches is that they tend to become not only inward-looking, but end up as communities where their social life becomes more important than the spiritual.
2. Theological. Expatriate churches that are inter-denominational in nature require a willingness to respect divergent theological views and the ability to compromise over secondary issues. Without this degree of tolerance and willingness to compromise, there are grounds for tensions and conflicts between people who hold different theological convictions...and a destabilizing threat to unity. In contrast, a denominational expatriate church does not the face the same danger. However, the challenge for such a church is that its denominational background excludes expatriates from different church traditions.

3. Sociological. One of the major sociological challenges to an expatriate church is what can be called the second generation problem. When expatriates decide to settle in their host country and become long-term immigrants, expatriate churches are presented with the problem of reaching the second generation who have grown up as third culture kids. Cultural assimilation among the second generation can easily estrange them from the expatriate church, and they may feel no need to attend a church for foreigners. Additionally, many members of expatriate churches are people in transition. This can create a double difficulty: integrating them into the church but without any real expectation of long-term commitment. There is the added danger that the regular departure of church members after a relatively short time can have a de-motivating effect on more settled members.
4. Geographical. Often, expatriate churches ministering to specific ethno-cultural groups have ministerial catchments which are much larger than a traditional parish. This has significant implications for pastoral work. Pastoral staff have to travel long distances to visit their church members and this is both time-consuming and costly. In addition to this traveling problem, wide catchment areas make it difficult to create a sense of community within the church and to establish contacts with the local community.
5. Leadership. Finally, for some expatriate churches, recruitment of pastoral staff becomes a critical issue. If the expatriate church is located in a less "attractive" location, it might struggle to find a pastor or youth worker for its congregation. As a result, an untrained and inexperienced church member is appointed as pastor. Expatriate churches which are part of a denomination in their home country usually do not face this chal-

lenge because they are provided with ministerial staff by their mother church. However, this arrangement can remove local control. The church has no real choice when it comes to appointing a pastor because candidates are often pre-selected by the church authorities in the home country.

Furthermore, pastors who are seconded serve only a limited time abroad, which can create further problems. Pastors need time to adjust to working in a foreign country and culture.

Summary: Pros and Cons

On the basis of what has been said above, there are six arguments that can be marshaled in support of the establishment of expatriate churches:

1. The Language Argument: Expatriate churches allow Christians lacking fluency in the language of the dominant culture to worship in their mother tongue.
2. The Social Network Argument: Expatriate churches give people the opportunity to meet people of the same ethno-cultural background and similar life experience.
3. The Cultural Argument: Expatriate churches can sustain home culture by offering language classes and by celebrating cultural festivals.
4. The Safe Place Argument: Expatriate churches provide a safe place from discrimination in wider society and indigenous churches.
5. The Evangelism Argument: Expatriate churches can evangelize members of their own ethnic group more effectively than indigenous churches.
6. The Pastoral Care Argument: Expatriate churches are better equipped to meet the pastoral needs of members of their own ethnic group than indigenous churches.

However, expatriate churches also face challenges which are specific to these churches and could be regarded as arguments against the establishment of such churches. These counter arguments can be summarized as follows:

1. The Limited Mission Argument: By focusing on members of their own ethno-cultural group, expatriate churches limit their mission and exclude other ethnic groups.
2. The Recruitment Argument: Expatriate churches may find it difficult to recruit qualified full-time pastoral staff, and, in consequence their ministry is undermined.
3. The Community Argument: Expatriate churches experience difficulties in creating a sense of community because their members are widely dispersed in huge catchment areas. In addition, expatriate churches are isolated from their local community. As a result, there is the danger that they become inward-looking.
4. The Second Generation Argument: Expatriate churches may find it difficult to serve and engage second-generation immigrants who have either adjusted to or become assimilated into the host culture.

Conclusion

The list of pros and cons shows that there is no definitive answer to the question posed about expatriate churches being a valid church model. Having served as a pastor of German and Chinese churches in Britain, I have experienced both the limitations and the advantages of such churches. I have, however, also encountered another church model that has proved to be useful in overcoming some of the restrictions outlined above.

I have found this model at Cornerstone Church, a large independent evangelical church located in Nottingham, England. In recent years, the church has not only experienced a constant growth in membership, but also a significant increase in international diversity.

It is normal for over thirty different nationalities to worship in this church. While seventy-five percent of those who attend the Sunday services are British, twenty-five percent have a foreign background. Diversity is also a feature of the church membership: fifteen nationalities are represented. Among the internationals who come to Cornerstone are both forced and voluntary migrants, such as students, scholars, doctors, and businesspeople. The largest groups among the internationals are Chinese, Persian, and Spanish-speaking Christians and seekers. All these groups have their own weekly Bible study or house group meetings. In addition, the Persian-speaking Christians meet for their own worship service on Sundays, which runs parallel to the main English service on the same premises. These internationals are supported by full-time pastoral workers and volunteers—both British and foreign—from Cornerstone.

In this model, expatriate Christians become part of an indigenous church and form a kind of church within a church. However, there are many points of contact for an expatriate and British Christians at Cornerstone. There are multilingual prayer meetings and evangelistic events, as well as social activities, such as church meals, retreats, soccer, golf, and badminton tournaments. There are Persian and Chinese New Year celebrations, which are attended by both expatriate and indigenous church members. Furthermore, the children from expatriate families are fully integrated in the church's English-speaking children's and youth programs. Since they are often fluent in English, they do not find it difficult to join the various church activities for children and young people.

Finally, there are many ministries at Cornerstone where expatriate and British Christians serve together. It is not unusual to have a postgraduate student from Singapore, a medical doctor from Germany, a refugee from Iran, and a British pensioner serving side by side as parking stewards on a Sunday morning or leading evangelistic Bible studies for international students on a Monday night. The church within a church model that can be found at Cornerstone not only allows expatriates to worship in their own language and in a way that is culturally relevant to them, it also offers them an indigenous safe haven. It provides them with the opportunity to make friends with indigenous Christians, fellowship with their own second generation in the same church, and reach out with the gospel of Jesus Christ to members of their host culture. In addition, indigenous Christians benefit greatly from their contact with expatriate believers as it helps them to experience that the Church of Christ is indeed God's colorful international family.

Thorsten Prill is a missionary with Africa Inland Mission (AIM), lecturing at Namibia Evangelical Theological Seminary in Windhoek. He was pastor of two expatriate churches in the English Midlands and international chaplain at the University of Nottingham, England.

MissioNexux **https://tinyurl.com/y5lb4763**

Reprinted by permission. Source: EMQ October 1, 2009. (www.missionnexus.org/emq).

Several articles on international churches by David Fresch may be found at **https://tinyurl.com/y6n87cej**

Previously published articles by the author

Union Churches in Latin America

By Kenneth D. MacHarg

They came from Sao Paulo, Mexico City, Maracaibo, Santo Domingo—but they shared a common dilemma. When pastors of Union Churches in Latin America converged on San Juan, Puerto Rico, for their annual conference in February, they heard Colombia theologian Rafael Avilia warn that Union Churches are likely to be symbols of U.S. imperialism in Third World nations. The tendency of some of these English-speaking churches to withdraw from the people and customs around them can become a way of ignoring or escaping the struggles of peoples worldwide.

Point of Contact

Despite this tendency toward self-isolation, however, the pastors at the conference were well aware that Union Churches are for many foreign residents the point of contact, dialogue and involvement with the "host" culture. Far from providing merely a shelter and sanctuary, many of the English-speaking congregations are involved in language courses, transcultural dialogue, relationships with indigenous churches and organizations, and the raising of ethical issues with diplomats, businessmen, students, missionaries. Still other churches help sponsor ecumenical programs such as CIDALA (Committee for Intercultural Dialogue and Action in Latin America) as an attempt to minister to the whole community while bringing change to business and social relationships.

As part of their continuing effort to relate to the struggles of their host countries, the Union Church pastors also explored together current trends in sociology and theology in Latin America. A presentation by Ted Katchel of Earlham College in Indiana outlined the activity of both technology and bureaucracy as carriers or modernity to developing regions. While the relationship of technology to capitalism was seen as a relatively inflexible pattern and the relationship of bureaucracy to socialism a more adaptable one, liberation theology in reaction to both was pointed to as a way in which Third World people can approach the modern age on their own terms—protecting their present values while reaping the benefits of change and development. Another important facet of the conference as at past meetings, was the working toward and understanding of the local environment-in this case through sessions with church and political leaders to discuss the future of Puerto Rico.

Prototype of the Future

To obtain an overall picture of the shape and style of this unique ministry outside U.S. borders, a survey will be conducted in all 37 Latin American Union Churches during the coming year. At the conference a trial run of the survey form revealed that the ministers present felt considerable frustration in the practice of those aspects of faith which are more social and political, especially given their common predicament of being "guests" in host countries; more often than not in these overseas churches, faith is expressed in the form of traditional congregational participation. The ministers saw their congregations' future needs to be of a nurturing and service nature, while institutional survival was viewed as less important. Seventy percent of those attending anticipated that membership in their church would remain somewhat steady; 20 percent foresaw a decline; only 10 percent projected growth. These opinions were reinforced by reports reaching the conference that the U.S. presence overseas is diminishing and that some of the existing churches are lively to move toward part-time programs and staffs.

Conferences such as this are especially valuable to Latin American clergy in the Union Churches because they are not only widely separated from each other but also somewhat isolated from their colleagues on the local scene. At the 1977 conference in Lima, Peru, these ministers plan to continue their evaluation of the Union Churches' ministry by taking a hard look at the data to be produced by the survey, and again they will come to grips with theological developments in the region. At this year's conference, the ministers reaffirmed the concept developed at Bogotá in 1975 that Union Churches overseas—as international, interracial, intercultural, inter-denominational congregations-are a prototype of the church of the future. That give them the challenging role now of being testing grounds for the shaping of those future religious communities. ***The Christian Century*, April 28, 1976 Copyright © April 28, 1976 by the *Christian Century*. Union Churches in Latin America by Kenneth D. MacHarg is reprinted by permission from the April 28, 1976 issue of the *Christian Century*.**

An unusual breed; Expats seek familiar worship in foreign setting
By Kenneth D. MacHarg

They're called expatriates—expats for short.

An unusual breed of people, they live outside of their home country, working, studying, serving, running, seeking.

Several million U.S. citizens call Mexico, South Africa, Thailand, France and a host of other foreign locations home.

Most of them are conventional expats. They are people who go abroad with a definite purpose for a defined length of time. They are diplomats sent by their governments, business executives deployed by international companies, students and professors pursuing educational goals, engineers and technical people working for oil companies or other organizations, relief and development experts seeking to improve the world and missionaries sent to serve the Lord.

Then there are the unconventional expats. These are people who are running from a bad marriage or family dispute, running from a failed business, running from the law, running from themselves, hoping to find a better way somewhere else. With these are an increasing number of retirees who seek a less-expensive way of life in a tropical climate.

They number in the millions—over one million U.S. expats live in Mexico alone. Most live in or near big cities or in coastline housing developments. Still others live near oil fields, in tropical agricultural areas or remote villages where they serve with non-profit endeavors.

Those who have lived outside of their native land form a unique culture with worldwide ties. They are known as Third-Culture people. In one sense they belong nowhere and in another sense they belong everywhere. Living in another culture, they never really become a part of their adopted land, even if they marry someone from their new home. They are always foreigners to some extent, set apart by language, cultural and political backgrounds and styles of life.

However, having lived outside of their native land, they view the world differently and find it very difficult to return home and fit into the isolationist patterns they discover that they left behind. They understand international air fares, visa regulations and international issues that no one at home knows or cares about. They have seen political coups, eaten exotic foods, traveled to remote beaches and mountains and experienced events not even imagined by their former neighbors and friends.

This culture has its own set of struggles, questions, successes and failures. They are often lonely in the midst of a big city, lost in another culture, cut-off from the familiar with a longing to return yet a resistance to going back home. And, they, like everyone else, are seeking for the answers to cosmic questions. They need the Lord.

A recent men's prayer breakfast sponsored by an interdenominational, international, English-speaking church in a Latin American capital highlighted the diversity and struggles of this eclectic bunch of expats.

David comes from the conventional expat group. A British citizen born and raised in Uruguay, he lived in Mexico for a while and has called this Central American country home for over 25 years. He and his wife have several children, one working with him in his small business, the other married and living in a South American country. He is a faithful member of the church, has served in leadership positions and plans on staying in Latin America for the rest of his life.

Ryan is a young missionary, working with English-speaking youth in a local private school. Single, he struggles with loneliness and cultural adaptation. His ministry is successful, but he is concerned about his effectiveness and how long he should stay outside of his home country.

James is married to a local woman and relocated to her country just over a year ago. He has opened a small service business, but struggles with the culture and would rather be "back home." But family ties for now keep him overseas. An evangelical Roman Catholic, he attends the men's Bible studies and has led it at times.

Sean is a young businessman with a spirit of adventure who decided that a foreign land offered new opportunities. But, unscrupulous business people who often escape the law by setting up their operations in other countries where there are fewer legal entanglements and little or no enforcement of laws have all-but stolen his business from him and he is returning to the U.S. discouraged and frustrated. At least there he will be closer to his children who live with his ex-wife.

Emmanuel spent much of his life growing up in Central America. Now in his early 20s and a late bloomer, his parents have insisted that he join them in the U.S. where he can work and determine his future. Not sure he wants to go, but with no other source of income, he is reluctantly leaving within the next week.

For the pastor of this international congregation, it is a challenge and a blessing to deal with all types of expats who come to church seeking help, seeking people from their own culture who will understand them, seeking fellowship among people who speak the same language, seeking the will of God for their lives.

They need help adapting to a new culture, getting used to friends leaving for new assignments, facing the uncertainty of moving themselves to another country and another way of life, dealing with frequent travel or frequent absences of their spouse who travels regularly, helping children as they change schools and friends every few years, living with political, social and security uncertainty and seeking to know the Lord in a different religious context or a church that's different from the one back home.

Psalm 137 asks: How can we sing the songs of the Lord while in a foreign land? How can expats seek counsel, find a place to worship, and meet fellow expats who understand them and their life?

The over 1,200 international churches provide that kind of place and the support and encouragement that they need. Situated in capital cities, business centers, oil fields, retirement communities and anywhere that expats live, the international churches offer a much-needed outreach to Christians and non-Christians alike who find themselves living in a foreign land.

About one-third of those churches are denominationally-related, many of them Baptist, Presbyterian, Lutheran or Anglican. The others are intentionally interdenominational representing a broad diversity of worship style and programmatic approach.

They range from over 1,000 members to several dozen. Many meet in their own building, others rent space from local churches, hotels, international schools or meet in member's homes.

International churches vary in their ministries and theology. Most of them are evangelical while others represent a more moderate traditional denominational style. Most offer worship and study opportunities as well as fellowship programs, counseling services, youth ministries and mission service.

Serving as a pastor of those churches offers an unparalleled challenge and opportunity to minister in a unique setting to some of God's very special people. To serve, one must be willing to participate in a multi-denominational setting while remaining faithful to the Gospel.

Pastors need to learn the third-culture, expatriate style of life and recognize that while the majority of members may be from the United States, the churches are international and often involve members from Europe, Africa, Asia and Latin America who bring their own perspectives.

Mostly, as elsewhere, pastors serving international congregations will learn to love their congregation, to thrive on their diverse backgrounds, and to proclaim the Word of the Lord in a foreign land.

Kenneth D. MacHarg is the Interim Pastor of Escazú Christian Fellowship in San José, Costa Rica.

English-language churches serve expats in foreign lands
By Kenneth D. MacHarg

How can we sing the songs of the Lord while in a foreign land? Psalm 137:4 NIV

The service is comfortingly familiar: hymns and choruses; shared prayer concerns and a sermon developing a theme from scripture. What is remarkable is that the service is in English and the church is located in a setting far from America's shores. Stretching from Islamabad to Istanbul, Ecuador to Estonia, nearly 600 overseas English language churches serve expatriates not only from the United States but other English-speaking countries as well who find themselves far from home for a period of time. Ranging from charismatic to liberal, contemporary to traditional, these churches provide a home away from home for diplomats, missionaries, soldiers, students, businessmen, travelers and others living abroad.

"The main distinctive of an overseas church is that many of the members are transients," said David Chism, pastor of Mexico City's Capital City Baptist Church. "They know when they arrive that they will be in the city for a short period of time. It may be weeks or years, but they are not permanent residents and they know it from the beginning." Dave Petrescue, pastor of the ecumenical Maadi Community Church in Cairo, Egypt agreed. "There is a distinct sense of the temporary. We are sojourners," he said.

International congregations often appear to be a mini United Nations in their make-up. "We are known for the many ethnic people who attend our church from about 20 nations," said Richard G. Boss, a missionary with Latin America Mission (LAM) who is Pastor of the International Evangelical Church of Lausanne, Switzerland. From Cairo, Pastor Petrescue said that his congregation counts members from 32 nationalities and over 50 different denominations. "To serve the diverse expatriate population well, the church must be broad enough to include people from various cultures and denominations without losing its focus and doctrinal base," Petrescue said.

International is an important characteristic shared by all overseas English-speaking churches whether denominational or independent according to Arthur O. F. Bauer, Director of the International Congregations and Christians Abroad office of the National Council of Churches. International congregations "testify to a willing embrace of all persons into one community in Christ," he said. The National Council of Churches does not operate any of the overseas churches, but relates to around 160. "Independence is a strong aspect of these churches," Bauer said.

Despite the diversity, most pastors say that they preach the same message they would back home. "Spiritual needs and problems are basically the same the world around. The Word of God is applicable to all people and situations and most if not all of our activities as a church are geared to help people draw closer to God," Boss said.

"The Berlin International Church is an evangelical church, but it seeks to be sensitive to all denominational distinctives and practices," said Pastor Henry Paasonen. While his church has ties to the Christian and Missionary Alliance denomination, Paasonen said that his congregation "invites all who come to be considerate of believers from other denominational flavors, especially in Sunday congregational worship. Within our small group emphasis, we encourage the expression of biblical practices which may not come to be expressed on Sunday morning."

Typically, the overseas interdenominational churches have to struggle with different practices. "We need to find a way to accommodate the varying worship styles and theological stances of a variety of denominations," said Charis Geisinger, a member of the International Christian Fellowship of Managua, Nicaragua who has also attended international churches in Thailand, Venezuela, Costa Rica and Russia during her husband's long diplomatic career. "There have been discussions from how often to serve communion, what to call it when we serve it (Communion or the Lord's Supper), to whether women can be allowed to bring a sermon and fill leadership roles."

Americans abroad and the churches they attend have particular needs not always seen in stateside congregations. "We have found that expatriates have some unique problems because of their life in another country and the upheaval and adjustments necessary," said Boss, who served similar churches in Panama, Mexico and Colombia during his missionary service with LAM. "Because of the fact that they often are transferred in a few years, the counseling aspect of the ministry is very important."

Petrescue agrees, "In addition to all the expat issues of culture shock, change in lifestyle concerns and health issues, there is the added pressure of how to live out one's faith in a non-Christian environment."

Fellowship is important in these churches, said Bob Binden, pastor of the International Church of Budapest, Hungary (Southern Baptist). "Expatriates are looking for friendly faces for emotional support and networking," he explained.

In addition to the rapid turnover, many international churches face unusual situations. "There were two important age groups missing in the church," said John Adams, former Associate Pastor of Quito, Ecuador's English Fellowship Church. "College and career age young people (18-24 year olds) left to go to the U.S. Also, the retired age grandparents were missing. When a person retires, he or she normally returns to their homeland," he said.

"People in overseas assignments are generally chosen for their age, good health and general job effectiveness, said Fred Henry, pastor of Hope International Church in Paris. "Therefore we have much less visitation of the sick and in hospitals," he said.

Andy Fletcher, Deputy Director of Young Life's international schools ministry has been a member of international churches in Switzerland, Japan and France. He identified other challenges these congregations face including a lack of commitment by those who see their time abroad as a form of vacation, small, anemic youth groups and a lower level of spiritual maturity. In contrast, Adams observed that "The level of spiritual maturity in the (Quito) church membership was much higher than the average church in North America." Charis Geisinger reflected that the overseas churches spend less time in meetings, and involve members who are "committed and mature Christians." She said that their interdenominational nature leads to more openness and discussion and less of a dogmatic approach. "Our overseas churches have been much less structured and formal, meeting in rented facilities, having to set up for every service and tear down afterward." That lack of a physical facility has "served to emphasize that the church is not a building, but the people in it," she said.

Many overseas churches began as the outgrowth of mission work or the desire of expatriates to duplicate their worship experience from back home in a foreign setting. But that "chaplaincy" type ministry is changing according to Fletcher. "An exciting trend is found in those churches which are being planted deliberately to reach out into the community on a broader, more modern front," he observed. Referring to Crossroads church in Geneva, Switzerland, he said "The vision from the outset was to target the international community for evangelism and to appeal on a broader front to those who had little or no church experience or expectations."

The constituency for overseas churches may be changing in another way. In Mexico City, men in middle and upper management positions with corporations or the U.S. Embassy have headed most expatriate families. Now, according to Pastor Chism, many corporations have pulled upper level management people out of the country and replaced them with short-term technical people. If that trend continues, international congregations may find themselves having to change how they attract members and the way they minister to families who may only be in the country for a few months.

Whatever their nature, international overseas churches provide a needed ministry for those living abroad. "We have actually been more involved in our overseas churches than we were at home," Geisinger said. "These churches have been absolutely essential to our spiritual well-being. The fellowship is invaluable; always important in helping us keep our balance in a foreign setting."

Many who have participated in these congregations encourage churches back home to be supportive. "Expatriates or internationals overseas are an important people group that needs ministry," Paasonen observed. Geisinger agreed. "I believe that most denominational mission boards completely overlook the idea of ministry to English-speaking people serving overseas and see no need to send out and support pastors for such congregations," she said. "This is an important area for ministry and counseling."

English-language churches serve expats in foreign lands, Christianity Today, Feb 25, 1999

Expatriate Ministry: Inside the church of the outsiders

By David Pederson, published by Korean Center for World Mission, (also available through amazon.com), 1999, 201 pages.

Reviewed by Kenneth D. MacHarg, Missionary Journalist, Latin America Mission

Expatriate churches (also known as Union Churches or International Congregations) have always accompanied foreign travelers, diplomats, missionaries, business people and other exiles who found themselves a long way from home. While various articles have been written about them, and a few have turned out their own histories in book form, only now is a thorough study of these churches available in durable form.

David Pederson, a veteran pastor of overseas expatriate churches in Greece, Korea and the Philippines, has turned his doctoral thesis into a readable study of ministry, the expatriate population, church organization and polity, ecumenical relations, evangelism, church growth and other unique factors affecting these churches. Well-researched, the volume is filled with statistical studies, anecdotal notes and theological reflection that will serve to educate the academician and inform the would-be foreign pastor.

Pederson correctly discerns the trend among overseas expatriate congregations from serving simply as a chaplaincy, a haven for people out of their culture to becoming vital congregations reaching out primarily, but not limited to, the unevangelized expatriate population. Reflecting their interdenominational nature, he says that some International Congregations describe themselves as "evangelical-ecumenical."

Changes in the nature of the international churches leads Pederson to identify four areas of tension that may be unique to these congregations: Babel-Tribal, most often manifest in discussions as to whether the church should serve only expatriates or be open to citizens of the host country; Oasis-Launching pad, the divide over international churches functioning as a haven to escape from the local culture or as a bridge to open up the expatriate to new ways; Truth-Relationship, the ethics of how to relate to a host culture through a position of righteousness or tolerance (manifest in such issues as to whether to pay bribes), and Dependence-Independence, the struggle concerning whether a church should be autonomous or related to either a denomination "back home" or in the host country.

International Congregations serve a unique population, people who often cannot define where "home" is or where they will end up. Many use the overseas experience as a way to get away from the mores that shape their life while others find it a crisis in which they search for meaning and truth.

Pederson currently an Assistant Professor of Practical Theology at Torch Trinity Graduate School of Theology in Seoul, Korea, does an admiral job defining the participants, the dynamics, the needs and the expression of expatriate Christianity among the more than 1,000 overseas congregations and estimated 15 million Americans who live abroad. He concludes, "Now that the gospel has reached many parts of the world, the need for effective expatriate ministry is even greater than before.... On these margins, where strangers gather to share the commonness that they have as foreigners, the expatriate church will grow. However, the growth must not continue in a sectarian fashion.

Congregations and chaplaincies must remain focused upon providing a smorgasbord rather than fast food. The (International Congregation) is neither a beach house nor a social club….It has the making of a mosaic…a divine mosaic."

Expatriate Ministry: Inside the church of the outsiders, Evangelical Missions Quarterly, January 31, 2000

The Growing International Church Movement
By Kenneth D. MacHarg

"The Union Church of Istanbul has its beginnings in the early work of missionaries…and in the need they and some British residents…recognized for an English language church for themselves and their families."(1) That statement could easily be found in the history of most English-language, international congregations outside of the United States, especially those which were established twenty years or more ago.

With estimates of 15 million Americans living abroad, the overseas English-language church movement today is a growing enterprise, with some estimates of up to 1,000 churches overseas. (2) These congregations range from large, several-hundred member churches in major foreign cities such as Paris or Tokyo to a small handful of people gathered in a school auditorium, hotel conference suite or even an available living room for worship and Bible study. A few are related to denominations such as the Southern Baptist, Anglican, Christian and Missionary Alliance and Church of Scotland, but the majority are interdenominational.

Some have a long history. The Istanbul, Turkey church began in the early 1830s while the Seoul Union Church in South Korea traces its beginnings to 1885. (3) Others have sprung up as expatriates moved to a new area to open a business or begin missionary work or the changing winds of political fortune allowed a freedom of religion where none existed previously.

There is no doubt that the older churches began primarily as chaplaincies. "Most were formed by colonials in the colonies to import traditional forms of worship and church experience," said Andy Fletcher who is Deputy Director of Young Life International Schools Ministry in Colorado Springs. "Consequently, the primary attendees were those who were familiar with or comfortable by these styles of churches." Many served to provide either a bridge into the national community or to act as a buffer from the perils of culture shock.

That confined cultural island is changing as more English-speaking churches are being formed overseas to, as Fletcher put it, "deliberately reach out into the community on a broader, more modern front." The Crossroads Community Church in Geneva was "the first church planted to target the unchurched expats in any city," he said. "It was that emphasis that made it unique, an intentional desire to reach out into the international community and away from the resident Christian community in Geneva."

Christian Associates International (CAI) is also at work planting English-language churches designed to reach both the expatriate community and nationals with the gospel. Jon Freeman who is working with CAI in the Crossroads International Church of Amsterdam said, "Our goal is not to just reach expatriates living overseas, but to reach Europeans. We believe God has called us to reach this continent for Christ." Freeman said that his agency is now operating in 12 cities including Dublin, Barcelona, Lisbon, Berlin and Warsaw and hopes to be in 50 cities by the year 2010.

Some of the older English churches are also changing their emphasis to reflect a more diverse membership and a non-traditional outreach. The 30-year old First Baptist Church of Quito, Ecuador recently changed its name to International Baptist Church to signal a broader appeal. And at the Union Church of San Jose, Costa Rica, members are working to overcome a "rich gringo" impression by reaching out to Costa Ricans.

"Over the years it has been interesting to see the church evolve from being a congregation of English speakers, mainly foreigners, into a bilingual church which ministers primarily to permanent residents," said Rev. James McInnes, a missionary with Latin America Mission (LAM) who serves as the pastor of the Costa Rican church. "We are a bridge to the community and support many activities and ministries that reach out to people. We minister to leaders who have both social and spiritual ministries, everything from rescuing prostitutes to feeding children to Christian literature and evangelism," he said.

Rev. Arthur O. F. Bauer, director of the New York-based office of *International Congregations and Christians Abroad* lists six common characteristics of international congregations. These include Evangelical (focusing on the gospel), Ecumenical (multi-denominational), International, English as a common language, in the Context of another culture and Missional (bearing witness to God and His love). (4) Most of the 160 churches related to Bauer's office are older, interdenominational congregations with close ties to mainline U.S. denominations.

David Pederson, who served English-language congregations in Athens and Seoul, identifies six trends that are reshaping these churches. The current movement is from denominationalism to (interdenominational) associations, he wrote. Networks such as CAI will approach ministry from a particular "style" rather than from a denominational basis. Second, there will be increased International Church planting in all areas including mainline denominations. Third, growth will continue to outstretch the ability to track and identify all of the churches. (In Korea, he noted that while most lists identify five such churches, in fact there are around 85 currently active!). Fourth, the two-thirds world will increasingly assume leadership of the International Churches. Fifth, churches will continue to move from a national identity, i.e. American or British to international. Sixth, evangelicals will continue to grow, adding to both constituents and pastors. (5)

Along with their own programs, many of the overseas churches are banding together where possible to meet other needs of the English-speaking community. In Costa Rica, the Union church, along with Escazú Christian Fellowship and an English language Southern Baptist congregation are encouraging a ministry to expatriate women. "We call it an SOS—Save our Sanity—program, but underneath we are also wanting to "Save Our Souls," said Darlene Lauderbaugh, also an LAM missionary whose ministry is exclusively with English-speaking expatriates. "We help newcomers with orientation, bring together female missionaries for fellowship and support and hold a Bible Study for new Christians," she said.

In Quito, missions and English churches are reaching out through strategically placed missionaries to meet the needs of youth. As a "youth advocate," HCJB missionary Len Kinzel has linked with English Fellowship Church, the Alliance Academy and other mission agencies to "serve as either a conduit or a catalyst for youth in their most vital relationships," helping them to work through problems with parents, peers, school and others.

Meanwhile, Fletcher says that a broad ministry to English-speaking people is crucial. "We perceive…that the next generation of the world's leaders are attending international schools around the world, uniquely available to relational evangelism because they are either attending schools which educate in English or are learning it out of necessity," he said. "There are 1,100 international schools globally, in which are represented not only kids with the potential to be tremendously influential on a world scale later in life, but kids from every nation, every people group, every religion, from the 10-40 window and beyond, from places where it is illegal either to talk about Christianity or to change one's faith."

With the number of Americans and others growing overseas, the English language churches must continue to find a way both to minister to those who bring their cultural expectations with them and to reach both expatriates and nationals with the good news.

(1) Edmonds, Anna G., The Union Church of Istanbul, A History, Union Church of Istanbul, Istanbul, Turkey, 1986, p. 10
(2) (2) Andy Fletcher of Young Life maintains a list of 600 identifiable overseas English Language congregations.
(3) (3) Various, The Seoul Union Church History, Seoul, South Korea, 1985, (4) Bauer, Arthur O.F., Christians Abroad in International Congregations, paper distributed by IC/CA office, New York (5) Pederson, David, Expatriate Ministry: Inside the church of the outsiders, Seoul, South Korea, Korean Center for World Missions, 1999, p. 32 **https://tinyurl.com/y6fxzclh**

Missionaries minister to English speaking, expatriate communities

By Kenneth D. MacHarg
LAM News Service

Where do the approximately 15 million North Americans who live abroad attend church? The answers are varied, but many find their spiritual home in one of nearly 1,000 English language congregations around the world.

While many of these Union Churches or International Congregations were established as a chaplaincy to provide ministry to expatriates, today most have become multi-national as well as multi-denominational and are reaching out not only with pastoral care but in evangelistic ways as well.

"Our church has tended to be an island in the past," says Dick Boss, a missionary with the Miami-based Latin America Mission (LAM) who is currently the pastor of the International Evangelical Church of Lausanne, Switzerland. "In recent years there has been a greater recognition that there are Christians in other churches with whom we can have fellowship. So, the bridge is slowly being built, especially to the English-speaking of the third world."

The Lausanne church is typical of an overseas English-speaking congregation in that it draws parishioners from twenty-two countries and is multi-denominational. Boss says that while his church identifies itself as mainstream evangelical, it has occasionally attracted Catholic and Orthodox Christians as well as occasional Muslims and Buddhists.

Across the ocean, LAM missionaries Jim and Pat McInnis serve the Union Church of San Jose, Costa Rica where expatriates and local residents mix in a bilingual service each Sunday.

"It was primarily an expatriate church when we came here and we are still open to that," McInnis says. "However, I saw a need to serve expatriates who were married to Spanish-speaking Latins. They felt left out so we started to do things in Spanish to include them."

McInnis said that translating helped, but wasn't enough, so the church decided to become bilingual. "We tried two services, but we ended up with two congregations," he said.

Pastor McInnis, who is from Hamilton, Ontario, Canada, is bilingual but also uses a translator. "Sometimes when he is preaching he switches to Spanish and doesn't know it," McInnis' wife Pat says. "The translator just goes into English and everybody breaks up."

Jim and Pat McInnis both recognize that a three-hour, bilingual, charismatic service isn't for everybody. "At the same time the Lord was changing our vision, he made provision for other expatriates," says Stratford, Ontario born Pat, referring to the cross-town English-only Escazú Christian Fellowship located near the U.S. embassy.

Some overseas English churches closely resemble congregations back home, others are quite different. "Our church is different from a typical U.S. church in its multi-national make-up, its simple style of worship without cultural accretions and its concentration on the linguistic adaptation of the Gospel to people for whom English is often a second language," Boss says. However, "it's the same in that spiritual needs and problems are basically the same the world around, the Word of God is applicable to all people and situations, and all of our activities are geared to help people draw closer to God."

Boss, a native of Syracuse, New York, served similar international congregations in Colombia, Panama and Mexico before moving to the Swiss church a year and a half ago. "Why the Lord took two "retreaded" semi-retired former missionaries who speak Spanish and lived in the tropics for many years and sent them to French-speaking Switzerland and the cold winters, we're not sure we understand," Boss says. "But, we like the scenery and opportunities for ministry here."

Pastors of overseas churches find their ministry somewhat different than that back home. For one thing, members who retire or become seriously ill often return to their native country, thus there is less hospital visitation and funerals are rare. On the other hand, expatriates face problems of culture shock and challenges to their faith, so counseling and home visits are important.

"One of the frustrating aspects of this type of ministry is that there is a large turnover of people all the time," Boss says. "You have only a relatively short time to minister to some of them."

An important part of international ministry is reaching out to youth. While San Jose's Union church has its own Spanish language youth ministry, it also cooperates, along with the Escazú church and an English language Baptist church in AMCA, a LAM-related program for English speaking residents of San Jose.

AMCA also provides an outreach to expatriate women in the community according to Darlene Lauderbaugh, an LAM missionary working on the AMCA staff. "We help to convey Christ's love and caring to all expatriates living in the San Jose area with orientation and Bible studies," she explains.

International churches and their related ministries provide a needed service to those who live so far from home. "We have actually been more involved in our overseas churches than we were at home," says Charis Geisinger who until recently was a member of the International Christian Fellowship of Managua, Nicaragua and also attended international churches in Thailand, Venezuela, Costa Rica and Russia during her husband's long diplomatic career. "These churches have been absolutely essential to our spiritual well-being. The fellowship is invaluable; always important in helping us keep our balance in a foreign setting."

Missionaries minister to English speaking, expatriate communities, LAM News Service, June 14, 1999

Familiar worship in an unfamiliar setting—International congregations serve expats worldwide

By Kenneth D. MacHarg

The church service is comfortingly familiar: hymns and choruses, shared prayer concerns and a sermon. What is remarkable is that the service is in English and the church is located in a setting far from America's shores. Stretching from Islamabad to Istanbul, Ecuador to Estonia, over 1,000 overseas English language, international churches serve expatriates not only from the United States but other English-speaking countries as well.

Most of those congregations are multi-denominational as well as multi-national, though some were started by denominational groups such as Presbyterian, Lutheran, Baptist and Anglican.

These international churches function in English which is not normally spoken in the host country. They are made up primarily by people from other countries, i.e, expatriates, and they have a multi-cultural mix and diversity with a more global perspective than congregations in home countries.

According to UN statistics, more than 200 million people were living outside of their home country in 2010. However, this number also included economic migrants and refugees. The U.S. State Department estimates that 6.2 million American citizens were expatriates as of 2011.

Not only do these international congregations provide a place of worship and Christian education for expats, but they are also a source of counsel, stability and encouragement for those who try, often unsuccessfully, to adapt to life abroad.

Some experts estimate that up to 40% of people who relocate outside of their home country for work, study or pleasure fail at adapting and end up returning home.

In analyzing these trends in 2012, the *Talent Mobility Study* by Towers Watson, a New York City-based global professional services company, warned that assignment failures among expats can largely be attributed to job performance problems and family or personal situations.

The most common reason given for an assignment failure by Asian companies was the assignee's family (53%) while among U.S. companies family issues ranked second (52%) after job performance problems (68%).

Among other problems and stresses are the employee's inability to adapt to the host country's culture, language barriers and inadequate infrastructure (healthcare/schools) in the host country.

But, the report continued, most companies do not evaluate an employee's family situation when selecting candidates for international assignments, nor do they often provide support for the family as a means of minimizing assignment failures. Only 15 percent of U.S. companies and 14 percent of Asian companies take those situations into consideration.

The report concluded that companies need to develop innovative solutions and approaches to address the challenges.

Many international churches offer that kind of support to expats, whether business people, diplomats, NGO workers, educators, missionaries or others living overseas.

Some churches provide orientation to new expat residents. The 600 member Beijing International Christian Fellowship sponsors a several week *Welcome to Beijing* program following their Sunday service. The church also produces a *Welcome to Beijing* booklet with language tips, maps, lists of restaurants, government offices, and other information that would be of interest to new expatriate residents.

The American Church in Paris (France), where 700 people worship each Sunday, uses a similar methodology. They have been offering an orientation course to life in Paris called *Bloom Where You're Planted* for over 40 years, and they publish a book that is a survival kit encyclopedia of helpful information.

Needs are different among those who live abroad. Expatriates have some unique problems because of their life in another country and the upheaval and adjustment of culture shock. In addition, young adults, particularly those who are single, find the loneliness of living in a new city to be very difficult. Because of these problems and the fact that expats often are transferred in a few years, the counseling aspect of the ministry is very important.

Then there is often the added pressure of how to live out one's faith in a non-Christian environment.

The main distinctive of an overseas church is that many of the members are transients. They know when they arrive that they will be in the city for a short period of time. There is a distinct sense of the temporary.

International congregations often appear to be a mini United Nations. The International Church of Bishkek, Kyrgyzstan counted participants from 35 nations in a survey two years ago.

In addition, while around sixty percent of these churches consider themselves to be intentionally multi-denominational, even those that were established by a particular denomination usually find themselves ministering to a wide mix of people from varying church backgrounds.

To serve the diverse expatriate population well, an international church is usually broad enough to include people from various cultures and denominations without losing its focus and doctrinal base.

Typically, the overseas churches struggle with different practices, trying to find a way to accommodate the varying worship styles and theological stances of a variety of denominations. It is not uncommon to find children studying from an American Methodist Sunday school curriculum while adults use material provided by Scottish Presbyterians and newcomers prepare themselves for membership through Baptist material developed in Asia.

The demographic makeup of these churches can be quite different than back home. Unless the church is located in a city with a large foreign student population, college and career age young people may be absent because they left to go back to their home country. Also, the retired age grandparents are missing. When a person retires, he or she normally returns to their homeland. As a result, many overseas pastors find that they do less hospital visitation and fewer funerals than their colleagues back home.

While some IC pastors say that overseas members see their time abroad as a form of vacation and exhibit a lower level of spiritual maturity, others report that overseas churches spend less time in meetings, and more deeply involve members who are committed and mature Christians.

A large number of overseas churches are much less structured and formal than congregations in home countries. They meet in rented facilities such as school auditoriums or hotel banquet halls and thus have to set up for every service. That lack of a physical facility serves to emphasize that the church is not a building, but the people in it.

International overseas churches provide a needed ministry for those living abroad. "We have actually been more involved in our overseas churches than we were at home," an expat who lived in more than a half-dozen countries told me. "These churches have been absolutely essential to our spiritual well-being. The fellowship is invaluable; always important in helping us keep our balance in a foreign setting."

Via Wendy's or friends; The Lord is building an English-language church in Venezuela

By Kenneth D. MacHarg
LAM News Service

Valencia, Venezuela (LAMNS)-Missionary Dan Rambow may minister more at his local Wendy's restaurant than he does in the church where he serves.

For one thing, his congregation rents church space for only a few hours a week. And, as a pastor of Valencia Community Church, an English-language congregation in Venezuela, Wendy's or McDonald's is a natural place to meet English speaking, foreign residents.

"A woman came to church this past Sunday for the first time," Dan said recently. "I met her when I was just standing in Wendy's at noon and found the two girls in front of me talking in English. They said that they had been here for months and had been looking for a church."

Finding English-speaking residents in a foreign country can be both difficult and easy. On the one hand, there are usually no English language radio stations or newspapers in which to advertise and foreign residents can quickly disappear into the community. On the other hand, expatriate residents tend to congregate around the local English-language school and stand out in public places both physically and by their language.

Dan, who serves with the Latin America Mission, says that the church is beginning to look for new ways to reach out. "Our angle for evangelism is to get into the industrial community and find a target audience," he says. "I figure there are about 20,000 English-speaking people in the community who could attend the church and understand the message if they want to."

As with any pastor who serves in a multi-cultural, foreign setting, Dan is learning cultural sensitivities. "On Mother's Day, I wanted to hand out roses for the holiday, and I wanted to give out different colored roses, for example, white for single women," he remembers. "But, in this Venezuelan culture, the color coding is different. I ended up just getting one color."

"We have to study the different culture and learn to deal with different customs, such as for funerals," he explains. Members of the Valencia church come from a variety of countries such as the United States, Trinidad, Nigeria, Granada, England and Venezuela. "We also have people who come from different denominations, and I have to study church history and traditions to understand them," Dan says.

That diversity is hailed by many members of the Valencia church, says Michael Taylor who was born in Rangoon, Burma, and came to Venezuela via England. "It's good to have so many denominations within one church; it helps us to grow," he says.

Dan, who was born in Farmington Hills, Michigan, but now considers Boca Raton, Florida, as his home, is a new pastor, serving his first church. "I'm new at this," he reports. "Right now, I'm following where I sensed God has opened the door. We are following where the Lord is leading. God is training me."

His first week at the Valencia church last February could be described as a 'baptism by fire.' "When I first got here and was trying to unpack my bags, in one week we had five people in the hospital," he says. "I wasn't ready for it, I didn't have a telephone and nobody knew how to contact me."

Those obstacles didn't stop the church from mobilizing to help out. "It was neat to see how God took care of the hospitalization, a funeral and the birth of a baby," he says. "The church came together. God laid it on each person's heart to step in and take care of it. God was taking care of the big stuff!"

The Valencia church holds its Sunday service at 8:30 a.m. in the rented facilities of a local Lutheran congregation. "The early morning is a good time because of the heat in Valencia," Dan explains. "Sometimes we have birds fly right through the chapel."

The service is informal and contemporary with music accompanied by a CD and guitars and led by church members. Attendance hovers around 25 to 30. There was a time when the church counted between 200 and 300 in attendance, but much of the foreign industry has left Valencia and the number of expatriates has declined.

"On Sunday I get to preach, but I don't get to know the people," Dan says. "Wednesday nights I get to hear the people share as we study through books, Bible study material and other guides such as *Experiencing God.* It's a wonderful time when almost half of the people are a different group than come on Sunday." He says that through the Wednesday evening studies, people have made professions of faith and renewed their commitment to the Lord.

An English-language church in a foreign setting such as Valencia is a welcome institution for expatriates. "The church brings the Christian community together and it brings a little of home to me," says Jenna Nelson who is from Kansas City and teaches middle school classes at the local English-language international school. "The church has helped me to assimilate into the culture better and has given me a local family to call on."

Melissa Oberdiech from St. Louis says that she would rather attend an English language church overseas because she can participate more easily and understand what is going on.

While hanging around Wendy's has proven to be helpful, Dan is encouraged by the way the Lord is bringing people to the church. "One by one, people are showing up, calling. We are ready for God to use us. People come to us, that's where our biggest ministry has been."

Global Increases in Expatriates Challenge International Churches in Ministry

By Kenneth D. MacHarg

Exactly how many expatriates are there?

Of course, nobody knows for sure, but some good, educated guesses abound.

Whatever the true numbers are, a new report says certain sectors of the globe are expecting more in the coming years with challenging implications for those who minister to expats with international congregations.

Over 1,000 English-language congregations serve people living outside of their home country around the world. Most of those congregations are multi-denominational as well as multi-national, though some were started by denominational groups such as Presbyterian, Lutheran, Baptist and Anglican.

These international churches function in a language, usually English, not normally spoken in the host country. They have a majority of people from other countries, i.e, expatriates, and they have a multi-cultural mix and diversity with a more global perspective than congregations in home countries.

According to UN statistics, more than 200 million people were living outside of their home country in 2010. However, this number also included economic migrants and refugees.

In terms of outbound expatriation, as of 2009, the United Kingdom had the highest number of expatriates among OECD countries with more than three million British citizens living abroad according to *Wikipedia*. Some estimates point to 5.2 million U.S. citizens living outside their home country.

Over 43 percent of companies across Asia project an increase in cross-border traditional expatriate assignments in the next two years, according to an article in the Bangkok, Thailand, newspaper, *The Nation.*

And, 85 percent of them expect to send their staff to posts in neighboring Asian nations. Globally, 45 percent of all international companies expect to send an increasing number of employees abroad to all parts of the world.

Those statistics offer an expanding opportunity for outreach by international churches, but also present a challenge in formulating ministries to meet the unique needs of third-culture members.

In analyzing these trends the *Talent Mobility Study* by Towers Watson, a New York City-based global professional services company, warned that assignment failures among expats can largely be attributed to job performance issues and family or personal situations.

The most common reason given for an assignment failure by Asian companies was the assignee's family (53%) while among U.S. companies family issues ranked second (52%) after job performance problems (68%).

The newspaper reported that "Asian-headquartered companies identify the employee's inability to adapt to the host country's culture, language barriers and inadequate infrastructure (healthcare-schools) in the host country as significant causes of assignment failures as well."

But, the report continued, most companies do not evaluate an employee's family situation when selecting candidates for international assignments, nor do they often provide support for the family as a means of minimizing assignment failures. Only 15 percent of U.S. companies and 14 percent of Asian companies take those situations into consideration.

The report concluded that companies need to develop innovative solutions and approaches to address the challenges.

Many international churches already offer that kind of support to expats, whether business people, diplomats, NGO workers, educators, missionaries or others living overseas.

"Every Fall, when most of our new folks arrive, we have a several week *Welcome to Beijing* program following our Sunday services," said Pastor Mark Blair who serves as the pastor of the 600-member Zhong Guan Cun daughter church of the Beijing (China) International Christian Fellowship. "This is a sit down in a circle, have a coffee, sharing time with long-term residents who are church leaders. Often the chat time follows with going to lunch together in a near-by restaurant."

Mr. Blair said the church also produces a *Welcome to Beijing* booklet with language tips, maps, lists of restaurants, government offices, and other information that would be of interest to new expatriate residents.

There is what Blair called a "great economic boom" in China which has led to an increase in expats there in recent years. He also attributed the expansion to an interest in helping the growing church in China and the "generous amount of scholarships given by China to students from all over the world."

The Rev. Scott Herr, pastor of the American Church in Paris (France), where 700 people worship each Sunday, uses a similar methodology. "We have been offering an orientation course to life in Paris called *Bloom Where You're Planted* for the past 40-some years," he said. "We also publish a book that is a survival kit encyclopedia of helpful information."

Rev. Herr said that his church doubled in membership in recent years primarily by adding a third worship using contemporary music.

In Santiago, Chile, Pastor Samuel A. Mateer also reports growth in the expat population propelled by "the demand on copper from China and India which means the mining industry has great demand for management level and above workers."

"Our women spend time at the grocery stores listening for English spoken and at international women's groups, looking for ways to help the new ladies adapt to their new culture," Mr. Mateer reported. "They invite them to church and to the women's Bible studies to give them a sense of being loved."

"They provide them someone who can talk their language and understand what they are facing with a maid they cannot talk to, a husband extremely busy, and a school with new demands," the pastor explained.

Rev. Mateer said that at his 100 member San Marcos International Church (a Presbyterian congregation), "We lose one third of the congregation each year due to transfer in business and new postings with the U.S. embassy."

Jimmy Martin, an elder of the International Christian Fellowship in Oberursel (Frankfurt), Germany, affirmed the role of church women in helping expat spouses adapt to living in another country. "Finding a 'home away from home' in a loving group of women who understand many of your own challenges is a tremendous help to moms and wives," he said. Mr. Martin is also the General Secretary of the International Baptist Churches, an association of Baptist congregations in 27 countries.

Many overseas churches integrate cultural adaptation and expat issues into their regular weekly activities. Small groups, parenting and cross-cultural support ministries, counseling, language training and prayer groups all form a strong component of support for those who struggle with the issues of living and functioning well in a different culture. Many pastors also address those issues in sermons and study groups.

The International Church of Bangkok, Thailand, is one example where expatriate concerns are a natural part of its many ministries. "We address all these areas comprehensively and holistically through our worship and small groups ministries," explained Stewart Perry, the pastor of the 300 member congregation.

Among other issues frequently reported by pastors of expat churches are loneliness, culture shock, language-learning struggles, bureaucratic hassles and homesickness.

Links: http://www.towerswatson.com/research/7502

http://www.nationmultimedia.com/business/Expat-assignments-on-rise-in-Asia-30181090.html

Expat Clergy on the Front Line for Psychological Support

By Kenneth D. MacHarg
Jul 23, 2015 *The Wall Street Journal Expat Blog*

"Yes, we would like to talk about it." The long-term expat couple in Honduras was responding to my question about whether they would return to their home country or remain abroad. With aging parents back home and an urge to move on to something new, they were considering all options. They needed someone to help them reflect on their thoughts and uncertainty.

Another twenty-something member of the church I served in Costa Rica sat across the coffeehouse table from me. A vivacious person always surrounded with the teenagers from a local American school she had come to mentor, I assumed that her life was filled with social activities.

Tears formed in her eyes as she told me, "My best friends here are the people I see on television every night."

Expats are like anyone else: they struggle through times of trauma, disappointment, uncertainty, death and unfaithfulness as well as joy, fulfillment, success and celebration.

But they are also different: They deal with culture shock, loneliness, frequent moves, separation from friends and loved ones, great uncertainty and frustration that they would never experience back home.

In their home country they would most likely turn to a professional counselor, a psychiatrist or psychologist, a school counselor, a social worker, or a clergy person.

In a foreign land where there might not be a trained, English-speaking counselor, finding someone who can listen and advise professionally is often a struggle.

Enter one of the English-speaking pastors, priests, rabbis and other clergy who serve expats through international

"The most difficult are troubled people who really should be in their own country where there is a support system," said a North American pastor in a North African country who asked not to be identified for security reasons. "Recently a woman has been coming to church. She has suffered from depression. She needs help and may be bipolar. But she will not return to France because she has a boyfriend here."

"I consider us to be on the front-line of offering help," he observed.

Many pastors and priests provide initial, trouble-shooting counseling abroad as church members and community residents approach them with problems ranging from marital struggles or disturbed children to loneliness and difficulty with cultural adjustment.

"The main issues I encounter include guidance on whether to stay or leave or where to go," reported the Rev. Mark Blair of the 600-member Beijing International Christian Fellowship in China.

Rev. Blair also pointed to problems unique to expats, such as not knowing what is really happening with family back home or how to help aging parents or ill relatives.

Then there are temptations related to being far from familiar moral restraints, he said, as well as cultural confusion around dealing with local employers, landlords, and contracts.

In my years serving churches in the Bahamas, Costa Rica, Czech Republic, Ecuador, Panama, Kyrgyzstan, and now

Honduras, the problems I've seen most frequently are extreme loneliness, especially among single, young adult expats, and issues surrounding expats' frequent transitions.

Increasingly, international English-speaking churches are trying to establish a more formal counseling process for people seeking assistance.

In San Jose, Costa Rica, the Rev. Stacey Steck, who has served at the Escazú Christian Fellowship for nine years, helped his church establish a formal counseling program that was both English-language and faith-based. Adding more hours to his workweek, Rev. Steck says, was a way to gauge whether there was an even greater need for help, possibly through a counseling center with more staff.

In Beijing, the size of the city and the church means that counseling is already available there, says Rev. Blair. In addition to that, the church offers a support group for those with substance abuse problems.

Research proves that emotional issues can grow into bigger problems for expats. The 2012 Talent Mobility Study by Towers Watson, a New York-based global professional services company, warned that assignment failures among expats mainly come from job performance issues and family or personal situations.

Asian companies reported that 53 percent named problems with an employee's family as the reason an overseas assignment failed. In the U.S., family issues were ranked the second most significant reason for assignment failure, after job performance problems.

The report said that most companies do not evaluate an employee's family situation when selecting candidates for international assignments, nor do they often provide support for the family to limit problems. Only 15 percent of U.S. companies and 14 percent of Asian companies take those situations into consideration.

That's where international churches can help. As the pastor of several international congregations, I have worked at not only at identifying and inviting new expats in town to attend our church, but also to integrate them into the life of the congregation and to acquaint them with other, more settled expats.

A Mexican-American student who attended one of our churches told me of her difficulty in getting to know others and in dealing with her homesickness. To help, I asked two young women who had been in the city for a while to invite her to lunch or for a cup of coffee. I also matched her with a Mexican woman in the church who invited her over to make tortillas.

Other churches have developed specific programs to orient new arrivals to the city. "Every fall, when most of our new folks arrive, we have a several-week 'Welcome to Beijing' program following our Sunday services," said Rev. Blair. The church also produces a Welcome to Beijing booklet with language tips, maps, lists of restaurants, government offices, and other information.

The Rev. Scott Herr, pastor of the American Church in Paris, where 700 people worship each Sunday, uses a similar methodology. "We have been offering an orientation course to life in Paris called 'Bloom Where You're Planted' for the past 40-some years," he said. "We also publish a book that is a survival kit encyclopedia of helpful information."

Jimmy Martin, an elder of the International Christian Fellowship in Oberursel, near Frankfurt, Germany, said that women in the church can help. "Finding a 'home away from home' in a loving group of women who understand many of your own challenges is a tremendous help to moms and wives," he said.

Stewart Perry, the former pastor of the 300-member International Church of Bangkok, Thailand, explained that his church identified newcomers in the community and worked to integrate them into various activities.

Expats don't have to join a church to get some help. Many of the more than 1,000 English-speaking, international congregations worldwide open their doors to non-members in need of friendship or dealing with difficult adjustments and circumstance. Some of them can be found at www.internationalcongregations.com www.micn.org www.ibc-churches.org and www.internationalchurches.net.

A first-line source for help a long way from home
By Kenneth D. MacHarg

Businesses, organizations and the military which send employees abroad often don't realize the tremendous pressure and cost that these people and their families pay to live far away from home.

While some have initiated cultural adjustment programs, most are at a loss when it comes to dealing with an employee or family member who doesn't adapt well, falls into depression, or whose work and status may be threatened by family problems, the breakup of a marriage, or the inability of children to adapt to a new location.

Several recent articles in the *Wall Street Journal* and the *WSJ Expat Blog* highlight the stresses and pressures that expats find as they move from place to place around the globe. Divorce is high on the list of those whose marriages may already have experienced problems which are exacerbated by the move to another culture so far from the normal support systems at home.

What many expats and their employers may not realize is that help is readily available in most major international cities where expats are posted.

Just as back home, the pastors and priests of local churches provide the first line of counseling and support for those experiencing personal problems of almost any kind.

And, for those expats who speak English, that first-line help can be found at the more than 1,000 international, English-language churches that are situated close to the expat communities around the world.

Just like back home, most of the pastors of these unique congregations have been trained in qualified seminaries or Bible colleges, and their course of study included classes in counseling, psychology, marriage and family issues and other helpful topics.

Several years ago, *The Nation* in Bangkok reported that with the passing of the Great Recession, more companies were expected to send employees abroad. But, the newspaper reported, not all international moves were successful.

I wrote an article about that, including the following observations:

The *Talent Mobility Study* by Towers Watson, a New York City-based global professional services company, warned that assignment failures among expats can largely be attributed to job performance issues and family or personal situations.

The most common reason given for an assignment failure by Asian companies was the assignee's family (53%) while among U.S. companies family issues ranked second (52%) after job performance problems (68%).

The newspaper reported that "Asian-headquartered companies identify the employee's inability to adapt to the host country's culture, language barriers and inadequate infrastructure (healthcare-schools) in the host country as significant causes of assignment failures as well."

But, the report continued, most companies do not evaluate an employee's family situation when selecting candidates for international assignments, nor do they often provide support for the family as a means of minimizing assignment failures. Only 15 percent of U.S. companies and 14 percent of Asian companies take those situations into consideration.

The report concluded that companies need to develop innovative solutions and approaches to address the challenges.

Many international churches already offer that kind of support to expats, whether business people, diplomats, NGO workers, educators, missionaries or others living overseas.

"Every Fall, when most of our new folks arrive, we have a several week *Welcome to Beijing* program following our Sunday services," said Pastor Mark Blair who serves as the pastor of the 600-member Zhong Guan Cun daughter church of the Beijing (China) International Christian Fellowship. "This is a sit down in a circle, have a coffee, sharing time with long-term residents who are church leaders. Often the chat time follows with going to lunch together in a near-by restaurant."

Mr. Blair said the church also produces a *Welcome to Beijing* booklet with language tips, maps, lists of restaurants, government offices, and other information that would be of interest to new expatriate residents.

There is what Blair called a "great economic boom" in China which has led to an increase in expats there in recent years. He also attributed the expansion to an interest in helping the growing church in China and the "generous amount of scholarships given by China to students from all over the world."

The Rev. Scott Herr, pastor of the American Church in Paris (France), where 700 people worship each Sunday, uses a similar methodology. "We have been offering an orientation course to life in Paris called *Bloom Where You're Planted* for the past 40-some years," he said. "We also publish a book that is a survival kit encyclopedia of helpful information."

Rev. Herr said that his church doubled in membership in recent years primarily by adding a third worship using contemporary music.

In Santiago, Chile, Pastor Samuel A. Mateer also reports growth in the expat population propelled by "the demand on copper from China and India which means the mining industry has great demand for management level and above workers."

"Our women spend time at the grocery stores listening for English spoken and at international women's groups, looking for ways to help the new ladies adapt to their new culture,"

Mr. Mateer reported. "They invite them to church and to the women's Bible studies to give them a sense of being loved."

"They provide them someone who can talk their language and understand what they are facing with a maid they cannot talk to, a husband extremely busy, and a school with new demands," the pastor explained.

Rev. Mateer said that at his 100 member San Marcos International Church (a Presbyterian congregation), "We lose one third of the congregation each year due to transfer in business and new postings with the U.S. embassy."

Jimmy Martin, an elder of the International Christian Fellowship in Oberursel (Frankfurt), Germany, affirmed the role of church women in helping expat spouses adapt to living in another country. "Finding a 'home away from home' in a loving group of women who understand many of your own challenges is a tremendous help to moms and wives," he said. Mr. Martin is also the General Secretary of the International Baptist Churches, an association of Baptist congregations in 27 countries.

Many overseas churches integrate cultural adaptation and expat issues into their regular weekly activities. Small groups, parenting and cross-cultural support ministries, counseling, language training and prayer groups all form a strong component of support for those who struggle with the issues of living and functioning well in a different culture. Many pastors also address those issues in sermons and study groups.

The International Church of Bangkok, Thailand, is one example where expatriate concerns are a natural part of its many ministries. "We address all these areas comprehensively and holistically through our worship and small groups ministries," explained Stewart Perry, the pastor of the 300 member congregation.

Among other issues frequently reported by pastors of expat churches are loneliness, culture shock, language-learning struggles, bureaucratic hassles and homesickness.

Hopefully, those involved with placing employees outside of their home countries will be alerted by the *WSJ* story and will provide them with information concerning the international churches which can be of great service to expat workers whether they are Christians or not. **https://tinyurl.com/yxcon49h**

Eight Things to Know as the Pastor of an International Church

By Kenneth D. MacHarg

It all began as an aside in a mission class taught many years ago by Dr. Norman Horner at the Louisville Presbyterian Theological Seminary.

He was explaining the various ways in which a person could serve overseas such as via denominational mission boards, independent faith mission groups, ecumenical bodies and others.

Pausing for a moment, he remarked almost as an after-thought, “By the way, if you are interested in an English-language ministry overseas you might consider the Union Churches which serve expatriates living abroad.”

Dr. Horner went on to explain that these congregations brought people together from various denominations to worship in an international location where there weren’t enough English-speaking Lutherans or Methodists, Congregationalists or Pentecostals to form their own church.

That was a “light bulb” moment for me. While I had (and continue to have) an intense interest in global issues and missionary work, I had never considered learning a language and moving abroad to carry out ministry.

But discovering that there were, in those days, around 200 of those congregations in a diversity of countries set me to considering serving one of them.

Generally known as international Congregations (ICs) today, there are at least 1,500 such multinational, multi-denominational churches located in major cities around the world serving an ever-expanding cadre of expatriates. And, increasingly, pastors from the United States and other English-speaking countries are heading abroad to take up the pastorate of these churches.

If you are one of those, congratulations. You are about to embark on an exhilarating and profound experience as you take on serving a multi-denominational and multi-national congregation.

But, before you go, there are at least eight things for you to consider to successfully serve such a diverse group.

1. What works back home won't necessarily succeed in an IC. U.S. pastors are used to packaged programs for evangelism and discipleship that lay out several steps to achieving success. And, there are numerous types of church governing patterns or models (seeker and emerging churches, missional congregations, lay-led, elder-led) which may not be at all relevant to a congregation that involves people from diverse ecclesiastical backgrounds.

   Not everyone in an IC will respond well to these guided process. Some will resist having their church shaped in Australian, North American or European styles and assumptions. Others will see opportunities from a broader, international perspective. Better to develop programs for education, outreach or youth work that are more relevant to the broad make-up of the church you are serving.
2. Give up the idea of building a stable church with a growing membership.

   Just as soon as you begin to succeed, you will reach a year when a large percentage of the congregation is transferred out of the country or decides to go back home. Or, upheaval in the country or region will send many expats packing. The IC pastor will quickly learn that turn-over is a major factor that shapes much of his or her reoccurring work. (An IC pastor in South America told me that each year he loses around 50% of his participants due to transfers in the diplomatic and business communities). In international congregations, loyal, supportive members will leave sooner or later and new people will come in to take their place—and none of that is based on whether you are a dynamic preacher or a strong leader.

Turnover can best be addressed by learning how to integrate people into the life of a church quickly and completely. Assuring that they find a small group, asking them to lead in worship or teach Sunday school, using their musical abilities will encourage many to stay and provide immediate replacements for those who leave. While a church will want to get to know someone responsibly before placing them in certain positions, making them wait six months or a year while they are examined usually means they will go somewhere else or will leave without ever getting involved or feeling at home.

3. Be prepared for the lowest attendance Sundays of the year at Christmas and Easter.

   That makes no sense to a traditional pastor of a church in the home country. But the reality is that teachers, who may make up a large percentage of an IC, diplomats and some business people have extended vacations over those holidays and use them to travel home or take a vacation elsewhere in the region. Not only that, be aware that diplomats will frequently be gone for multiple weekends—they observe holidays from the host country and those from their home country. Attendance for some will be, at best, sporadic because many expats are regional directors or managers and must travel frequently.

4. Enjoy the opportunity to preach to an international audience.

They are serious about hearing good, biblical preaching and messages that resonate with the struggles of expat life. A never ending series of expository sermons that runs through a book or the whole Bible for months or a year may not be feasible or effective because of the attendance fluctuations and the sizable turnover during any given year. It's much better to keep series in a manageable length such as three to eight weeks.

Another challenge to your preaching: dare I say most of your tried and true illustrations from back home won't be relevant in an IC? Australians don't understand baseball nor North American football. Filipinos don't watch American or European TV programs and so won't understand who you are talking about. Latin Americans, Africans, Asians, Europeans cannot follow the twists and turns of U.S. primary elections and never will understand the Electoral College no matter how often you explain it. Pick and choose stories and illustrations that will communicate cross-culturally and internationally.

Oh yes, another caution: If you decide to celebrate the 4th of July, then—in fairness–be ready to celebrate the independence day of all the nations represented in your church. In one congregation we had people from 35 nationalities—making celebrating any national holiday impossible.

5. Your congregation may be in deep need of encouragement and emotional/spiritual support.

   Not only will they want counsel and understanding for those normal struggles they would have back home such as marital stress, concern about children and aging parents, drug and alcohol abuse and the like, but they will also require support for unique expat issues.

These might include frequent losses as they or friends relocate or move away after a short period of time, adjustment to another culture and learning other languages, responding to violence and insecurity, intense homesickness or loneliness or the fear of deportation or having to return to their home country and giving up the expat lifestyle. Good, biblically-based, need-oriented preaching can help build a basis for dealing with those issues, but many cups of coffee (or tea) at a local restaurant will be required as you help them work through these challenges.

6. Conflict can also arise in an IC.

   The issues are many, some of them different from what a pastor might expect: differing expectations between people coming from liturgical or non-liturgical backgrounds, conflict over preaching style from those who want what they had back home; tension between members from developed countries and those from developing nations; political differences in a very diverse congregation; stresses and a lack of understanding between missionaries and business people.

   While blending traditions and practices from multiple church backgrounds often works well, an IC pastor must be sensitive to differences among the members in such a diverse congregation. Learning to lead a congregation made up of liturgical Anglicans, middle of the road Baptists and expressive Pentecostals can be a joy while also challenging.

7. Learn four useful phrases which will provide counsel and understanding as you adapt and get along with both expats and people from the local culture.
   a. When dealing across cultures, if you remember that "your" assumptions are not necessarily "their" assumptions, you will get along well.

b. A successful expatriate has a good sense of humor and a poor sense of smell.
c. In another culture, you cannot say "you would think…" The reality is that you and they think and do things differently. Be quiet and learn from the way "they" do things.
d. Since you are there to preach the Gospel, taking a political stance in a diverse congregation can damage your personal relationships with people of various persuasions. Avoid discussing politics, especially those from your own country, with anyone. And remember, many of your members don't watch the same news channels you do (they are more likely to be tuned into the BBC World News or CNN International).

8. Be ready to be challenged, blessed, excited, fulfilled and satisfied.

   The reality is that there are no more interesting, challenging and fulfilling churches to serve than the international congregations. They are filled with fascinating people who have the most amazing and bizarre stories to tell; whose perspectives are far beyond those of most folks back home; who are deeply committed to the Lord and the work of His church; who will teach you more than you will ever teach them; who will appreciate your efforts and likely recommend you to serve their new church when they move half a world away.

Sidebar

Expatriate: Someone who lives outside of their own country. Also known as an Expat. Do not confuse an expatriate with an expatriot—someone who has given up citizenship in their country of origin. Sometimes known as a traitor.

Brexit Offers Opportunity for International Congregations in Europe

By Kenneth D. MacHarg

In a constantly changing world, economic and geo-political changes are an often-overlooked dynamic that can affect churches in terms of the ebb and flow of participants and the development of programming to meet new dynamics.

One needs to just remember the 25% increase in church and synagogue attendance after the attacks of September 11, 2001. Yet, that surge eventually dropped and participation in worship returned to the previous norm.

For the approximate 2,000 International Congregations (ICs) which serve English-speaking expatriates around the globe, worldwide politics, economics and social movements have historically affected their outreach and membership. During World War II many of these expat churches, especially in Asia, were forced to close as members fled approaching troops and bombing raids. In recent times, the massive exodus of oil executives and other expats from Venezuela has reduced the number of ICs in Caracas from a half-dozen or so to one or two today.

On the other hand, over the past 35 years the fall of the Soviet Union and the rise of Globalization which opened many previously-closed borders and encouraged many students, business people and retires to go abroad, have led to an astounding increase in the number of ICs in all parts of the globe.

A 2012 *Talent Mobility Study* by *Towers Watson*, a New York-based global professional services company, said that over 43 percent of companies across Asia projected an increase in cross-border traditional expatriate assignments within two years,

And, as the global economy improved after the Great Recession, 85 percent of them expected to send their staff to posts in neighboring Asian nations. Globally, 45 percent of all international companies were expected to send an increasing number of employees abroad to all parts of the world.

Those statistics offered an expanding opportunity for outreach by international churches, but also presented a challenge in formulating ministries to meet the unique needs of third-culture members. (A complete article can be read at **https://tinyurl.com/y45lglj3**)

Now, a new report from the Wall Street Journal highlights a similar opportunity throughout Europe due to Brexit, the recent vote by British citizens mandating that their country leave the European Union within the next few years.

That change will result in numerous business executives and their families leaving the United Kingdom to settle in European cities, according to the newspaper.

This projected change has brought concern to English-language expatriate schools across the continent as they attempt to gear up for the influx.

"There are (currently) just over 775,000 students attending English-language international schools in kindergarten through 12th grade throughout Europe, according to the International School Consultancy, which tracks the international schools market," the paper reported.

A challenge is that most of those schools report they are full, capacity is tight and government efforts to meet demand might not match the post-Brexit surge.

Shortly after the Brexit vote, France's prime minister Manual Valls said that the country would build as many English-language schools as needed. Similarly, German officials reported that their schools were full. (The complete WSJ article may be viewed here.)

While International Congregations may not have those overflow concerns, the impending wave of English-speaking expats to scattered European churches can be a unique opportunity for the ICs to expand their ministries, find new ways of service and grow their congregations.

As has been done in other locations, ICs which link with English-language schools can use that relationship to provide relocation and orientation services to newly arrived residents, offer counseling and family support as people make the transition, and advertise the availability of their church for worship, fellowship, Christian education and other services.

Those who do reach out, however, might be cautioned that the recruitment of new people moving because of changing political or economic circumstances can fall flat if the outreach and programming fail to meet incoming potential participant's needs.

Referring to the 9/11 spurt in church attendance, church researcher George Barna was quoted in a USA Today op-ed piece saying, "'After the attack, millions of nominally churched or generally irreligious Americans were desperately seeking something that would restore stability and a sense of meaning to life. Fortunately, many of them turned to the church. Unfortunately,' he said, 'churches succeeded at putting on a friendly face but failed at motivating the vast majority of spiritual explorers to connect with Christ in a more intimate or intense manner.'"

Since any large movement of English-speaking families to the continent may not be immediate, International Congregations have time to develop significant programs and extensive recruitment for potential new attendees.

Bibliography

Books

Allen, Cameron, (2013). Bloomington, IN. *The History of the American Pro-Cathedral of the Holy Trinity, Paris (1815-1980).* iUniverse books.

Bloemberg, G. Jacob (2017). *Love Your City; 5 Steps to City-wide Movements*. WestBow Press, a division of Thomas Nelson and Zondervan, 2020

Carlson, James, (2019). Hamilton, MA. *International Church Assessment: A Light to all Nations? Assessing the Missional Strength and Commitment of International Churches in Europe.* Independently published.

Duggan, Thomas E., (2002). New York City. *Opportunity to serve, The American Church in Paris, 1978-1992,* American and Foreign Christian Union.

Edmonds, Anna G., (1986). Istanbul, Turkey. *The Union Church of Istanbul, a History*. Union Church of Istanbul.

Ekhator, Dan, (Ed.). (2013) Rome, Italy. *Nestled in the Eternal City, Uniting the Nations for Christ*. Rome Baptist Church.

Hemphill, Robert F. (1980). Tokyo, Japan. *A Church For All Seasons, Tokyo Union Church, 1872-1980.*. Tokyo Union Church. (Also available online at https://tinyurl.com/y62dsgk4.

McConkey, Clarence, (Ed.). (1992). Balboa, Panama. *The Union Church of the Canal Zone, 1950-1992*. The Union Church of the Canal Zone.

Van Rensburg, Elaine. (2007). Istanbul, Turkey. *In God's House, 150 Years of the Union Church of Istanbul in the Dutch Chapel*. Dutch Chapel.

Packer, David. (2013). *Look Who God Let into the Church, Understanding the nature and sharpening the impact of a multicultural church.* Growth Points International Publications.

Packer, David, (Ed). (2015) *The International Pastor Experience*, Published privately.

Pederson, David. (1999) Seoul, South Korea. *Expatriate Ministry: Inside the Church of the Outsiders,* Korean Center for World Missions.

Rolofson, Robert H. (1950) Balboa, Canal Zone. *Christian Cooperation at the World's Crossroads,* The Union Church of the Canal Zone.

Stout, Herman and Herbert Stout. (Publishing date unknown, circa early 1960s). *Appointed by Christ Exclusively, A history of the Association of Baptists in Continental Europe, Forerunner of the European Baptist Convention*, Privately published.

Underwood, Brian. (2004) London. *Faith & New Frontiers, A Story of Planting and Nurturing Churches, 1823-2003.* Intercontinental Church Society.

Underwood, Brian (1994) London. *Faith without frontiers: Intercon 1969-1993*. Intercontinental Church Society.

Underwood, Brian. (1974) London. *Faith at the Frontiers: Anglican evangelicals and their countrymen overseas, 150 years of the Commonwealth and Continental Church Society,* Commonwealth and Continental Church Society.

Wahnschaffe, Mario. (2017). Bonn. *Building an International Church.* Kindle Edition.

Webber, Christopher. (Ed.). (1969). *Ministry to Laymen Abroad in Asia.* Hong Kong. Laymen Abroad.

Wald, Jack. (2016). St. Louis, MO. *Pastoring a Parade, A Guide to International Church Ministry,* Wildwood Press.

Theses

Dreessen, Paul. (In process) *How English-speaking, international churches reach, disciple and minister to their target audience.* Asbury Theological Seminary.

Klassen, Eugene. (2006). *Exploring the Missional Potential of International Churches: A case study of Capital City Baptist Church, Mexico City.* (Doctoral dissertation). Retrieved from place.asburyseminary.edu. https://tinyurl.com/y4oxsu9q

Young, David W. (2017) *Redirecting the International Church from an Oasis Paradigm to Missional Thought, Community and Practice*, George Fox University. (Doctoral dissertation). Retrieved from digitalcommons.georgefox.edu. https://tinyurl.com/y69da24d

Also see books above by David Peterson, Jacob Bloemberg, James Carlson and Jack Wald.

Excellent companion book

Relevant, concise, devotional reading for Expats

A book of biblical reflections and insight into those feelings and questions that expatriates have while living in a foreign land. Using the Bible as guidance, this book encourages expats and helps them to live a full life overseas.

Available at www.amazon.com

https://tinyurl.com/uaqxr7a

www.ingramcontent.com/pod-product-compliance
Lightning Source LLC
LaVergne TN
LVHW050921080826
845145LV00001B/162

* 9 7 8 1 6 3 1 9 9 5 7 7 4 *